Kant on Causation

SUNY series in Philosophy
George R. Lucas Jr., editor

Kant on Causation

*On the Fivefold Routes to the
Principle of Causation*

Steven M. Bayne

State University of New York Press

Published by
State University of New York Press, Albany

© 2004 State University of New York

All rights reserved

Printed in the United States of America

No part of this book may be used or reproduced in any manner whatsoever without written permission. No part of this book may be stored in a retrieval system or transmitted in any form or by any means including electronic, electrostatic, magnetic tape, mechanical, photocopying, recording, or otherwise without the prior permission in writing of the publisher.

For information, address the State University of New York Press,
90 State Street, Suite 700, Albany, NY 12207

Production by Kelli Williams
Marketing by Jennifer Giovani

Library of Congress Cataloging-in-Publication Data

Bayne, Steven M.
    Kant on causation : on the fivefold routes to the principle of causation / Steven M. Bayne.
        p. cm. — (SUNY series in philosophy)
    Includes bibliographical references and index.
    ISBN 0-7914-5901-2 (alk. paper) — ISBN 0-7914-5902-0 (pbk. : alk. paper)
    1. Kant, Immanuel, 1724–1804. 2. Causation. I. Title. II. Series.

B2799.C3B39 2003
122'.092—dc22
                                                                     2003190073

Contents

Acknowledgments	ix
Introduction	xi
1 Relationships	1
Concepts and intuitions	2
Kant's introduction to the problem of the Schematism and his introductory solution	3
Kant's true task in the Schematism	4
Leibniz	4
Hume	5
Leibniz, Hume, Kant, and applicability	7
The importance of the Schematism	9
A problem with Kant's account of the Schematism	10
The transcendental deduction and the principles	13
Principles of Understanding and Principles of Reason	16
Analogies of Experience	22
Kant and Hume	26
Hume's Doubt	28
Hume's reasons for doubting the possibility of demonstration	30
Transcendental proof and Kant's proof of the causal principle	32
2 The Causal Principle	35
The principle of the second analogy.	35
Evaluation of Possible Interpretations of the Formulation of the Causal Principle	39
The Same-Cause-Same-Effect thesis	39
The Every-Event-Some-Cause thesis	43
3 The Fivefold Routes to the Principle of Causation	45
Possible Argument Strategies	45
Evaluation of Argument Strategies	51
The Veridical Strategy	52
The Event/Object Strategy	55
The Event/Event Strategy	58
The Justification Strategy	67

4 The Irreversibility Argument — 75
Lovejoy's Position — 76
Strawson's Position — 81
Bennett's Position — 87
Melnick's Position — 89
Guyer's Position — 92
The house, the ship, and irreversibility — 97

5 Objects of Representations — 103
The principle of the Second Analogy — 104
Subject to a rule — 107
Objects of representations and being subject to a rule — 108
Irreversibility revisited: Are successions of appearances subject to a rule? — 112
An example for the official definition — 116
Successions of appearances must be subject to a rule — 118
Problems and Defense — 120
    The requirements for a succession of appearances' being subject to a rule — 120
    Are my requirements too strong? — 121
    Are my requirements too weak? — 123
        Repeatability — 123
        Necessary Order — 126
    Textual Worries — 128
        Repeatability — 128
        Necessary Order and Necessity — 130
        Is this really a causal theory? — 135

6 Hume Revisited — 137
A brief review — 137
Transcendental proof and the mistake strategy — 139
A problem with Kant's transcendental proof and mistake strategy — 143
The implications of this problem — 144
Turning the copy thesis on its head — 146
Problem: Drawing the distinction between a beginning of existence and a cause of existence — 148
Final Status of Kant's Answer to Hume — 150

Conclusion — 153
On the Guide(s) to the Discovery of the Route to the Principle of Causation — 153
The house, the ship, and irreversibility — 154

The nature of the principle of the Second Analogy	157
Synthetic and *a priori*	157
Constitutive versus regulative	158
Objects of representations	160
Object of Experience Strategies	162
Bibliography	167
Index	173

Acknowledgments

I would like to thank Lee Brown, Charlie Kielkopf, George Pappas, and Ralf Meerbote for their helpful comments on the philosophical predecessors to some sections of this book. I would like to thank the anonymous referee for the *Journal of the History of Philosophy* who back in 1993 forced me to begin to come to grips with my position on the nature of the necessity involved in Kant's causal principle. I would like to thank the reviewers from the State University of New York Press: Anonymous Reviewer A and Eric Watkins (formerly Anonymous Reviewer B) whose extensive comments on the manuscript were invaluable in my attempt to make this a better book.

Portions of chapters 1 and 6 include material first published in my article "Kant's Answer to Hume: How Kant Should Have Tried to Stand Hume's Copy Thesis on Its Head," in the *British Journal for the History of Philosophy* 8(2) 2000: 207–24. Chapters 2 through 5 include material first published in my article "Objects of Representations and Kant's Second Analogy," in the *Journal of the History of Philosophy* 32, No. 3 (1994) 381–410. I am grateful to the editors of these journals for their kind permission to reproduce this material here.

I would like to thank my colleagues at Fairfield University, because without their support over the years I do not believe this book would have ever been written. I would like to thank Tony and Helen Chirakos as well as Pierluigi and Laurie Miraglia for their friendship throughout the preparation of this book. I would like to thank my parents Paul and Myra Bayne, because without their help I would never have become more than a *possible* object of representations. Finally, I would like to thank my wife Laura S. Keating for her sustained philosophical as well as emotional support—without her I would be a much less happy object of representations.

Introduction

Causation was an important topic for Kant. In fact, if we take him at his word, then perhaps, in terms of his order of discovery, it was the most important topic for him. Of course, Kant famously confessed that "the recollection of David Hume was just the thing which many years ago first interrupted my dogmatic slumber, and gave my investigations in the field of speculative philosophy a completely different direction" (*Prolegomena*, 260).[1] What was it in Hume's writings that affected Kant so powerfully? It was Hume's treatment of cause and effect. Kant tells us that "Hume started principally from a single but important concept of metaphysics, namely that of the *connection of cause and effect*" (*Prolegomena*, 257). Kant sees Hume as presenting us with a dilemma. From a pre-critical framework,[2] there were two ways we could think about the concept of cause and effect. On the one hand, the connection of cause and effect could be a conceptual connection produced through reason. In what should have been a startling result,[3] however, Kant tells us that

> Hume proved incontrovertibly that it would be completely impossible for reason to think such a combination *a priori* and from concepts, because this contains necessity. However, it cannot be seen how, because something exists, something else must also necessarily exist, and thus how the concept of such a connection can be introduced *a priori*. (*Prolegomena*, 257–58)

Kant's first step out of his dogmatic slumber was to realize that Hume was right. That is, concepts alone cannot give us any necessary connection between objects and so concepts alone cannot be the source of our concept of cause and effect. So the concept of cause and effect must come from somewhere else.

---

1. All translations from the *Prolegomena* are my own. The text used is from *Werke* Volume III, ed. Wilhelm Weischedel (Wiesbaden: Insel-Verlag, 1956), however the page number references are to the standard page numbers of volume IV of *Kants gesammelte Schriften*, ed. Königlichen Preußischen Akademie der Wissenschaften (Berlin: Walter de Gruyter & Co., 1902).
2. That is to say, the philosophical framework shared by all thinkers before Kant developed his new philosophical framework as first presented in the *Critique of Pure Reason*.
3. I say *should have been* a startling result here because Kant does not believe others were startled by Hume's conclusion because they did not actually understand Hume's conclusion. In this regard Kant particularly mentions Reid, Oswald, Beattie, and Priestly. See *Prolegomena*, 258–59.

So what is the other horn of the dilemma? Kant puts this quite colorfully. He tells us since reason cannot produce the connection of cause and effect through concepts, then this, in turn, led Hume to conclude

> that reason is altogether deceived with regard to this concept, which she falsely thinks of as her own child, yet it would be nothing other than a bastard of imagination that, impregnated through experience, brought certain representations under the law of association, and substituted a subjective necessity arising from it, i.e., habit, for an objective [necessity] from understanding [*Einsicht*]. (*Prolegomena*, 258)

Although Kant recognizes the force of Hume's conclusion that it is only through the force of habit that we are able to make the connection between objects, he is simply unwilling to accept this conclusion. This is Kant's second step out of his dogmatic slumber.

Now, he may be making progress, but Kant realized that he still needed to find a way to solve Hume's problem. With this in mind, he set out to determine whether Hume's problem was unique. That is, whether the concept of causation was the only one subject to Hume's criticisms. Kant tells us that he quickly realized it was not unique at all. For he

> soon found that the concept of the connection of cause and effect is by far not the only one through which the understanding thinks *a priori* the connection of things, but rather that metaphysics consists entirely of this. (*Prolegomena*, 260)

This of course does not solve anything. On the contrary, there is a clear sense in which this just makes things worse. From a pre-critical framework, this would simply subject *all* of metaphysics to a generalized version of Hume's dilemma concerning cause and effect. Kant quickly realized that since through concepts alone, reason cannot make *any* connections between objects *a priori*, then this generalized version of the dilemma stands with full force and so this leaves him with only the other horn of the dilemma. Just like Hume, he would be forced to regard "all supposed *a priori* principles of our understanding to be imaginary" and forced to find "that they are nothing but a habit arising from experience and its laws" (A765/B793).[4] This of course Kant was unwilling to do.

---

4. For quotations from the *Critique of Pure Reason (Kritik der reinen Vernunft)* I have consulted both the Raymund Schmidt edition (Hamburg: Felix Meiner Verlag, 1993) and the Wilhelm Weischedel edition (Wiesbaden: Insel Verlag, 1956), although I give only the standard academy pagination from *Kants gesammelte Schriften*, ed. Königlichen Preußischen Akademie der Wissenschaften. (Berlin: Walter de Gruyter & Co., 1902). All translations are my own.

Introduction

In some ways we can think of Kant's refusal to subject all of metaphysics to such humean conclusions to be the final step in his waking from dogmatic slumber. For it is this refusal that ultimately leads to Kant's revolutionary changes. If Kant refuses to accept either horn of the dilemma, then what options are left? The only option is to attack the framework that is presupposed by the dilemma. That is, in order for Kant to be able to vindicate metaphysics, then rather than simply accept the pre-critical framework on which the only two types of cognition are *a priori* reasoning based solely on concepts and habitual connections based on experience, he must reject it and develop a new framework. This new framework must contain a third alternative for cognition—an alternative that allows for the possibility of *a priori* cognition that is not based solely on concepts. That is to say, this revolutionary new framework must enable us to explain how *synthetic a priori* cognitions are possible. Spelling out this new framework and explaining how synthetic *a priori* cognitions are possible is one plausible way to describe the main task of Kant's *Critique of Pure Reason*. Now, although the concept that got things started must give up center stage to the more general investigation of how synthetic *a priori* cognition is possible, as a synthetic *a priori* concept of metaphysics, the concept of causation will still have its place within the framework of synthetic *a priori* cognition that Kant develops. This is where this book comes into the picture.

In the *Critique of Pure Reason* the main place we look for Kant's views on causation is in the Second Analogy. It is important to keep in mind, however, that although the Second Analogy may be the main place Kant writes about causation in the first *Critique,* it is not the only place. Of course, Kant writes about causation in works other than the *Critique of Pure Reason* as well. This is significant, because it is important not to regard the Second Analogy as the be-all and end-all with regard to Kant's views on causation. Although in this book I will focus mainly on the Second Analogy, the completion of Kant's theory of causation will require us on a number of occasions to investigate important texts from later in the first *Critique* as well as crucial passages from Kant's *Critique of Judgment*. We must remember that the Second Analogy is one piece that must fit into the broader context of Kant's critical philosophy. Kant's attempted proof of the principle of causation in the Second Analogy is certainly the first part of his views on causation, but it is not until we investigate the broader context that we get the completion of his theory of causation.[5] We do, however, need to begin with this first part, so it is time to turn our attention to the Second Analogy.

The Second Analogy contains Kant's attempt to prove the principle of causation. It should not be surprising that there is disagreement concerning

---

5. For more on this point see the section "Principles of Understanding and Principles of Reason" in chapter 1 as well as the second half of chapter 5.

the success of Kant's attempted proof—that is, whether or not it truly amounts to a successful proof of the causal principle. After all, evaluations of Kant's proof have run the gamut from its being considered the crown jewel of his critical philosophy to its being considered "one of the most spectacular examples of the *non-sequitur* which are to be found in the history of philosophy."[6] On the other hand, what should be surprising, I think, is that there is even a great deal of disagreement over the exact nature of the principle Kant attempts to prove. That is, not only do commentators disagree about whether Kant's proof is successful, they even disagree over what it is that Kant is trying to prove. Since we cannot even agree on the nature of what Kant is trying to prove, I think it will now come as no surprise that commentators cannot even agree about the exact nature of Kant's intended proof strategy for the causal principle. When we put these three disagreements together what we find is that we can't agree whether Kant successfully proved, by whatever method he was trying to use, whatever it was he was trying to prove. This certainly calls for some clarification. So the nature of Kant's causal principle, the nature of his proof for this principle, and the status of his intended proof are three of the main topics I examine in this book.

When we think about the nature of Kant's causal principle in the Second Analogy, there are two main things to be clear about. The first is that the Second Analogy is not a self-contained section of the *Critique of Pure Reason*. It stands in complex relationships of dependence with the sections that come before it in the first *Critique,* so we must pay careful attention to the context in which the Second Analogy appears. If we take it out of this context and treat the Second Analogy as if it were a stand-alone text, it will be extremely difficult to achieve a proper understanding of the nature of the principle for which Kant intends to argue. The Second Analogy's context within the *Critique of Pure Reason,* will be one of the main subjects of chapter 1.

The second thing we need to be clear about with regard to the nature of the causal principle concerns a distinction Kant develops in the "Appendix to the transcendental dialectic" in the first *Critique* and in the *Critique of Judgment*. This is the distinction Kant draws between constitutive principles of understanding and regulative principles of reason. Each type of principle plays an important role in Kant's critical philosophy, but each type of principle serves a specific purpose and so has its own unique set of requirements. The causal principle in the Second Analogy is supposed to be a constitutive principle of understanding. Once we realize this, we must be vigilant in resisting the common temptation to include features in this causal principle that would only be appropriate if it were a regulative principle of reason. This

---

6. Arthur O. Lovejoy, "On Kant's Reply to Hume," reprinted in *Kant: Disputed Questions,* ed. Moltke S. Gram (Chicago: Quadrangle Books, 1967), 303.

topic will be first discussed in chapter 1, but it will also come up at numerous other points throughout the book.

When we turn from the nature of the causal principle to the nature of Kant's intended proof for that principle, we will find that the key to understanding the nature of his proof is his discussion of objects of representations. Ordinary physical objects (such as a house, or a ball) are standard examples of objects of representations. In the Second Analogy Kant makes it clear that he holds events (such as a ship floating downstream or water freezing) to be objects of representations as well. We will see that it is through his investigation into the requirements for something's being an object of representations combined with his realization that events are objects of representations that Kant is able to develop his proof for the causal principle.

Once we make clear the emphasis Kant places on the consequences of his taking events to be objects of representations, then we will see that any interpretation of his proof for the causal principle that does not take this as the basis of his argument cannot be correct. Four standard interpretations of Kant's proof that fail for this reason are those that take the basis for his argument to be either (1) the distinction between veridical representations and dreams, or (2) the criterion we use in order to determine whether or not what we have perceived are successive or coexistent states, or (3) the ability to determine the temporal positions of distinct events in relation to one another, or (4) the requirements for the justification and/or knowledge that a particular event occurred. The nature of Kant's proof will be the main topic in chapters 3, 4, and 5.

Finally, when we come to think about the status of Kant's proof, one of the main things we often worry about takes us back to where we began this introduction—that is, to Hume's problem. It was the recollection of Hume's views about the connection of cause and effect that woke Kant from his dogmatic slumber. So even though Kant's project quickly became much bigger than the initial dilemma about the origin of cause and effect, it still seems legitimate to ask whether his proof of the causal principle constitutes an answer to Hume's skepticism concerning causation. In chapter 1 we will see that Kant correctly understood the nature of Hume's doubts about causation and we will introduce Kant's intended answer to Hume. In chapter 6, after we have examined Kant's argument for the causal principle, we will then be in a position to resume our evaluation of Kant's answer to Hume. After some interesting complications we will find, once we correctly understand Kant's proof of the causal principle, that Kant has available to him an answer Hume would have to accept in order to remain consistent with two of his own fundamental philosophical principles.

Chapter One

Relationships

In this chapter I will deal with relationships. In particular, I will examine five relationships that are important for preparing the ground for the treatment of the Second Analogy proper. The first is the one between concepts and intuitions. In particular we will focus on the worries about the applicability of concepts (the pure concepts in particular) to sensible intuition that Kant expresses in the Schematism Chapter. In order to properly understand the nature of the principle of the Second Analogy we must heed the lesson of the Schematism Chapter.

The second is the relationship between the Transcendental Deduction and the Principles of Understanding. The Principles of Understanding do not stand on their own. Instead they fit as an integral part of a whole task whose other main part is the Transcendental Deduction. In order to properly understand the principles, then, we must have some understanding of how they are connected to the task of the deduction of the categories.

The third relationship I will examine is the relationship between principles of understanding and principles of reason. Since Kant utilizes both types of principles in his work, then in order to put things in the proper context, we need to be clear about the distinction between these two types. We also must be clear about which type of principle the Second Analogy is.

The fourth relationship is the relationships we find within an analogy. The Second Analogy is one of the three principles named analogies. Kant tells us there is a reason for this name and in this third section I will examine his reasons for calling them analogies.

The final relationship that must be discussed is the relationship between Kant and Hume. When dealing with the Second Analogy it is easy to overemphasize the importance of the relationship between Kant and Hume. The

Second Analogy is often regarded as the central text in which Kant attempted to answer Hume's skepticism concerning the causal principle, so naturally the relationship between Kant and Hume will be important when dealing with the Second Analogy. We should be clear, however, about two interrelated things. First, the Second Analogy alone cannot stand as a complete answer to Hume's position on the causal principle.[1] The Second Analogy itself is not a self-contained argument. The argument of the Second Analogy, especially when viewed as an answer to Hume, relies on crucial conclusions from other sections of the *Critique*. Secondly, the Second Analogy is more than simply a passage that Kant intended as an answer to Hume. The Second Analogy has a systematic role to play in the *Critique* as a whole. Overemphasizing its role as an answer to Hume tends to obscure this important role.

CONCEPTS AND INTUITIONS

The Schematism, along with the Metaphysical Deduction, is one of the most maligned sections of the first *Critique*. The Schematism Chapter, however, is an important one for Kant. According to Kant the Schematism makes possible the transition from the Pure Concepts of Understanding (categories) to the Principles of Pure Understanding.[2] Some commentators, however, believe that the distinction between categories and principles is artificial and unnecessary. Since this distinction seems to be Kant's reason for developing the Schematism in the first place, some argue that the Schematism too can be set aside as artificial and unnecessary. I argue, however, that the Schematism is far from being artificial or unnecessary. Instead it is best seen as a requirement of Kant's general theory of concepts.[3] Kant develops this theory as an alternative that he takes to be more plausible than the theories of either the Rationalists (as typified by Leibniz) or the Empiricists (as typified by Hume). Unfortunately, the Schematism's role in this important project is easily overlooked because of the often confusing way Kant expresses his task in the opening four paragraphs of the Schematism Chapter.

---

1. Of course it should also be clear that the Second Analogy cannot stand alone as Kant's resolution of his general disagreement with Hume. The scope of Kant's criticisms of Hume go way beyond Hume's views on causation. Of course Kant's criticisms of Hume's position on the status of the causal principle are *part* of his disagreement with Hume. Kant did believe that Hume's mistake with regard to causation was symptomatic of the shortcomings involved with Hume's empiricism. So the criticisms of Hume's position on causation will be an important part of the overall criticism of Hume's position, but they cannot be the whole story.
2. For more on the difference between categories and principles see the section titled "The transcendental deduction and the principles" later in this chapter (p. 13ff).
3. I say general theory of concepts here in order to indicate that it is not just something he invents to deal with pure concepts. Instead, as we shall see below, it is something that must be utilized for all concepts.

Kant's introduction to the problem of the Schematism and his introductory solution

At the beginning of the Schematism Kant introduces a problem that he suggests poses a threat to the task of the Analytic of Principles. The problem develops out of Kant's brief explanation of the general procedure through which one could find out whether some concept has application to experience (i.e., appearances). Kant tells us in the Schematism that we would do this by showing that some object (or objects) is (are) subsumed under the concept. That is, we must show that what is *conceptually* represented in a concept is *intuitively* represented in an object (A137/B176). Now, in order for this to be done, says Kant, "in all subsumption of an object under a concept, the representation of the former must be *homogeneous*[4] with the latter" (A137/B176). Kant's example of how this works involves the concept of a plate and the concept of a circle. Kant tells us that "the empirical concept of a *plate* has homogeneity with the pure geometrical concept of a *circle*" (A137/B176). This is so, Kant writes, because "the roundness that is thought in the former can be intuited in the latter" (A137/B176).[5] The problem is supposed to be, however, that this general procedure for subsuming objects under concepts will not work with the pure concepts of understanding.

For we must remember that the pure concepts of understanding are special sorts of concepts for Kant. Unlike empirical concepts, pure concepts (categories) cannot *all by themselves* be applied to appearances. For the

> pure concepts of understanding are, in comparison with empirical intuitions (indeed with sensible intuitions in general), quite heterogenous[6] and can never be met with in any intuition.... For no one will say that a category, e.g., causality, could also be intuited through sense and is contained in appearance. (A137–3/B176–77)

So, how do we show that the pure concepts apply to appearances? Well, Kant claims we need to find some third thing that can mediate between the pure concepts and appearances. That is, something that is homogeneous with both the pure concepts and with appearances. Kant believes this third thing to be time. (A138/B177) So, by relating the pure concepts to time, they can then be related through time to appearances. The vehicle through which the pure concepts are related to time is the Schematism. So, according to Kant, it is

---

4. *gleichartig*—"*gleichartig*" in all its forms will be translated by some form of "homogeneous."
5. I should note that I do not in any way intend to suggest that I think Kant's illustration here is very helpful in making clear the nature of subsumption.
6. *ungleichartig*—"*ungleichartig*" in all its forms will be translated by some form of "heterogeneous."

possible to show, in the Analytic of Principles, that the individual categories have application (let alone necessary application) to experience only if the Schematism is utilized. So, the need for the Schematism, according to Kant's introduction, seems to arise because of the special heterogeneity of the pure concepts of understanding and sensible intuitions.

Kant's true task in the Schematism

In the introduction to the Schematism, Kant focuses on the heterogeneity pure concepts are supposed to have with sensible intuitions, but we must not let that distract us from the bigger purpose lurking in the background. That is, in the Schematism Kant will be concerned with solving the problem of the applicability of not just the pure concepts, but of *all* concepts to sensible intuition. The application of pure concepts will turn out to be just a special case of the more general applicability problem. Perhaps the most important thing that gets obscured in all this is that it is because Kant has developed a new treatment of concepts that there is an applicability problem in the first place. The theories of concepts Kant rejects (i.e., those of Leibniz and Hume) have no applicability problem. It is only because Kant rejects their theories that, on the one hand, the applicability problem becomes an issue at all and, on the other hand, that the Schematism must be developed in order to solve the applicability problem created by Kant's theory of concepts.

To make the case for this position, there are three things that must be spelled out: First, we need to examine the theories of concepts utilized by Leibniz and Hume. Second, we need to examine Kant's rejection of their theories and see how this leads to there being an applicability problem. Finally, we must figure out how the Schematism is supposed to be utilized in order to solve the applicability problem. Once these have been spelled out we will be in a position to explain why this is important for Kant's proofs of the Principles of Understanding.

Leibniz

According to the view attributed to Leibniz by Kant and a number of commentators,[7] concepts have a real homogeneity with perceptions. Concepts and

---

7. Whether or not Leibniz actually held the view that has been attributed to him remains, in my mind, an open question. As far as I can see Leibniz's writing on this matter does not provide us with any clear verdict one way or the other. Kant seems to attribute such a view to Leibniz in a number of places, but two examples are in § 8 in the Transcendental Aesthetic (A42ff/B59ff) and in the Appendix (The amphiboly of the concepts of reflection) to the Transcendental Analytic (A260ff/B316ff). Among the commentators who attribute such a view to Leibniz are Paton (see "Kant on the errors of Leibniz," in *Kant Studies Today,* ed. L. W. Beck [La Salle, Ill.: Open Court, 1969], 72–87) and Kemp Smith (see his *A Commentary to Kant's Critique of Pure Reason* [New York: The Humanities Press, 1950], 600–606).

perceptions are homogeneous in the sense that they are ultimately the same type of thing as each other. Perceptions are for Leibniz simply confused concepts. That is,

> sense experience, in its intrinsic nature, is nothing but pure thought. Such thought, owing to the inexhaustible wealth of its conceptual significance, so confuses the mind which thus generates it, that only by prolonged analysis can larger and larger portions of it be construed into the conceptual judgments which have all along constituted its sole content. And in the process, space, time and motion lose all sensuous character, appearing in their true nature as orders of relation which can be adequately apprehended only in conceptual terms.[8]

It should be clear that Kant cannot accept such a view concerning the relation of concepts and intuitions. One of Kant's most fundamental assertions is that "experience contains two very heterogeneous elements, namely, a *matter* for cognition from the senses and a certain *form*, to order it, from the inner source of pure intuition and thought" (A86/B118). Intuitions and concepts are, according to Kant, the two distinct necessary elements of all of our cognition. The difference between these two elements "does not merely concern their form, as being clear or confused, but rather it concerns their source and content" (A44/B61–62). Intuitions arise from our sensibility, while concepts arise from our understanding. Sensibility, for Kant, is the capacity we have that enables us to become aware of objects. Understanding, on the other hand, is the capacity we have that enables our awareness of objects to be organized. Neither sensibility nor understanding can perform the function that is performed by the other. No matter how clear and distinct our intuitions are they can never function as concepts. No matter how confused and indistinct our thinking is concepts can never function as intuitions.

Hume

For Hume, ideas and impressions are genuinely similar to each other. They are similar in two main ways. First of all, both ideas and impressions are imagistic—that is, both impressions and ideas can be thought of as being a type of picture.[9] The difference between these "consists in the degrees of

---

8. Kemp Smith, *Commentary*, 605.
9. John Yolton is a commentator who argues against this traditional view of impression and ideas. Yolton argues, in "Hume's Ideas," in *Hume Studies* volume VI number 1 (April 1980) that although ideas are "exact representations" of impressions, ideas need not be likened to images or pictures. This is clearly a minority position, however.

force and liveliness, with which they strike upon the mind."[10] Impressions enter the mind with the "most force and violence," while ideas are "the faint images" of impressions.[11] According to Hume, ideas are similar to impressions in a second way as well. Each idea is a copy of some set of impressions. In this vein, Hume writes that the contents of the mind are doubled. What first appears in the mind as an impression is then duplicated in the mind as an idea. According to Hume all impressions and ideas are either simple or complex. Simple impressions and ideas are atomic. That is, they cannot be resolved into a collection of simpler impressions or ideas. All complex impressions can be resolved into collections of simple impressions and all complex ideas can be resolved into collections of simple ideas. According to Hume, all simple ideas exactly resemble simple impressions. That is, the content of a simple idea is an exact copy of the content of some simple impression. Since each complex idea can be resolved into some set of simple ideas,[12] and each simple idea is an exact copy of some simple impression, it follows that the content of a complex idea is an exact copy of the content of some *set* of simple impressions. So, ideas are similar to impressions in that each idea has the same content as some set of impressions.[13]

Kant, however, can accept neither that concepts have the same content as some set of intuitions nor that concepts and intuitions are both imagistic. Kant cannot accept that concepts have the same content as some set of intuitions, because, as we have seen above, according to Kant the difference between concepts and intuitions "does not merely concern their form, as being clear or confused, but rather it concerns their source and content" (A44/B61–62). Sensibility and understanding perform two different functions, both of which are necessary for cognition. Our intuitions provide the specific and determinate content in our cognition, while a concept "is always something general, and that serves as a rule" for unifying representations (A106, see also A69/B94). If a concept, however, has the same content as some set of intuitions, then its content would be *specific* and hence it would not be something general and so it could not serve as a rule for unifying

---

10. David Hume, *A Treatise of Human Nature*, Second Revised Edition by P. H. Nidditch (Oxford: At The Clarendon Press, 1978), Bk. I, pt. I, § I, 1. Henceforth cited simply as *Treatise*.
11. *Treatise* Bk. I, pt. I, § I, 1.
12. At *Treatise* Bk. I, pt. I, § I, 4. Hume writes that "we find, that all simple ideas and impressions resemble each other; and as the complex are formed from them, we may affirm in general, that these two species of perception are exactly correspondent." In the *Enquiry* (*An Enquiry Concerning Human Understanding*, ed. Eric Steinberg [Indianapolis: Hackett Publishing Company, 1977]) Hume writes that "when we analyse our thoughts or ideas, however, compounded or sublime, we always find, that they resolve themselves into such simple ideas as were copied from a precedent feeling or sentiment" (§ II, 11).
13. Hume, *Treatise*, 2–4. See also § II of the *Enquiry*, 9–13.

representations. Since this is precisely the role concepts play, according to Kant, then he could not consistently hold that concepts have the same content as some set of intuitions.

Now, this can also be turned very quickly into an argument that Kant cannot allow both intuitions and concepts to be imagistic. Kant makes it clear that he believes that images are not themselves general, and thus in the Schematism Chapter Kant writes:

> No image *[gar kein Bild]* of a triangle would ever be adequate to the concept of a triangle in general. For it would not attain the generality of the concept, which makes it valid for all triangles, . . . Still even less does an object of experience or an image of the same ever attain the empirical concept. (A141/B180)

So according to Kant, if a concept were an image, then its content would be specific and not general at all. If a concept were not something general, then it could not serve as a rule for unifying representations. Since this is precisely the role concepts play, according to Kant, he cannot consistently hold that concepts, like intuitions, are imagistic.

Leibniz, Hume, Kant, and applicability

The important thing to notice is that on both Leibniz's and Hume's theories when it comes to apply concepts to sense perceptions we end up connecting two things of the same type. That is, in Leibniz's case, once we break sense perceptions down, we are ultimately comparing one concept (or set of concepts) to another. In Hume's case we end up comparing one image (or set of images) to another. The formats or structures of both things we are connecting are of the same type, so there is no special problem of the applicability of one to the other. When we turn to Kant's theory of concepts, however, it is a different story.

In general, according to Kant, concepts serve as rules that are used to organize (unify) our thought. Sensible intuitions, however, can be thought of as being imagistic (pictorial) representations. Now, when the question of application arises (Which intuitions, if any, are subsumed under this concept? Which concept[s] does this intuition fall under?) we may be at a loss for direction. Intuitively we might think that I must somehow compare some concept to some sensible intuition in order to see whether the content of the concept, which is represented discursively in the concept, stands in the appropriate relation to the content of some intuition, which is represented pictorially in the intuition. Yet this may not be so easy. For when I try to compare some particular concept with some particular intuition, I am not exactly sure what to do. If I were comparing one intuition to another intuition or one concept to another concept, then I can see how to proceed—for the things I am comparing are of the same type. When I am asked to compare a discursive representation to an intuitive one, the task is not so easy. Yet there must be some way to make this comparison if we hold the three following claims (as Kant does): (1) sensible intuitions and concepts are two distinct types of mental representation, (2) it is sometimes the case that what is discursively and in a general way represented in a concept is correctly correlated with what is pictorially and concretely represented in some sensible intuition, and (3) we can tell when it is the case that a concept is correctly correlated with some sensible intuition.

Kant believes that this comparison can be and is in fact made via a general method of transforming the content of the rule for the organization of our thought (a concept) into something with pictorial content (an image). It is, then, the image that was developed from the concept that can be compared directly with the sensible intuition. This role of translator is precisely the role Kant believes is filled by schemata. The schema of a concept is the "representation of a general procedure of the imagination for providing a concept with its image" (A140/B179–80).

In the introduction to the Schematism Chapter Kant seems to imply that it is *only* pure concepts that require the services of schemata. There he implies that empirical concepts can be *directly* applied to sensible iintuitions while pure concepts cannot. Pure concepts can be applied to sensible intuitions, but not directly. That is, pure concepts require an *indirect* method of application. This indirect method of application requires the use of what Kant calls a schema. It is the schema that "mediates the subsumption of appearances under the category" (A139/B178).

It is only a few paragraphs later, however, that we come to realize Kant's real position is that pure sensible concepts (i.e., mathematical concepts) and empirical concepts require the use of a schema as well. Kant tells us that "in fact it is not images of objects, but schemata that lie at the foundation of our pure sensible concepts" (A140–41/B180). "Still even less," Kant continues,

> does an object of experience or an image of the same ever attain the empirical concept, but rather this is always directly related to the schema of the imagination, as a rule for the determination of our intuition, in accordance with a certain general concept. (A141/B180)

So it turns out that neither mathematical concepts nor empirical concepts stand in immediate relation to sensible intuitions, but like pure concepts they too are "always directly related to the schema of the imagination" (A141/B180).

Schemata for mathematical and empirical concepts are rules for producing spatial images that are correlated with the concept. It is this spatial image, derived from the concept through its schema, that can then be directly compared with sensible intuitions. Schemata for pure concepts, on the other hand, are not rules for producing spatial images. For "the schema of a pure concept of understanding is something that cannot be brought into any image at all" (A142/B181). Rather than being correlated with a spatial image, a pure concept is correlated with a transcendental time determination. That is, the pure concepts are correlated with distinct temporal structures or relationships—*temporal* images if you like.[14]

In the last few sections we have seen that in the *Critique of Pure Reason* Kant is committed to an explanatory account of concepts that is different than the account given by either Leibniz or Hume. Concepts and intuitions are distinct types of mental representations and neither can be reduced to the other—while intuitions are imagistic, concepts are rules for the organization of thought. In the Schematism Chapter itself we find Kant doing two main things toward developing his theory of concepts. First, he argues that thinking of concepts as being imagistic is inadequate.[15] Second, and more importantly, he *sketches* a solution to a problem that seems to arise because of his theory of concepts: the problem of the application of concepts to intuitions.[16]

The importance of the Schematism

So why is all of this important? There are two main reasons. The first has to do with the criticism raised at the very beginning of this section. That is, the criticism that since the Schematism was devised simply to make the artificial and unnecessary transition from categories to principles, then this makes the Schematism itself artificial and unnecessary. Once it has been shown, however, that the Schematism plays a crucial role in the development of Kant's

---

14. It may be worth noting here that this distinction between the product of the schema of a pure concept and the product of the schema of an empirical or mathematical concept is what can provide us with a way of technically preserving Kant's distinction between concepts that have or lack homogeneity with sensible intuitions. If an image can be produced through a concept's schema, then this concept is said to be homogeneous with sensible intuitions. If no image can be produced through a concept's schema, then the concept is said to be heterogeneous with sensible intuitions.
15. Note that here in the Schematism Chapter Kant does not spend any time arguing against the Leibnizian side of this coin. That is, in the Schematism Chapter itself Kant does not argue against the claim that sensible intuitions can ultimately be reduced to concepts.
16. For more on the reasons for using the word *sketches,* see the subsection "A Problem with Kant's Account of the Schematism" below p. 10ff.

theory of concepts, this criticism is easily deflected. For regardless of what we think about the legitimacy of Kant's distinction between categories and principles, given Kant's theory of concepts, the Schematism is needed in order to make the application of concepts to intuitions possible.

A second reason this is important is that in seeing the Schematism as presenting a crucial aspect of Kant's theory of concepts we should think of Kant as arguing for a crucial premise in his criticism of Hume.

Kant has argued that thinking of concepts as being images of what is given through sensation is not an adequate way to think of a concept. This is not even an adequate way of thinking of our empirical or mathematical concepts. In the case of empirical or mathematical concepts we can get by with this mistaken conception, because with these a spatial image can always be produced from our concepts via schemata. So, there will always be some spatial image that can be confusedly taken to be the concept itself. So when we come to the question of the applicability of empirical or mathematical concepts to experience we will be able to answer this question successfully, because we will always end up comparing the spatial image that can be derived through the schema of the concept to sensible intuitions. It will not make any *practical* difference that we have mistaken this derived spatial image for the concept itself.

With the pure concepts, however, we cannot even get by with this mistaken conception, because no spatial image can be produced from the pure concepts. So when it comes time to determine whether or not pure concepts have (or must have) application to sensible intutions, then since there will not be any spatial image that we can compare to our sensible intuitions and because we do not recognize the need for schemata we will not be able to determine what we are supposed to look for. That is, in the Schematism Chapter we should see Kant are arguing that Hume *could not have realized* that the pure concepts have (or must have) application to sensible intuitions, because he failed to realize the necessity of something like schemata. For, according to Kant, it is only after we come to accept this more adequate theory of concepts along with the Schematism that it even becomes *possible* for us to properly determine whether or not the pure concepts have application (let alone necessary application) to sensible intuitions.

A problem with Kant's account of the Schematism

Earlier, I said that in connection with the development of what he took to be a more adequate theory of concepts, in the Schematism Chapter we find Kant doing two main things. First, he argues that thinking of concepts as being imagistic is inadequate. Second, he *sketches* a solution to a problem that seems to arise because of this new treatment of concepts: the problem of the application of concepts to intuitions. I use the word *sketches* here partly to highlight the limited success of the Schematism Chapter with regard to this second task. We cannot regard Kant's solution to the problem of the application of concepts to intuitions as being truly successful, because Kant does not provide us with all of the necessary details of this process of schematizing. He argues that there must be such things as schemata if concepts are going to be applicable to intuitions. Kant does tell us that schematizing is done through the imagination, but the particular process of the imagination involved will differ depending on the type of concept involved. In the case of empirical concepts he tells us that an image is produced from the schema and it "is a product of the empirical ability *[Vermögens]* of the productive imagination" (A142/B181). With mathematical concepts, the schema "signifies a rule of the synthesis of imagination with regard to pure shapes in space," and "is a product and as it were a monogram of the pure imagination *a priori*" (A141–42/B180–81). With pure concepts of understanding, the schema is

> the pure synthesis, . . . which the category expresses, and is a transcendental product of the imagination, which concerns the determination of inner sense in general, according to the conditions of its form (time) in regard to all representations, in so far as these are to be connected *a priori* in one concept in accordance with the unity of apperception. (A142/B181)

Unfortunately, when it comes time to spell out the details of how images, pure shapes in space, or transcendental time determinations are produced from concepts via schemata Kant waves his hands and mentions something about the Schematism being "a hidden art in the depths of the human soul" (A141/B181).

In the case of mathematical concepts and some empirical concepts the schematizing process doesn't *seem* like a big mystery. In fact, Kant's first example of placing "five points next to one another . . . . . ," (A140/B179) as an illustration of the method by which we produce an image for the number five is reassuring, but in reality I think this only gives us a false sense of security. Even in this case Kant does not spell out any of the details of the procedure for producing some particular image from the concept of five. Something about this example seems familiar to us, so the lack of detail doesn't really bother us and so more importantly the lack of detail doesn't lead us to question our understanding of this process of schematizing. The regularity with which we actually connect things such as the concept of five with five dots in a row, or the concept of a triangle with a triangle, or the concept of dog with dogs and/or images of dogs (to complete Kant's trio of examples), is the reason we don't find this process of schematizing to be any big mystery. The fact that we regularly make connections of this sort, however, doesn't mean we really understand or can explain the details of the schematizing process. We should not let our *ability* to schematize fool us into thinking we *understand* or *can explain* the schematizing process.

Perhaps some less standard cases of empirical concepts will illustrate just how few details of the Schematism have been explained. For example, how do we deal with concepts such as "bark," "loud," or "whisper"? What will be the product of schematizing such concepts as these? Will it be a spatial image, will it be a temporal structure? Perhaps to deal with concepts such as these we will have to develop what we might call a sound image. Maybe even more troublesome are such empirical concepts as "intelligent," "stupid," "impatient," "friendly," "stolid," etc. I'm not sure we understand the details of schematizing sufficiently to even know where to begin with concepts such as these. It may be that the ability to schematize is "a hidden art in the depths of the human soul," but without understanding the details of this process of schematizing, how will we be able to determine in any given case that the schematizing has been done correctly? If we don't understand the details of schematizing and someone presents us with a schema candidate for a concept, then how will we know whether this schema is the correct one?

This worry becomes particularly acute when we realize it is not just a problem for empirical concepts, but it is a problem for any concept that requires the use of a schema. In other words, it is a problem for *all* concepts, since according to Kant, all concepts, whether they be mathematical, empirical, or pure, require the use of a schema. The point is, that without the details of the process of schematizing before us, how can we be sure that the schema someone provides for a concept is the right one? For our immediate purposes the truly important question is: without understanding the details of the schematizing process, then how can we be sure that the schemata Kant (or anyone else for that matter) provides for the pure concepts of understanding are the right ones?

The clear path to determining whether or not the proposed schemata for the pure concepts are correct is by way of the details of the process of schematizing. Once we understand the details of schematizing we can then proceed to show how this process generally applies to pure concepts. This will finally put us in a position to show how this leads to the particular formulation of the schema for each particular category.

Unfortunately, this is precisely what we do not find in the Schematism Chapter. In fact, Kant seems to sidestep the whole issue. When he is prepared to give the particular schemata for the pure concepts, Kant tells us that

> rather than our being held back by a dry and boring analysis of what would be required for transcendental schemata of pure concepts of the

understanding in general, we would prefer to present them according to the order of and in connection with the categories. (A142/B181)

Yet this "dry and boring analysis" is exactly what would be needed in order to justify the particular formulation of the schema for each pure concept. What we end up with instead is simply a list of the schemata for the pure concepts of the understanding without any argument for its correctness.

Given the importance of the Schematism for the formulation of the Principles of Understanding (as we will see below) and for laying some very basic groundwork for Kant's ability to respond to Hume's challenges (as we saw above and will return to below), this lack of argumentation for the specific formulations of the schemata can be disconcerting. In many respects it is similar to the situation we find in the Metaphysical Deduction, where with little or no argument Kant makes the crucial transition from the table of judgments to the table of categories. Here in the Schematism, with little or no argument, Kant makes the crucial transition from the table of categories to the list of schemata. Now of course this doesn't mean that Kant has made a mistake in his list of schemata, but it does mean that his list of schemata requires further justification.

The path for this justification is clear before us. On Kant's behalf we would have to spell out the details of the process of schematizing from the sketch he offers and then we would have to spell out how this applies in the case of the pure concepts of understanding. However, completely unlocking the mystery of the schematism is a very big task and one that goes far beyond the scope of this project. So unfortunately the justification for the particular schemata of the pure concepts will have to remain a promissory note rather than actual currency.

THE TRANSCENDENTAL DEDUCTION AND THE PRINCIPLES

In the Transcendental Aesthetic Kant believes he has shown that space and time are the pure *a priori* forms of sensible intuition, and that space and time are themselves pure *a priori* intuitions.

In the Metaphysical Deduction Kant believes he has shown that what takes place when various representations are united in a judgment is the same operation (or type of operation) that takes place when various representations are united, through a concept, in an intuition. It is, Kant claims, the understanding that performs this (these) task(s). This being the case, the table of judgments will correspond to another table—the table of concepts. That is, the table of the pure concepts of the understanding—the categories. Hence, based on the table of judgments we can discover the table of categories.

In the Transcendental Deduction Kant believes he has shown that a consciousness cannot be conscious of a representation unless that representation is unified—that is, the representation is one organized unit. It cannot be an unorganized set of various unconnected parts. Furthermore, Kant argues that a representation must get its unity from the understanding because there is no combination in representations apart from the understanding.[17] According to Kant, then, a representation gets its unity through the pure concepts of understanding (that is, the categories). The categories are what make a representation as an object of consciousness possible. An intuition is a particular type of representation and as such it must have unity. The intuition gets its unity through the pure concepts of the understanding. A sensible intuition is an intuition that we become conscious of through our sensibility. Sensible intuitions are still of course representations and as such they must have unity and this unity comes through the categories. Kant of course isn't interested in stopping here. It is a step in the right direction to show that all sensible intuitions are made possible through the categories, but ultimately it is not the sensible intuitions themselves, but the content of these sensible intuitions (that is, objects of experience) Kant is interested in. That is, Kant wants to show that all objects of experience are made possible only through the categories.

According to Kant the contents of human sensible intuitions are subject to the conditions of the pure forms of human sensibility—that is, space and time. So according to Kant it will turn out that the content of our sensible intuitions are objects in space and time. That is, our objects of experience are spatiotemporal objects. Must such objects of experience be subject to the categories? Well, Kant draws upon his conclusions from the Transcendental Aesthetic to prove that they must be. In the Aesthetic Kant has argued not only that space and time are the pure *forms* of human sensible intuition, but that space and time are also themselves *intuitions*. To be more precise, space and time are pure *a priori* intuitions. Given, as we saw above, that all intuitions are subject to the categories, space and time are themselves, as intuitions, also subject to the categories. Finally, since all objects of experience are subject to the conditions of space and time and space and time are in turn subject to the categories, objects of experience too are subject to the categories. That is, objects of experience are made possible only through the categories.[18]

---

17. See §15 of the B Deduction B129–31.
18. Of course, this is nothing more than a bare statement of Kant's task in the Transcendental Deduction. I make no pretense of giving any arguments for this statement. A significant discussion of Kant's transcendental deduction is in itself a monumental task and as such goes way beyond the scope of this book. For getting started the following works may be of some use. Dieter Henrich, "The Proof-structure of Kant's Transcendental Deduction," *Review of Metaphysics* (June 1969): 640–59; Henry E. Allison, *Kant's Transcendental Idealism* (New Haven: Yale University Press, 1983); Paul Guyer, *Kant and the Claims of Knowledge* (Cambridge: Cambridge University Press, 1987); Eckart Forster, ed., *Kant's Transcendental Deductions: the Three 'Critiques' and the 'Opus Postumum'* (Stanford: Stanford University Press, 1989; Paul Guyer, "The transcendental deduction of the categories," in *The Cambridge Companion to Kant*, ed. Paul Guyer, 123–60 (New York: Cambridge University Press, 1992).

What is the relationship between the categories and the Principles of Understanding? This question might also be put this way: what is the difference between the Transcendental Deduction of the categories and the transcendental proofs for the Principles of Understanding? One straightforward way to think of the difference between them is the level of abstraction. The principles are the concrete and the categories are the abstract. As Kant puts it just before he introduces the table of principles, "The table of categories gives us the entirely natural instructions for the table of principles, because these are nothing other than rules for the objective use of the former" (A161/B200). The categories make up the general framework that applies to all sensible intuition regardless of the specific nature of the sensibility involved. The principles make up the framework that applies to all sensible intuition of the spatiotemporal variety. With the deduction of the categories Kant has proven that objects of experience are possible only through the categories, but the specific nature of these objects is left undetermined. The nature of these objects will also depend on the type of sensibility a being has. So it is only once we combine the categorial framework with a form of sensibility that we can give specific details about the requirements for objects of experience. In the deduction Kant proves the categories are required for the possibility of experience, but with the principles collectively Kant is concerned with showing what is specifically required for experience of beings like us. In the principles what Kant will do is to explain the specific requirements for spatiotemporal experience (that is, the requirements for the kind of experience we have). In other words he will uncover the specific requirements for spatiotemporal objects (that is, the objects we are aware of through sensibility).

Of course this task does not begin completely anew with the table of the principles. As we saw in the previous section, it is in the Schematism Chapter where this work begins.[19] It is there where Kant gives us the transcendental schemata for the categories. In the principles Kant begins with these so-called schematized categories, formulates principles, and then develops transcendental proofs for each of the principles.

Since these are not the only type of principles Kant deals with, however, before moving toward a positive view of how this works for the particular principle we are concerned with, we first need to be clear about the

---

19. In fact we might even think Kant begins this task even earlier than in the Schematism Chapter. With the introduction of the second edition revisions of the Transcendental Deduction, it looks as if Kant has begun this task as early as in the second step of the deduction. There where he utilizes the dual nature of space and time (as both forms of intuition and pure *a priori* intuitions) Kant makes it clear he is concerned with our specific sensible intuition and not just sensible intuition in general. Nonetheless, even if it is clear as early as the second step of the B deduction that the categories are requirements specifically for spatiotemporal objects, it is not until the Schematism and principles that we get the specific details of these requirements.

general distinction between the type of principles we find here in the Transcendental Analytic of the *Critique of Pure Reason* and other types of principles Kant utilizes.

PRINCIPLES OF UNDERSTANDING AND PRINCIPLES OF REASON

In an investigation of the Second Analogy's causal principle, we need to be careful to draw a distinction between two types of principles that are utilized in Kant's critical philosophy. These two types are principles of understanding and principles of reason. Since these are different types of principles each with its own unique purpose and requirements, it is important to carefully distinguish between them so that we do not inadvertently attempt to impose the purpose and requirements of one type of principle on the other. We can see that a confusion of this sort is not so difficult to fall into when we realize that in particular cases both types of principles may be concerned with the same basic subject matter. What will set two such principles apart from each other will be the purposes for which they are formulated and the specific requirements in light of these purposes. So we will end up with two different principles that cover the same subject matter. So what are the purposes and requirements of these two separate types of principles? In short, the difference between them is that principles of understanding are constitutive principles while principles of reason are regulative principles.

The employment of the understanding is constitutive. When we are dealing with something that is required for the possibility of experience, such as the categories, this will be constitutive. As Kant puts it in the Appendix to the Transcendental Dialectic (A642ff/B670ff): "These dynamical laws[20] are admittedly constitutive in regard to *experience,* as they make possible *a priori* the *concepts* without which no experience takes place" (A 664/B692). The regulative use of reason, however, "is not a principle of the possibility of experience and the empirical cognition of objects of sense, consequently not a principle of understanding" (A509/B537). Instead, a regulative principle of reason is one that can be used as a guide for carrying out our investigations of experience. For example, Kant tells us it is through a regulative principle of reason that we come to suppose that comets have parabolic courses. Reason guides us to this conclusion through the principle that whatever explains the motions of the planets will also explain the motions of comets. More generally speaking, Kant says, we conclude that the motions of all celestial bodies are explained by the same principle (i.e., gravitation).[21]

---

20. These are the six principles of understanding under the headings of *Analogies of experience* and *Postulates of empirical thought in general.* See A160–62/B199–202.
21. See A663/B691.

Such principles are not empirical principles, but instead they are *a priori* principles. They clearly are not *constitutive a priori* principles, for they are not required for the possibility of experience. That is, experience would still be possible if the explanation of the motions of comets were not the same as the explanation of the motions of planets or more generally the explanation of the motions of one type of celestial object were different than the explanation of the motions of any other type of celestial object. If these principles are not constitutive, then what do they do? Kant tells us that these

> as synthetic *a priori* principles have objective but uncertain validity, and serve as a rule for possible experience, also in dealing with experience they may be used with good success as heuristic principles, still one cannot manage a transcendental deduction of them. (A663/B691)

In other words, although such principles are not prerequisites for experience (as constitutive principles are), they do legitimately serve as rules for guiding our research into and extending our cognition of experience. So, in the case of comets we are led to a proper understanding of their paths by utilizing the orbits of planets as our guide. That is, our investigation of comets is advanced by seeking for their paths according to the laws that explain the orbits of planets.

With a second case we can see a direct comparison of a particular principle of reason with what would be a constitutive principle dealing with the very same materials. In section eight of the Antinomy of Pure Reason, Kant discusses the regulative principle of pure reason in relation to the cosmological ideas, which were presented in the four antinomies. Here Kant calls the appropriate regulative principle of reason connected with the cosmological ideas the cosmological principle of totality. This principle

> is a principle of the greatest possible continuation and extension of experience, according to which no empirical boundary must be valid as an absolute boundary. Thus it is a principle of reason, which, as a *rule,* postulates what should be done by us in the regress and *does not anticipate,* what is given *in the object* itself before all regression. Therefore I call it a *regulative* principle of reason, where on the other hand the principle of the absolute totality of the series of conditions, as being given in the objects (the appearances) themselves, would be a constitutive cosmological principle. (A509/B537)

In this section[22] Kant uses the search for human ancestors as an example. When tracing back ancestors the rule of reason tells us no matter how far back we

---

22. See A511ff/B539ff.

have gone, we must always seek for a further ancestor. Kant tells us that in tracing ancestors "I can always go still further in the regression, because no member is empirically given as absolutely unconditioned, and thus a higher member may still always be admitted as possible" (A514/B542). That is, when we come to a particular ancestor there has been nothing in our experience to lead us to expect that this will be the absolutely first ancestor. We may not have a current record of this ancestor's parents, but the regulative principle of reason requires us to seek for her parents. This regulative principle cannot require that there *must* be further ancestors in this series, because with a regulative principle a series is not given in its entirety beforehand. We are given a particular member (or members) of the series and then through a regulative principle we are able to spell out the series only step by step indeterminately (or *possibly* infinitely) far back. With a constitutive principle, however, the series would be given in its entirety even before our step by step investigation of the series. Kant's first example here is the division of a body.

Kant tells us that a material body is contained within determinate boundaries and "consequently it is given in empirical intuition with all of its possible parts" (A513/B541). This means the completed series of parts is given prior to any step by step investigation of the series. Analogous to the search for a further ancestor, in the case of the division of parts of a body no part of this series is given as absolutely unconditioned. There is nothing in our experience that could lead us to expect that this particular part will be the absolutely first part of the division. That is, there is no empirical justification for accepting this part to be indivisible. So, just as at each stage we must inquire after further ancestors, here with each division we can inquire after further divisions. The difference is that here we may proceed constitutively. Not only is it always possible to inquire about further members of the division, it is certain that there will be further divisions. Kant tells us, when we are only given one member of a series "it is always *necessary to inquire* after more,"[23] but when an infinite series is given in its entirety (as it is with the division of a body), then it is "*necessary to find* more members of the series."[24] Kant tells us that a regulative principle of reason "cannot say *what the object is*, but only *how the empirical regression is to be conducted* in order to reach the complete concept of the object" (A510/B538).

If we take the principle concerning ancestors as constitutive, we would end up with a correlate of the first part of the antitheses of the First Antinomy[25] and hence it would be a constitutive cosmological principle. Such a

---

23. A514/B542; italics on "necessary" added.
24. A514/B542; italics on "necessary" added.
25. "The world has no beginning and no boundaries in space, but is infinite in regard to both time and space" (A427/B455).

principle would posit the entire series of ancestors along with all its possible parts as given in the object, hence the completed series of ancestors would be given prior to any step by step investigation of the series. In this case it would no longer be necessary to inquire after further ancestors, because since the entire series is given prior to the investigation of the series, there *must be* further members. Of course, there are differences here from what we had in the case of the divisibility of a body—the body is contained within precise boundaries and it is given in empirical intuition. These differences, however, are precisely the reason Kant finds constitutive principles of reason to be problematic. What we find with a cosmological principle of this sort is "a *constitutive principle* of reason for extending the concept of the sensible world beyond all possible experience" (A509/B537). The nullity of just such a principle, Kant tells us, he hopes to indicate through the distinction between constitutive and regulative principles "and thereby prevent, what otherwise unavoidably happens (through transcendental subreption), the attaching of objective reality to an idea that serves merely as a rule" (A509/B537).

If we are to avoid mistakenly taking regulative principles for constitutive ones, then we need to be clearer about the scope of these principles. In our case, since we will be focusing on the system of principles of understanding and the Second Analogy in particular, we must focus on the relationship of both types of principle to nature. That is, what will count as being constitutive of nature and what exactly will not be constitutive of nature? Of course, the easy answer is to say that the categories and principles of understanding are what Kant takes to be constitutive of nature and everything else would be regulative. This turns out not to be very helpful. It might be helpful if we already have a clear understanding of the nature of categories and principles of understanding, but a clear interpretation of principles of understanding (well, at least one of them anyway) is the very thing we are trying to achieve here. A clear interpretation of principles of understanding in large part itself depends on a clear understanding of Kant's distinction between constitutive and regulative principles. So, being clearer about what counts as constitutive of nature not only will help us avoid mistakenly taking a regulative principle for a constitutive one, but it will help serve as a basis for the correct interpretation of the principles of understanding. The *Critique of Judgment* contains a helpful discussion for this investigation.

In the third *Critique* Kant stresses the difference between what is required for nature and what is required for an *order* of nature. Those things required for nature are constitutive while those things required to produce an order of nature will be regulative. The constitutive things are again categories and principles—things that are required for the possibility of experience. Kant often calls these "universal *[allgemeiner]* laws of nature." In addition to this, understanding develops rules for explaining particular aspects of nature.

For example, one of the rules from the discussion on the paths of comets above: planets have circular orbits. These rules are ones we come to know through experience, but because of a further requirement, understanding "must think these rules as laws (i.e., as necessary)."[26] This further requirement is that understanding "also requires a certain order of nature in its particular rules"[27] (*CJ*,184). Again for an example, think of the discussion about the paths of comets: the paths of comets will be explained by the same principle that explains the orbits of planets. We cannot know before doing our research that the rule for comets is the same as (or akin to) the rule for planets, but we investigate on the presumption that it will be the same. Here in the third *Critique* Kant grounds this supposition on something stronger than its being useful for heuristic purposes:[28] He tells us that

> although understanding can determine nothing *a priori* in regard to these (objects), it must still, in order to investigate these empirical so-called laws, lay as a foundation for all reflection about nature an *a priori* principle, namely that according to these laws a discernable *[erkennbare]* order of nature is possible. (*CJ*, 184–85)

And again:

> This agreement of nature to our cognitive ability is presupposed *a priori* by the power of judgment for the purpose of its reflection on nature according to empirical laws, while at the same time the under-

---

26. *Critique of Judgment,* AK 184. All quotations from the *Critique of Judgment* are from the Vorländer edition (Hamburg: Felix Meiner Verlag, 1993), although I give only the academy pagination from volume 5. All translations are my own. Henceforth, I will cite this in the text as *CJ*.
27. Kant tells us, we must think of these particular rules as laws, "because otherwise no order of nature could be determined" (*CJ* 184).
28. Even in the passage from the *Appendix to the Transcendental Dialectic,* Kant has stronger justification in mind. Even there it is not *just* that such regulative principles are useful tools, but they are an integral part of the function of reason. Kant tells us that "to produce the unity of all possible empirical acts of the understanding is a business of reason, just as the understanding connects the diversity of appearances through concepts and brings it under empirical laws" (A664/B692). Further, as we saw in the passage from the Antinomy, the regulative principle is not optional. As with the series of ancestors Kant tells us it is necessary to inquire after more. Here reason tells us *"how the empirical regression is to be conducted* in order to reach the complete concept of the object" (A510/B538). Of course, saying that even in the first *Critique* Kant has stronger justification for a regulative principle of reason than its merely being useful still does not mean the justification is the same as we find in the third *Critique*—after all, Kant makes it clear in the first *Critique* that there are no transcendental deductions for regulative principles of reason.

standing objectively recognizes it as contingent, and only the power of judgment ascribes it to nature as transcendental purposiveness (in relation to the cognitive ability of the subject) because without this presupposition we would have no order of nature according to empirical laws, consequently no guide for an experience with all its diversity and investigation into it. (*CJ*, 185)

Our main concern here is with seeing how much (or how little) this principle of reason brings to the equation. Once we see which things fall under the scope of the regulative principle of reason, then we will have a good start at defining what falls under the scope of constitutive principles of understanding. That is, by seeing how far the regulative principle extends, we can see how much room is left for constitutive principles.[29] In short, the scope of the regulative principle of reason is far and wide.

Both the *comprehensibility* and *connectedness of experience* appear to fall under the scope of the regulative principle of reason. Even something as basic as that nature contains a hierarchy of species and genera falls under the scope of the regulative principle. So for example, Kahlua is a miniature pinscher, miniature pinschers are dogs, dogs are mammals, mammals are animals, or Boy is a parakeet, parakeets are parrots, parrots are birds, birds are animals. The constitutive principles of understanding do not guarantee that there will be hierarchies of species and genera in nature nor that if there are hierarchies they will be connected in the way these two are under a common genus. To the understanding such hierarchies and the connections between them are contingent and are only known empirically.[30] The second example Kant lists will be directly relevant for our discussion of the Second Analogy. Kant writes:

> [T]o our understanding it initially appears inevitable that for the specific variety of natural effects just as many different types of causality must be assumed, nevertheless they may stand under a small number of principles, with the search for these we have to occupy ourselves. (*CJ*, 185)

The constitutive principles of understanding do not guarantee that the force that causes the motion of De Chéseaux's comet of 1744, for example, is the

---

29. At this point this start toward a definition of the constitutive principles will be the best we can do. We can't positively define the constitutive principles without a thorough examination of the appropriate passages in the first *Critique*. By setting some ground rules, however, this negative definition will help immensely when we come to positively define the constitutive principles (well, again at least one of them—the causal principle of the Second Analogy) later on.
30. See *CJ*, 185.

same as the cause of the motion of any other body. It is only through regulative principles that we come to the

> unity of the cause of all laws of their motion (gravitation), from which we later expand our conquests, and also seek to explain all varieties and apparent deviations from these rules from the same principle, eventually even ... uniting the distant parts of, for us, an unlimited world system, that is connected through one and the same moving force. (A663/B691)

So it is not understanding, but the regulative principle of reason that allows us to say:

> Nature specifies its universal *[allgemeinen]* laws according to the principle of purposiveness for our cognitive ability i.e., to the appropriateness for human understanding in its necessary business to find the universal *[Allgemeine]* for the particular which is presented to it by perception, and on the other hand connection in the unity of the principle for variations. (*CJ*, 186)

Without the regulative guidance of reason,

> the specific variety of the empirical laws of nature together with their effects nevertheless could be so great that it would be impossible for our understanding to discover a comprehensible order, to divide its products into genera and species, in order to also use the principles of explanation and understanding *[Verständnisses]* of the one for the explanation and understanding *[Begreifung]* of the other and from such confused materials (actual infinite diversity, our power of comprehension could not measure) to make a connected experience. (*CJ*, 185)

With this discussion of the scope of regulative principles of reason we should have a clearer idea of what would not be not included in the constitutive principles of understanding and this will serve us well as we once again move forward in our positive understanding of one of these principles of understanding.

ANALOGIES OF EXPERIENCE

In the third section of the system of principles, Kant states that the names of the four groups of principles were "carefully chosen so that the differences, with regard to the evidence and the execution, of these principles is not left unnoticed" (A161/B200). Kant may have intentionally chosen the names of the four groups of principles, but his explanation of his reasons for making these choices, it seems to me, is not much more than a hint. In this section I will try to formulate (from Kant's hints) an explanation of the significance of the term *analogy of experience*.

The first hint at an explanation of the significance of the term *analogy of experience* comes when Kant gives his comparison of mathematical analogies with philosophical analogies (A179–80/B222–23). In a mathematical analogy we assert that the relation of one number to a second number is the same as the relation of a third number to a fourth number. Mathematical analogies allow us to determine any one of the four numbers if we already know the other three. So for example if we know that $1:3 = x:9$, then we know that $x = 3$. So, a philosophical analogy, we might expect, would allow us to determine any one of the four members if we already know the other three. But, Kant tells us, philosophical analogies will *not* allow us to determine the fourth member given the other three. For "in philosophy analogies signify something very different from what they represent in mathematics" (A179/B222).

According to Kant, mathematical analogies assert that the relation in which one item stands to a second item is *quantitatively* the same as the relation in which a third item stands to a fourth item. Philosophical analogies, however, assert that the relation in which one item stands to a second item is *qualitatively* the same as the relation in which a third item stands to a fourth. The difference between quantitative relations and qualitative relations is an important one. For it is

> only the concept of quantities that allows of being constructed, that is, exhibited *[darlegen]* a priori in intuition. Qualities, however, can be exhibited *[darstellen]* in no other intuition than empirical intuition. (A714–15/B742–43)[31]

Now, "mathematics does not only construct magnitudes (*quanta*) as in geometry, but also mere magnitude (*quantitatem*) as in algebra" (A717/B745). So, with mathematical analogies if three of the quantities are given, then the fourth quantity can be constructed *a priori* in intuition.

With philosophical analogies, however, "from three given members we can cognize and give *a priori* only the relation to a fourth, not *this* fourth *member* itself" (A179–80/B222). For qualities cannot be constructed *a priori*

---

31. See also Section III of the Introduction of the *Jäsche Logic*—although there it is suggested that qualities cannot be exhibited in intuition at all. There Kant writes: "The reason, however, why in mathematics we consider quantities more, lies in that quantities can be constructed in intuition *a priori*, qualities on the other hand cannot be exhibited *[darstellen]* in intuition."

in intuition. So, a philosophical analogy does not give us the means to construct the fourth member *a priori* in intuition,[32] but rather it gives us the knowledge that a fourth member that stands in the specified relation to the three given members is to be found in experience.

The problem with this hint at the meaning of "analogies of experience" is that although we are told what philosophical analogies are not (i.e., they are not mathematical analogies), it doesn't really give us anything positive about analogies in philosophy. One of the things we most want to know about philosophical analogies is where we come up with *two* relations. In the general statement of the Analogies of Experience[33] Kant brings up one relation with which the analogies will deal and with principles of understanding it will be the main relation with which we will be concerned. This is the relation of one perception (*appearance* in A) to another (A177/B218). If this is the first relation, what is the second relation to which it is equal?

One suggestion concerning the source of this second relation is that we should look to the *unity of apperception* as the source of the second relation. Kant himself suggests that "the general principle of the three analogies rests on the necessary *unity* of apperception" (A177/B220). Furthermore, in what is usually considered to be part of one of Kant's early attempts at a transcendental deduction, we find the suggestive remarks that

> [a]pperception is the consciousness of thought, i.e., of representations as they are placed in the mind. In this there are three exponents: (1) the relation to the subject, (2) the relation of succession among one an-

---

32. This is the sense in which the analogies (and postulates) "are admittedly constitutive in regard to *experience*, as they make possible *a priori* the *concepts* without which no experience takes place," but they are not "constitutive as regards intuition" (A664/B692). The principles of the analogies and the postulates (and all principles of understanding for that matter) are in Kant's standard sense constitutive principles in that they are required for the possibility of experience. That is, they make experience possible. In this section Kant is using "constitutive" in an unusual way. He is not using "constitutive" and "regulative" in regard to experience, but rather in regard to intuition. Something counts as constitutive *here* only if the object can be constructed *a priori* in intuition. Here Kant includes only the axioms of intuition and anticipations of perception as constitutive in this special sense. "Since these cannot be constructed, they will only concern the relation of existence and can provide nothing other than merely regulative principles. Thus here neither axioms nor anticipations are to be thought, but if a perception in a time relation to another (although undetermined) is given, then it cannot be said *a priori*: *which* other and *how big* a perception, but how its existence is necessarily connected to the first in this mode of time" (A179/B221–22). When I use "constitutive" and "regulative" in this book I will use them in the standard Kantian sense as spelled out earlier in this chapter and not in the special sense we find here.

33. "All appearances stand, as regards their existence, *a priori* under rules of the determination of their relation to one another in one time" (A176–77). "Experience is possible only through the representation of a necessary connection of perceptions" (B218).

other, (3) of collection. . . . The three relations in the mind require therefore three analogies of appearance, in order to change the *subjective functions* of the mind into objective ones and thereby make them into concepts of the understanding, which give reality to the appearances. (*Reflexionen*, 4674–75)[34]

I take this to suggest there is an analogy between the mind and appearances (experience). That is, we should expect to find an analogy between the organization of the items united in one consciousness and the organization of the items united in one experience. In consciousness we will be concerned with connections of representations in general, while in experience we will be concerned with connections of perceptions. This is suggested in the second edition statement of the principle of the analogies as well as at A177/B220. Just as representations, which make up one consciousness, must stand in the three relations to one another, there will be three analogous relations in which perceptions that make up one experience must stand to one another.

This suggestion is supported and made more explicit by a second possible source for this second relation. This second suggestion is that we look to the *unity of concepts* as the source of the second relation. Kant writes that we are, "through these principles, justified in combining appearances only according to an analogy with the logical and general unity of concepts" (A181/B224). Of course, it is not just any concept that he has in mind here. He is thinking of the categories (specifically the categories of relation) in their strictly logical employment—that is, the *un*schematized categories. "The category," Kant says, "contains a function that is restricted by no sensible condition" (A181/B224). Such a concept can only be employed as "the unity of the thought of a manifold in general." "Through a pure category . . . no object is determined, but rather only the thought of an object in general, according to various modes, is expressed" (A247/B304).

In the principles, however, we are concerned not with thought in general, but with the contents of human sensibility. What Kant thinks we need from the principles is a function that is, unlike a pure category, restricted by sensible conditions, but nonetheless remains *analogous* to the pure category. In order to get both of these, the principle must provide a formula for the unity of a given sensible manifold. The principle will thus be restricted by sensible conditions, but it will also be analogous to the category, because the category provides a formula for the unity of the thought of a manifold in general. The principle will attain this twofold goal by utilizing the *schema* of a pure concept of understanding. An analogy, in particular, will attain this twofold goal by utilizing the schema of the appropriate category of relation.

---

34. *Kants gesammelte Schriften*, Volume 17, 647–48.

As we saw above, a schema of a pure concept of understanding expresses a determinate temporal structure. For the categories of relation in particular the schema will express a determinate temporal relation between representations. By following the formula of the schema we would thus ensure that we were staying within the bounds of appearances (i.e., we would be restricting ourselves to sensible conditions), because we will always be concerned with some determinate temporal relation. This is precisely what occurs in the principles. It is not the pure concept that Kant invokes in each principle, but it is the *schema* of the pure concept. So by sticking with the schema in the principles it is guaranteed that the principles are restricted to sensible conditions.

The use of the schema in the principles also ensures that the principles are analogous to the pure concepts. Again as we saw above, the schema of a pure concept translates into a determinate temporal structure what was, in the pure concept, only a determinate structure of thought. So, when in the principles we utilize the schema of a pure concept we will be dealing with a determinate temporal structure that is the sensible analog of the determinate structure of thought that is found in the pure concept. For the analogies, in particular, when we utilize the schema of a category of relation we will be dealing with a determinate temporal relation that is the sensible analog of the determinate relation of thought that is found in the appropriate pure concept.

Thus, in the analogies the use of the schema not only provides the conditions that restrict the use of the analogies to experience, but it also reveals the source of the second relation. For the use of the schema in the analogies allows the three relations of items in sensible intuition (as expressed in the analogies) to be equated with the three relations of items in thought (as expressed in the categories of relation).

KANT AND HUME

The Second Analogy is often regarded as the central text in which Kant attempted to answer Hume's skepticism concerning the causal principle. Evaluating the success of the Second Analogy in this regard is not a particularly easy task. This evaluation is complicated in large part by the controversial choices one must make in order to begin to evaluate the Second Analogy as an answer to Hume. Two claims that generally are not regarded as being controversial are these: there is some causal principle that Hume in some way doubted, and in the Second Analogy Kant intends to prove some causal principle that Hume in some way doubts. This is where widespread agreement ends. From this point in order to evaluate how Kant's proof of the causal principle stands as an answer to Hume we must be clear about three main things.

First is the nature of Hume's doubt. Naturally, if we hope to solve anything we must be clear about which causal principle (or principles) Hume doubts. We must also be clear about the precise nature of Hume's skepticism concerning the causal principle(s) in question.

Second is the nature of Kant's arguments in the Second Analogy. In terms of Kant's arguments in the Second Analogy, we first must be clear about the precise nature of the principle Kant intends to prove. We must also be clear about the strategy Kant uses to prove this causal principle, and of course we must be clear about whether or not Kant's proof is any good.

The third thing we must be clear about is the way Kant's arguments relate to Hume's doubt. In order to be clear about the relationship between Kant's arguments and Hume's doubts there are three further things we must be clear about. First of all it will be helpful to determine what Kant takes Hume's doubt to involve. Naturally, if Kant misunderstands Hume's doubt, it will be less likely that his argument in the Second Analogy constitutes a successful answer to Hume. Secondly, we need to decide whether or not the causal principle Kant argues for is the same as at least one of the principles that Hume doubts. Clearly, if Hume doubts one principle while Kant proves a different principle, this will make it extremely unlikely that Kant's argument constitutes a successful answer to Hume. Lastly, we must be clear about what sort of "answer" we are looking for. On the one hand, we might think an argument provides an answer to someone's position in the sense that the argument provides a sound refutation of the person's position. For an answer in this sense what counts is simply arguing validly from true premises to a conclusion that is inconsistent with the other person's position. On the other hand, we might think an argument provides an answer to someone's position in the sense that the argument provides a refutation which that person does or should (if that person wants to maintain a logically consistent position) accept. That is, for an answer in this sense what counts is arguing validly from premises that the other person accepts as true to a conclusion that is inconsistent with the other person's position. It should be clear that Kant believes his answer to Hume is an answer in the first sense—that is, it is a sound refutation of Hume's skepticism concerning the causal principle. It is important to keep in mind, however, that it does not appear Kant intends to provide an argument that is an answer to Hume *only* in the first sense. As Lewis White Beck suggests, Kant intends for his proof of this causal principle to be one that proceeds from premises that Hume does or should (if he is to remain consistent with himself) accept.[35] In this book when I focus on how Kant's argument stands as an answer to Hume I will focus more on

---

35. See "A Prussian Hume and a Scottish Kant," in *Essays on Kant and Hume* (New Haven: Yale University Press, 1978), 111–29.

whether Kant's argument is an answer in the second sense than on whether it is an answer in the first sense.

Hume's Doubt

At the beginning of his discussion of cause and effect Hume writes that he will examine two questions concerning this idea:

> First, for what reason we pronounce it *necessary,* that everything whose existence has a beginning, should also have a cause?
> Secondly, why we conclude, that such particular causes must *necessarily* have such particular effects; and what is the nature of that *inference* we draw from the one to the other and of the *belief* we repose in it?[36]

The causal principle that is to be the subject of Hume's doubt and Kant's proof is the principle mentioned in the first of these two questions. That is, as Hume puts it, the principle that "whatever begins to exist, must have a cause of existence."[37] This is reminiscent of the formulation we find in the first edition version of the principle of the Second Analogy, where Kant states the principle he is going to prove as, "Everything that happens (begins to be) presupposes something upon which it follows *according to a rule*" (A189).

When we say that this is the principle that is the subject of Hume's doubt and Kant's proof, we need to be clear about exactly what is at issue. It is often thought that what is at stake is simply the truth of this causal principle. As it turns out, however, this is not right. Hume writes:

> 'Tis a general maxim in philosophy, that *whatever begins to exist, must have a cause of existence.* This is commonly taken for granted in all reasonings, without any proof given or demanded. 'Tis suppos'd to be founded on intuition . . . but here is an argument, which proves at once, that the foregoing proposition is neither intuitively nor demonstrably certain.[38]

It is the possibility of demonstrating this causal principle that Hume doubts. That is, Hume denies that the "Principle, *that whatever begins to exist must have a Cause of Existence* . . . was founded on *demonstrative* or *intuitive Certainty.*"[39] It is not the principle itself that Hume doubts, but

---

36. *Treatise,* Bk. I, pt. III, § III, 78.
37. Ibid.
38. Ibid., 78–79.
39. *A Letter from a Gentleman to His Friend in Edinburgh,* ed. Eric Steinberg (Indianapolis: Hackett Publishing Company, 1977), 118. See also Hume's claim at *Treatise* Bk. I, pt. III, § III, 82.

Hume doubts that this principle is subject to a rational demonstration.[40] Hume is emphatically clear on this point. In responding to criticism of his supposed denial of this principle in the *Treatise,* Hume writes that

> it being the Author's Purpose, in the Pages cited in the Specimen, to examine the Grounds of that Proposition; he used the Freedom of disputing the common Opinion, that it was founded on *demonstrative* or *intuitive Certainty;* but asserts, that it is supported by *moral Evidence,* and is followed by a Conviction of the same Kind with these Truths, *That all Men must die,* and that *the Sun will rise To-morrow.* Is this any Thing like denying the Truth of that Proposition, which indeed *a Man must have lost all common Sense to doubt of?*[41]

It is interesting to note that on this score Kant gets Hume exactly right. That is, Kant realizes that what is at stake is not the principle itself, but rather the rational grounding of that principle. Kant writes that for Hume

> the question was not whether the concept of cause was right, useful and, in view of the whole of natural cognition *[Naturerkenntnis]*, essential, for Hume had never called this into question, but whether it could be thought through reason *a priori.* . . . It was only a question of the source of this concept not the indispensability of its use. (*Prolegomena*, 258–59)

It appears that Hume also has doubts concerning the principle that "particular causes must *necessarily* have such particular effects"[42] Again it looks to me that Hume does not doubt the principle itself, but he doubts that the inference we draw from cause to effect is grounded in reason. Instead, " 'Tis only from experience and the observation of their constant union, that we are able to form this inference; and even after all, the inference is nothing but the effects of custom on the imagination."[43] We will see in chapter 5 that whatever Kant thinks about this principle in general, proving this principle does not figure in as part of his proof in the Second Analogy. So answering Hume's doubts about this principle will not play a role in his response to Hume *in the Second Analogy.*

---

40. Of course, if we believe that the causal principle is false, then this would give us reason to doubt there could be a demonstration of the causal principle (on the assumption that nothing false can be demonstrated), but this is not, as we will see below, Hume's reasons for doubting the causal principle can be demonstrated.
41. *A Letter from a Gentleman to His Friend in Edinburgh,* 118.
42. *Treatise,* Bk. I, pt. III, § III, 78.
43. Ibid., Bk. II, pt. III, § I, 405.

Hume's reasons for doubting the possibility of demonstration

According to Hume, a belief can be grounded in one of two ways: either we can provide a demonstration for it or else it is founded on observation and experience. According to Hume, the opposite of any belief that can be given a demonstration is itself impossible. That is, the negation of any belief that can be demonstrated implies a contradiction or absurdity.[44] In the case of the causal principle it is the possibility of a demonstration that is at issue. To demonstrate the causal principle, we have to be able to demonstrate that every beginning of existence must have a cause of existence. Demonstrating this requires that the opposite of the causal principle be impossible. That is, it must be impossible for there to be a beginning of existence that does not have a cause. In order to show this we would have to show that the possibility of a beginning of existence without a cause implies some contradiction or absurdity. Hume argues, however, that the possibility of a beginning of existence without a cause does not imply any contradiction or absurdity. Hume's argument for this relies on his separability thesis.

Hume introduces his separability thesis when he argues against the view that abstract ideas can represent a multitude of different things equally well, because abstract ideas are themselves general—that is, the features of the ideas are themselves imprecise.[45] Hume's separability thesis consists in the following four claims: (1) "whatever objects[46] are different are distinguishable," (2) "whatever objects are distinguishable are separable by the thought and imagination," (3) "whatever objects are separable [by the thought and imagination] are also distinguishable," and (4) "that whatever objects are distinguishable are also different."[47] Hume's argument against the possibility of demonstrating the causal principle utilizes the first two claims of the separability thesis.

Hume argues that the idea of a cause and the idea of a beginning of existence are distinct ideas, because " 'twill be easy for us to conceive any

---

44. Hume's views on the results of demonstrations can be found in a number of places. See for example the Abstract of the *Treatise*, 650, The beginning of Section IV of the *Enquiry*, the end of Section IV of the *Enquiry*.
45. *Treatise*, Bk. I, pt. I, Section VII. Hume's argument in this section is more simply, but less straightforwardly labeled his argument against abstract ideas. Whenever I refer to Hume's argument against abstract ideas this should be taken as shorthand for referring to Hume's argument against the view that abstract ideas can represent a multitude of different things equally well, because the features of the ideas are themselves general.
46. It may be worth reminding ourselves that, at least here when dealing with the separability thesis and the argument against abstract ideas, when Hume writes about an object he means an object that can appear to the senses—that is, an impression. So the *objects* in the separability thesis will not be some third division along with the *impressions* and *ideas* of the copy thesis because the *objects* in the separability thesis just are the *impressions* of the copy thesis.
47. *Treatise*, Bk. I, pt. I, § VII, 18.

object to be non-existent this moment, and existent the next, without conjoining to it the distinct idea of a cause or productive principle."[48] Since a cause and a beginning of existence are distinct ideas, according to the first part of the separability thesis, it follows that they are also distinguishable ideas. Since the idea of a cause and the idea of a beginning of existence are distinguishable ideas, according to the first part of the separability thesis, it follows that they are also separable by the thought and imagination. Hume then concludes that since the idea of a cause and the idea of a beginning of existence are separable by the thought and imagination, so too can a cause be separated from a beginning of existence in reality. In order to reach this conclusion Hume utilizes his copy thesis in much the same way as he does in his argument against abstract ideas.[49]

Hume's copy thesis requires that (1) "All our simple ideas in their first appearance are deriv'd from simple impressions, which are correspondent to them, and which they exactly represent,"[50] (2) "every simple impression [has] a correspondent idea,"[51] and (3) all complex ideas are composed of simple ideas.[52] As a result, according to Hume "impressions and ideas differ *only* in their strength and vivacity."[53]

In his argument against abstract ideas Hume argues that all of our impressions (that is, the objects that "can appear to the senses")[54] must appear in the mind in a precise degree of quantity and quality. In order to apply this same conclusion to ideas, Hume utilizes this result of the copy thesis. Since the conclusion that all of our impressions must appear in the mind in a precise degree of quantity and quality "is not founded on any particular degree of vivacity,"[55] the same must be true of our ideas—that is, ideas must appear in the mind in a precise degree of quantity and quality. *Here* Hume will argue, since the argument for the separability of the idea of a cause and the idea of a beginning of existence "is not founded on any particular degree of vivacity," there is nothing to keep us from applying this argument to the objects that can appear to the senses (that is, impressions). Since the idea of

---

48. Ibid., Bk. I, Pt.. III, § III, 79.
49. See note 45 above in this chapter.
50. *Treatise*, Bk. I, pt. I, § I, 4. There are italics in the original text.
51. Ibid., 3.
52. At *Treatise*, Bk. I, pt. I, § I, 4, Hume writes that "we find, that all simple ideas and impressions resemble each other; and as the complex are formed from them, we may affirm in general, that these two species of perception are exactly correspondent." In the *Enquiry* Hume writes that "when we analyse our thoughts or ideas, however, compounded or sublime, we always find, that they resolve themselves into such simple ideas as were copied from a precedent feeling or sentiment." (§ II, 11).
53. *Treatise*, Bk I, pt. I, § VII, p. 19, italics added.
54. Ibid.
55. Ibid.

a cause is separable from the idea of beginning of existence, so too can a cause be separated from a beginning of existence in reality.

Now, since it is possible that a cause is separated from a beginning of existence in reality, the supposition of "the actual separation of these objects is so far possible, that it implies no contradiction nor absurdity."[56] Since the possibility that there is a beginning of existence without a cause does not imply any contradiction or absurdity, it will not be possible to demonstrate that every beginning of existence must have a cause.

Transcendental proof and Kant's proof of the causal principle

Kant agrees with Hume that the causal principle cannot be proven (demonstrated) exclusively by use of the principle of contradiction. That is, Kant agrees that the negation of the principle does not imply a contradiction. The possibility of an uncaused beginning of existence does not imply any contradiction. The negation of the principle would imply a contradiction only if the principle was what Hume would call a relation of ideas and Kant would call an analytic claim. According to Kant, in an analytic claim the concept of the predicate is in some sense contained within the concept of the subject. In other words, it does not extend the concept of the subject. The causal principle is not analytic, so Kant agrees with Hume that the concept of a cause is not included in the concept of a beginning of existence.

According to Hume, if the causal principle is not a relation of ideas, then it must be a matter of fact. According to Kant if the causal principle is not analytic, then it must be synthetic. For a synthetic claim the concept of the predicate is not contained within the concept of the subject. That is to say, concept of the predicate extends (goes beyond) the concept of the subject. Whether or not the concept of the predicate is rightly applied to the concept of the subject cannot be determined by simply examining the content of either or both of the two concepts. Since the correctness of a synthetic judgment cannot be determined solely by the content of one or both of the two concepts, something else is required for determining correctness. In order to prove a synthetic claim, we need some "third thing" to test our claim against. Typically, we need some intuition in which the subject and the predicate are connected as claimed.

If this is Kant's position, it begins to look as if he must simply give in to Hume and accept that the causal principle can only be proven through observation and experience. For, on the one hand, Hume says that there are only two types of proof: demonstrations and proofs based on observation and experience. Since Kant believes no contradiction is implied by the negation

---

56. *Treatise*, Bk. I, pt. III, § III, 80.

of the causal principle, then as Hume says there cannot be any demonstration of the causal principle. Hence, it looks as if Hume can argue that the causal principle must be based on observation and experience just as he thought. Kant believes, however, this conclusion can and must be avoided. Clearly Hume would be right if demonstrations and proofs from observation and experience actually were the only two possibilities. Kant argues, however, that as a result of his limited empiricist framework, Hume failed to realize there is a third type of proof—*transcendental* proof.

Transcendental proofs have something in common with each of the other two types of proof. Like proofs based on observation and experience, transcendental proofs are used to prove synthetic claims. So like proofs based on observation and experience, transcendental proofs require some third thing to make the connection between the subject and the predicate. In the case of some claims, such as those of mathematics, this third thing is still some intuition as it was for proofs based on observation and experience, but it is an *a priori* intuition. We give proofs in mathematics by making reference to the features of the pure intuitions of space and time. We can demonstrate the connection between the subject and predicate by showing that they are properly connected in the pure intuition of space and time. For some other claims, however, this third thing is not simply the *a priori* intuitions of space and time. Transcendental proofs of these claims instead appeal to what is required for the *possibility of experience*. In order to demonstrate these claims we must show that unless the subject and predicate are connected in the appropriate way, experience itself is not possible. That is, we must show that no possible experience is one in which the subject and predicate are *not* connected in the appropriate way.

Although transcendental proofs are used, like proofs from observation and experience, to prove synthetic claims, they are also similar in some ways to demonstrations. Transcendental proofs are like demonstrations in that transcendental proofs provide necessity. That is, the conclusion of a transcendental proof must be true. For transcendental proofs that depend on *a priori* intuition to make the connection between subject and predicate, the necessity comes in because the intuition is *a priori*. For transcendental proofs that depend on the possibility of experience, the necessity comes in because in order for experience to be possible, the subject and the predicate must be connected in the specified way.

According to Kant, the causal principle is one of these synthetic claims that must, if it is to be proven at all, be proven through a transcendental proof that depends on the possibility of experience. The causal principle is demonstrated through a transcendental proof and so is not proven through observation and experience. At this point, in order to complete the evaluation of Kant's argument as an answer to Hume's skepticism about the causal principle, we must examine the details of his transcendental proof. Happily, this is one of the main purposes of this book. Unhappily for the continuity of the discussion in this section, the examination of the proof will take the next four chapters to complete. It is only at that point that we will be able to revisit Kant's relationship to Hume. But for now it is time to turn to the details of the argument of the Second Analogy.

Chapter Two

The Causal Principle

THE PRINCIPLE OF THE SECOND ANALOGY

First, for what reason we pronounce it *necessary*, that every thing whose existence has a beginning, should also have a cause?
 Secondly, why we conclude, that such particular causes must *necessarily* have such particular effects; and what is the nature of that *inference* we draw from the one to the other and of the *belief* we repose in it?[1]

In the second edition Kant states the principle he will prove this way: "*All alterations [*Veränderungen*] take place in accordance with the law of the connection of cause and effect*" (B232). In the first edition the principle is stated as follows: "Everything that happens (begins to be) presupposes something upon which it follows *according to a rule*" (A189). There are two differences between the A and B formulations. The first change Kant made in the B formulation was to replace the phrase "everything that happens (begins to be)" with the phrase "all alterations." The second change is the replacement of the phrase "presupposes something upon which it follows according to a rule," with the phrase "take place in accordance with the law of the connection of cause and effect."

Kant, however, did not intend for these changes to create any significant difference in meaning between the two versions of the principle. The first

---

1. *Treatise,* Bk. I, Pt. III, §III, 78.

change does not alter the meaning because it only makes explicit something Kant claimed in the First Analogy. In the First Analogy Kant has claimed that the only things that begin to be (or cease to be) are states (or determinations) of substances. Substances themselves do not begin or cease to be—they are permanent. Substances do, however, undergo alterations. An alteration is Kant's name for when "a certain determination [of a substance] ceases and another begins" (A187/B231). So in speaking of alterations Kant is still speaking of the same thing as he was when speaking of things that begin to be.

With regard to the second change the only difference between the two versions is that Kant left unanalyzed in the second edition (i.e., "the law of the connection of cause and effect") that which he spelled out a bit more precisely in the first edition. In the second edition Kant merely mentions the law of the connection of cause and effect, whereas in the first edition he actually states his basic formulation of that law. Just as with the first change, this second change does not provide us with any reason to think that the two versions of the principle differ in meaning.

Well, so what exactly is the meaning of this causal principle Kant hoped to prove in the Second Analogy? There are two main possibilities. The first possibility is the Every-Event-Some-Cause thesis.[2] This first possibility is simply the principle that each event has some cause.

EESC = For every event e there is some event c and c causes e.[3]

The second possibility is the Same-Cause-Same-Effect thesis. This is the principle that has been taken by some Kant commentators to be what is expressed in Hume's second question from the quote above.[4] It is the principle we get if we add to EESC the clause that if one individual event causes a second individual event, then whenever any event of the first type occurs, an event of the second type will follow.[5]

---

2. The names I have assigned to these two possibilities are basically the same as those used by L. W. Beck. See "A Prussian Hume and a Scottish Kant," 120.
3. Commentators who have adopted the EESC formulation include the following: Allison, *Kant's Transcendental Idealism*; Beck, "A Prussian Hume and a Scottish Kant"; Kemp Smith, *A Commentary to Kant's Critique of Pure Reason*; Robert Paul Wolff, *Kant's Theory of Mental Activity*, Reprint (Gloucester, Mass.: Peter Smith, 1973); and Graham Bird, *Kant's Theory of Knowledge* (New York: Humanities Press, 1962).
4. I do not intend to endorse this reading of Hume's second question. At the very best, this could be an accurate reading of only the *first clause* of the second question, but it is not clear to me that it is even an adequate reading of the first clause of the second question.
5. This statement should be taken to have the same meaning as the second clause in the formalized version below. What the formalized version makes clear is that this formulation should not be taken to require that there is a true generalization that connects every event type of which c is an instance with every event type of which e is an instance. This formulation only requires that there be at least one such generalization.

SCSE = (1) For every event *e* there is some event *c* and *c* causes *e*, *and* (2) If *c* causes *e*, then there is some event type *C* of which *c* is an instance and some event type *E* of which *e* is an instance such that whenever an event of type *C* occurs an event of type *E* will follow.⁶

Although neither of these formulations of the causal principle requires a great deal of explanation, it will be helpful to take note of some of the similarities and differences between them.⁷ The first point of importance is that of these formulations EESC is the only one that deals exclusively with particular events. That is, EESC makes no mention of event types. This is important because any claim that asserts that some causal generalization does or does not hold must be a claim that mentions not only particular events, but also event types.⁸ So, according to EESC, a successful proof of the causal principle will leave all options concerning causal generalizations open. That is, proving the causal principle, on this reading, will not guarantee that there are any true causal generalizations, nor will it rule them out. Proving the

---

6. Commentators who have adopted the SCSE formulation include the following: Jonathan Bennett in *Kant's Analytic* (Cambridge: At The University Press, 1966); Paul Guyer in *Kant and the Claims of Knowledge*; William Harper in "Kant's Empirical Realism and the Distinction between Subjective and Objective Succession," in *Kant on Causality, Freedom, and Objectivity*, ed. Harper and Meerbote (Minneapolis: University of Minnesota Press, 1984); Arthur O. Lovejoy in "On Kant's Reply to Hume," in *Kant: Disputed Questions,* ed. Moltke S. Gram (Chicago: Quadrangle Books, 1967); Arthur Melnick in *Kant's Analogies of Experience* (Chicago: The University of Chicago Press, 1973); H. J. Paton in *Kant's Metaphysic of Experience* (New York: The Humanities Press, 1936); Carl J. Posy in "Transcendental Idealism and Causality: An Interpretation of Kant's Argument in the Second Analogy," in Harper and Meerbote; P. F. Strawson in *The Bounds Of Sense* (London: Methuen & Co. Ltd., 1966); James Van Cleve in "Another Volley at Kant's Reply to Hume," in Harper and Meerbote.

7. I should note that it is theoretically possible to have a third interpretation that corresponds *only* to the *second clause* of the SCSE formulation. This formulation would be a conditional claim that would require that *if* there were any causal connections they would be such that if *c* is the cause of *e*, then whenever an event of type *C* occurs, an event of type *E* always follows. This, however, would not require that there actually are any causal connections. If this were the principle Kant proved, then he would still not have proven that the category of causality and dependence (cause and effect) must have application to experience. Given that one of Kant's explicit goals is to prove that cause and effect must have application to experience, it is difficult to see why Kant would want to argue for this third possibility. As far as I know no one has argued that the second clause of SCSE is the complete causal principle Kant tries to prove.

8. This will be true as long as we take causes and effects to be particular events. If, however, we take causes and effects to be not particular events, but particular states or particular conditions, then of course causal generalizations may not make any use of event types. Yet in that case EESC would have to be reformulated in terms of particular states or particular conditions and then what held for event types on the original formulation will hold for either state types or condition types and the same point about causal generalizations will then hold in regard to either of these.

causal principle, then, will only guarantee that for any particular event there is some particular event that causes it.

It will also be noted, from what has just been said, that the EESC formulation will, since it makes no claim one way or the other concerning causal generalizations, allow for the possibility that on one particular occasion event a of type A causes event b of type B but on some other occasion (perhaps even in similar circumstances) event a^* of type A occurs without causing any event of type B.

These two features of EESC, if this is what Kant successfully proves in the Second Analogy, would not, of course, require Kant to hold either (1) that it is impossible to guarantee that there are any true causal generalizations, or (2) that single case causation[9] is possible. If EESC is what Kant successfully proves in the Second Analogy, then all that follows from this is that if Kant wants to rule out the possibility of single case causation, or guarantee that there are true causal generalizations, then he must do it by utilizing something other than the causal principle he intends to prove in the Second Analogy.

Unlike EESC, SCSE mentions both particular events as well as event types. Unlike EESC, if SCSE is what Kant proves in the Second Analogy, then proof of the causal principle would guarantee that there are true causal generalizations. This is so because SCSE guarantees that for every true particular causal claim, there is a true corresponding causal generalization. Now it should be noted that although according to SCSE Kant is committed to holding that there are true causal generalizations, it does not follow from SCSE either that a true causal generalization is a necessary truth, or that a true causal generalization is a contingent truth. So, if SCSE is what Kant successfully proves in the Second Analogy, *and* if Kant wants to hold that true causal generalizations are necessary truths, then he must argue for this utilizing something other than the causal principle.[10]

---

9. By single case causation I just mean cases as I just described above where on one particular occasion event a of type A causes event b of type B but on some other occasion (perhaps even in similar circumstances) event a^* of type A occurs without causing any event of type B.

10. As we saw in chapter 1, Kant tells us that the understanding must think of its particular "rules as laws (i.e. as necessary)" (*CJ*, 184). There are two things to keep in mind: First, as we saw in the previous chapter, it is the regulative use of reason that requires this. To understanding these rules "can only be known empirically, and in its view are contingent" (*CJ*, 184). So here where we are dealing with constitutive principles of understanding, we would not expect to find a requirement that causal laws are necessary truths. Secondly, even with this quote we need to be careful. Saying these rules are laws (i.e., as necessary) is not necessarily the same thing as saying they are necessary truths.

EVALUATION OF POSSIBLE INTERPRETATIONS OF THE FORMULATION OF THE CAUSAL PRINCIPLE

The Same-Cause-Same-Effect thesis

As I see it SCSE has two major advantages. The first advantage is that a successful proof of SCSE would provide Kant with an answer to both aspects of Hume's doubt. In the *Treatise* Hume attempted to discover a satisfactory answer to the following two questions:

> First, for what reason we pronounce it *necessary*, that every thing whose existence has a beginning, should also have a cause?
> Secondly, why we conclude, that such particular causes must *necessarily* have such particular effects; and what is the nature of that *inference* we draw from the one to the other and of the *belief* we repose in it?[11]

It is typically thought, however, that Hume did not find any satisfactory answer to either of these two questions. If Kant intends to prove both that every event has a cause as well as that if c is the cause of e, then whenever an event of type C occurs, an event of type E always follows, and he is actually successful, then it appears he would be able to supply a satisfactory answer to both of Hume's questions.[12] If, on the other hand, Kant successfully proves the EESC formulation, it appears he could only provide a satisfactory answer to the first of Hume's worries.

A second advantage that the SCSE formulation has is due to the fact that it includes a repeatability requirement as its second clause. A repeatability requirement is often taken to be a feature that must be included in any adequate theory of causation. Since EESC does not include any repeatability requirement SCSE will better fit the expectations we might have for a theory of causation. So if Kant is successful in proving SCSE, he will have made substantial progress toward developing a fairly substantial theory of causation.

SCSE, however, does have a number of disadvantages. The first disadvantage SCSE has is that it conflicts with the intended nature of the principle of the Second Analogy. As we saw in the previous chapter, Kant intends for all of the Principles of Understanding to be constitutive not regulative. In the previous chapter we uncovered what it means for something to be constitutive—mostly by seeing what constitutive is not. Here in the Second Analogy

---

11. *Treatise*, Bk. I, Pt. III, §III, 78.
12. Once again, I do not intend to endorse the claim that the second clause of SCSE is an adequate reading of Hume's second question.

itself, however, Kant gives us some specific positive guidance. He tells us that "understanding is required by all experience and its possibility, and the first thing it does is not that it makes the representation of objects distinct, but that it makes the representation of an object possible at all" (A199/B244). The causal principle then, would *not* be required in order to make the representation of an event distinct. Instead it is required to make the representation of an event possible in the first place. If we think about how we come to learn that repeatability holds, then we will see that it is not a requirement for making the representation of an event possible.

Whether or not a repeatability requirement is met is a matter for empirical investigation of actual events. That is, in order to determine whether or not an instance of one event type is always followed by an instance of another event type we must examine the particular instances of the event types in question. So for example, when I hit a baseball into a window and this causes the window to break, I certainly want to know whether this is repeatable. So what do I do? I must observe other instances of baseballs hitting windows in order to see whether the same effects are repeated. If they are, then after a while I will conclude: Baseballs hit into windows cause them to break—repeatability holds.

Such an investigation fits Kant's description of the hypothetical use of reason. In the hypothetical use of reason,

> several particular cases, all of which are certain, will be tested by the rule in order to see whether they follow from it and in these cases when it appears that all of the given particular cases follow from the rule, then the universality of the rule is inferred, but afterwards from this all cases, even those that are not in themselves given, are inferred. (A646–47/B674–75)

The judgment that in a particular case a repeatability requirement is met is not an *a priori* judgment. The universality of such a rule is the *result of* empirical investigation, hence it is not a rule that we must accept *before* empirical investigations can proceed. For "the hypothetical use of reason,"

> is actually not *constitutive*, . . . but rather it is only regulative, in order to bring unity into the particular cognitions, in so far as it is possible, and thereby to *approximate* the rule to universality. (A647/B675)

As I see it a repeatability rule is extraordinarily useful in terms of the comprehensibility and connectedness of experience. If particular cases of events don't fall under repeatability rules what would our comprehension of experience be like? Kant himself tells us: If there are no regularities then "for the specific variety of natural effects just as many different types of causality must be assumed" (*CJ*, 185). In short, without a repeatability requirement then "the specific variety of the empirical laws of nature together with their effects nevertheless could be so great that it would be impossible for our understanding to discover a comprehensible order" (*CJ*, 185). As we saw in the previous chapter, however, this is precisely where the regulative principle of reason comes in. Kant tells us:

> The power of judgment thus also has an *a priori* principle for the possibility of nature, but only in a subjective respect, in which it does not prescribe a law for nature (as autonomy), but for itself (as heautonomy) for the reflection on the former, ... the principle of purposiveness for our cognitive ability i.e. to the appropriateness for human understanding in its necessary business to find the universal *[Allgemeine]* for the particular which is presented to it by perception, and on the other hand connection in the unity of the principle for variations. (*CJ*, 185–86)

A repeatability requirement is useful and even necessary, but it is necessary as part of the regulative principle of reason *not* as part of a constitutive principle of understanding such as we have in the Second Analogy. SCSE includes a repeatability requirement in its second clause, but this means it cannot be the correct interpretation of the principle of the Second Analogy.

The second disadvantage SCSE has is that, as we will see, both in his examples in the Second Analogy and in each of his positive statements of his argument in the Second Analogy Kant's remarks are limited to a discussion of *individual* events. If the causal principle for which Kant is arguing includes a repeatability clause, then we would have good reason to expect his examples as well as his positive arguments to include significant reference to event *types* as well as individual events. Such an expectation, however, is left unfulfilled.

In the discussion of the similarities and differences of the house and ship examples there is no mention either of other physical objects that are of the same type as the house or of other events that are of the same type of event as the ship floating down the river. These are Kant's main illustrative examples. Surely it is reasonable to expect event types to show up here if Kant intends for the causal principle to include a repeatability clause. Furthermore, event types do not show up in any of Kant's other examples of events in the Second Analogy (i.e., the stove heating the room, the leaden ball denting the cushion, and the water filling the glass) nor do they play a role in any of Kant's positive arguments for the causal principle.

Event types do show up, however, in the paragraph that begins on A195/B240 and ends on A196/B241. Yet the discussion here does not concern

Kant's own theory, but rather it concerns a position that Kant *rejects*. Furthermore, the expressions that Kant uses in this passage *do not reappear* in his discussion of his own theory.[13]

A third disadvantage is really a promissory note. As I spell out the details of the proper understanding of the argument of the Second Analogy in chapter 5 it will become clear that SCSE conflicts with Kant's actual proof in the Second Analogy. Kant bases his proof on the requirements that must be met in order for a succession of appearances to be an object of representations. In chapter 5 I show that a repeatability requirement is not something that is required in order for a succession of appearances to be an object of representations. So repeatability does not play any role in Kant's proof of the causal principle. Since SCSE does contain a repeatability requirement, there will be a problem with accepting SCSE.

A fourth disadvantage of SCSE is also a promissory note. This concerns the degree to which it can be supported by any one of the five general proof strategies discussed in chapters 3 and 5 below. As I will show in chapter 5, SCSE conflicts with the Object of Experience Strategy and thus cannot be supported by it. Although SCSE does not conflict with the other four proof strategies, I will argue, in chapter 3, that no successful proof for SCSE can be developed from any one of these four strategies. So, SCSE, I argue, cannot be supported by any one of the five interpretations of Kant's general proof strategy.

Of course this fourth disadvantage would not be enough *all by itself* to make SCSE unacceptable. For it may be that Kant intended to prove the SCSE formulation of the causal principle by utilizing one of these five strategies, but he failed to realize that SCSE cannot successfully be proven on the chosen strategy. It might also be the case that none of these five strategies actually is Kant's intended strategy and SCSE can be successfully proven on his actual strategy.[14]

I take this disadvantage, however, to have the following force. In the absence of Kant's clear assertion that he intends to prove the SCSE formulation, if SCSE cannot be successfully proven on any of the strategies that are plausibly attributed to Kant, then this gives us reason to reject the SCSE formulation.

Furthermore, if there is some other formulation of the causal principle that *can* be proven on one or more of the strategies that are plausibly attributed to Kant and as long as there is no compelling textual reason to reject this

---

13. For a more detailed discussion of this point see chapter 5 in the section labeled "Textual Worries" pp. 128ff.
14. Of course, it might be that none of these is Kant's actual intended strategy, but nonetheless SCSE still cannot be successfully proven on his actual strategy. I take this case to be essentially the same as the first possibility mentioned above.

other formulation, then if SCSE cannot be successfully proven on any of the strategies that are plausibly attributed to Kant, this gives us a *strong* reason to reject the SCSE formulation. In chapter 3 I will argue that the circumstances are such that this disadvantage does provide us with a reason to reject the SCSE interpretation. In chapter 5 I will argue that this disadvantage provides us with a strong reason for rejecting SCSE.

The Every-Event-Some-Cause thesis

The EESC formulation has a number of advantages, but my discussion of these will be relatively brief at this point. Most of these advantages are promissory in nature and so the details of these advantages will be spelled out in chapters 5 and 6.

The first major advantage is that the EESC formulation of the causal principle would allow the principle to be, as Kant intends it to be, a principle that is constitutive with regard to experience. Unlike SCSE, no part of EESC aims at making the representation of objects distinct, which is a regulative task of reason, but it aims solely at making the representation of objects (namely, particular events), possible. As we will see in chapter 5, in order for an event to be an object of representations it must be subject to EESC.

A second advantage, as I argue in chapter 5, is that the EESC formulation is the only one that can be proven on the Object of Experience Strategy. Since as we will see in chapter 3, none of the other proof strategies is successful, this then shows that, unlike SCSE, EESC can be proven on one of the proof strategies plausibly attributed to Kant. Since, as we will see in chapter 5, the Object of Experience Strategy is Kant's intended strategy, this will additionally show that EESC alone can be proven on Kant's intended strategy.

A third advantage is that EESC would provide Kant with an answer to Hume that begins with premises that Hume would have to accept. For as traditionally construed Hume claimed there was no way to prove *either* that every event must have a cause *or* that like causes must have like effects. So if Kant proves EESC, then he will have shown that Hume was wrong about the first disjunct, because Kant will have proven that every event has some cause. Furthermore, as I will argue in chapter 6, the proof Kant gives for EESC would provide him with an answer to Hume that Hume would have to accept on pains of inconsistency. So, Kant will have shown that Hume was wrong about the first disjunct *and* he will have done so in a way that would be able to provide him with a proof that uses only premises that Hume would have to accept.

The major obstacle for EESC concerns Kant's use of phrases such as "follows according to a rule" *(folgen nach einer Regel),* "is subject to a rule" *(einer Regel unterwerfen sein),* and "stands under a rule" *(stehen unter einer*

Regel). It is initially plausible to interpret such phrases as invoking some type of causal generalization and thus it is initially plausible to interpret such phrases as invoking the second clause of SCSE. If this is the correct interpretation of such phrases, then, since it does not include any repeatability clause, this would pose serious difficulties for the EESC formulation of the causal principle.

We will see in chapter 5, however, that although such an interpretation of these phrases is initially plausible this interpretation simply *cannot be supported by the text*. We will find instead that Kant's discussion of being subject to a rule in the Second Analogy, the Schematism, and elsewhere in the *Critique*, *forces* us to interpret being subject to a rule to be intimately connected with the requirements for being an *object of representations*. In fact, being subject to a rule is a necessary requirement for being an object of representations. Furthermore, we will see that repeatability (and hence causal generalization) plays no role in the requirements for being an object of representations. Thus, we will find that, phrases such as "being subject to a rule" do not invoke the second clause of SCSE, and hence such phrases do not pose any difficulties for the EESC formulation of the causal principle.

A second disadvantage for EESC is that since it does not include a repeatability clause, if this is what Kant proves in the Second Analogy, then it appears he will be unable to provide a complete theory of causation in the Second Analogy. Again this is because it is often thought that a full-fledged theory of causation must include a repeatability clause. Now, this disadvantage will pose a problem only if it was Kant's intention to formulate a full-fledged theory of causation in the Second Analogy and a full-fledged theory of causation must include a repeatability clause. As we have already seen above, however, the Second Analogy is not the only place in which Kant deals with causation. He deals with the topic of causation in other parts of the first *Critique* as well as in other works, so we should not expect the Second Analogy to be Kant's last or complete word on the topic. In the Second Analogy Kant spells out the basic constitutive features of the causal principle of understanding. A full treatment of causation will surely require the introduction of features that are invoked through the regulative function of reason, but for a discussion of these features we must look somewhere other than the Second Analogy. So the fact that something we would expect to find in a full-fledged theory of causation is left out of the Second Analogy would be no real obstacle unless this feature is left out because it is inconsistent with some feature of the causal principle introduced in the Second Analogy. Clearly EESC does not conflict with causal regularities, it is simply neutral with regard to them.

Chapter Three

The Fivefold Routes to the Principle of Causation

POSSIBLE ARGUMENT STRATEGIES

Although there is significant disagreement concerning Kant's goal in the Second Analogy, there is even more disagreement concerning the general strategy Kant employs in his attempt to prove the causal principle. In this chapter I will examine the five main strategies that have been attributed to Kant.

The first main strategy is suggested by Arthur O. Lovejoy in his article "On Kant's Reply to Hume."[1] Lovejoy claims that Kant simply adopts Wolff's general strategy for proving the causal principle. Through this strategy Wolff and Kant attempt to prove the causal principle by first showing

> the supposed necessity of assuming that principle as the basis of the distinction between merely subjective, and objectively valid, perceptions of change, between veridical representations and "mere dream."[2]

That is, they attempt to show that without the causal principle it would be impossible to make the distinction between veridical representations and dreams.[3] Kant is then supposed to show that "we actually make [the distinction] between purely subjective phenomena and the world of objective realities."[4] From this Kant is supposed to conclude that the causal principle is true.

---

1. "On Kant's Reply to Hume," 284–308.
2. Ibid., 296.
3. Ibid., 290.
4. Ibid., 290.

I will call this the Veridical Strategy and I will represent it as follows:

1. If the causal principle is false, then it is not possible to make the distinction between purely subjective phenomena and the world of objective realities.
2. We do, as a matter of fact, make the distinction between purely subjective phenomena and the world of objective realities.
3. If we actually make the distinction, then it is possible to make this distinction.

Therefore, the causal principle is true.[5]

We can take our clue for the second main strategy from Peter Strawson. Strawson argues that Kant begins by establishing a criterion for distinguishing between our successive perceptions of events and our successive perceptions of coexistent objects. According to Strawson, Kant holds that in the case of our perceptions of objective successions (events) "the order they have is a necessary order."[6] In cases of coexistent objects, however, our perceptions possess "order-indifference." That is, "they could have occurred in the opposite order to that in which they in fact occurred."[7] So according to Strawson's Kant, the

> lack or possession of order-indifference on the part of our perceptions is . . . our criterion—whether we reflectively realize the fact or not—of objective succession or co-existence.[8]

So according to Strawson, Kant's

> idea is that we could not empirically apply . . . the concepts of objective change and objective co-existence without implicitly using the notions of a necessary order, and of order-indifference, of perceptions.[9]

The crucial point on Strawson's reading is that the fact that we successfully employ this criterion will in the end provide the grounding for the causal principle. According to Strawson, Kant holds there is a close connec-

---

5. As far as I can tell Lovejoy is the only commentator who argues that Kant adopted the Veridical Strategy.
6. Strawson, *The Bounds of Sense,* 134.
7. Ibid.
8. Ibid.
9. Ibid., 137.

tion between the concepts of a necessary order and of order-indifference and the causal principle. For "these notions in turn could have no application unless the relevant causal principles applied to the objects of the perceptions."[10] So according to Strawson we should see Kant as arguing that I can distinguish between an objective coexistence and objective change only if I can apply the concept of a necessary order of perceptions. Yet in order to apply this concept, the relevant causal principles must apply to the objects of my perceptions. For, according to Strawson, Kant argues that "to conceive this order of perceptions as necessary is equivalent to conceiving the transition or change from A to B as *itself* necessary, as falling, that is to say, under a rule or law of causal determination."[11]

Since according to Kant we can distinguish between objective coexistence and objective succession, the causal principle is true.

This second main strategy I will call the Event/Object Strategy, and I will represent it as follows:

1. If the causal principle is false, then it is not possible to use the irreversibility of perceptions as a criterion for distinguishing between successive perceptions of events and successive perceptions of coexistent objects.

2. The irreversibility of perceptions is the criterion we actually use in order to distinguish between successive perceptions of events and successive perceptions of coexistent objects.

3. If we actually use the irreversibility criterion, then it is possible to use this criterion.

Therefore, the causal principle is true.[12]

The third strategy is suggested by Arthur Melnick. Melnick argues that according to Kant "it must be possible for a subject who judges about what is given temporally to determine the position in time of what is given."[13] In the Second Analogy, since we are dealing with objective succession, this means it must be possible for us, since we do make judgments about these temporally given items, to determine the position in time of a given succession. According to Melnick, once Kant has shown that we cannot determine when an event

---

10. Ibid.
11. Ibid., 138.
12. Among the commentators who argue that Kant adopted the Event/Object Strategy are Strawson, and C. D. Broad in *Kant: An Introduction*, ed. C. Lewy (Cambridge: Cambridge University Press, 1978).
13. Melnick, *Kant's Analogies of Experience*, 85.

occurred (i.e., determine its temporal position in relation to other events) by relating the states of the succession to absolute time or on the basis of perception alone, he proceeds to argue that the determination of temporal position must be based on features of the events perceived. "What is required," argues Melnick, "is some way of connecting two events or states x and y . . . on the basis of what kind of events x and y are."[14] This connection between events must enable us "to order events temporally as asymmetric . . . on the basis of what kind of events they are (and the circumstances of their occurrence)."[15] According to Melnick, Kant holds that this connection between events is provided by causal laws. That is, causal laws are what enable us to determine the temporal ordering of events. According to Melnick, *given* that we know what types of events x and y are and *given* that we know the relevant features of the circumstances in which x and y occur, a causal law is what enables us to infer either that x is prior to y or y is prior to x. Melnick says:

> Kant's claim may be put as follows: Causal laws are rules that license inferences from features of events to the temporal ordering of events ("inference tickets" in Ryle's terminology). When we determine the temporal order of events in terms of a causal law, we are using the law as a license.[16]

To determine the temporal order of events we figure out the order that is in accordance with the appropriate causal laws (i.e., the laws that apply to events of this type in the appropriate type of circumstances) and we judge that this required order is the actual order.

This third strategy I will call the Event/Event Strategy and I will represent it as follows:

1. If the causal principle is false, then it is not possible to determine the temporal positions of distinct events in relation to each other.

2. It is possible for us to determine the temporal positions of distinct events in relation to each other.

Therefore, the causal principle is true.[17]

The fourth main strategy turns on the claim that in the Analogies "Kant is dealing strictly with the principles that would have to be appealed to in the justification of empirical claims to knowledge."[18]

---

14. Ibid., 89.
15. Ibid., 90.
16. Ibid., 133.
17. Among the commentators who argue that Kant adopted the Event/Event Strategy include the following: Bennett, Melnick.
18. Guyer, *Kant and the Claims of Knowledge,* 258–59.

That is, in the Analogies Kant is concerned with the necessary conditions "for the *justification, verification, or confirmation* of the judgments about empirical objects that we make on the basis of our representations of them."[19]

Paul Guyer argues that in the Second Analogy Kant's aim is to show how it is possible to justify a judgment that a particular event has occurred. According to Guyer, Kant first argues that the judgment that a particular event has occurred cannot be justified by any direct appeal to the temporal positions of the states that make up the event, "for the temporal positions of the objective states themselves are not directly given."[20] So, the judgment that a particular event occurred must be justified on some other basis.

According to Guyer, Kant ultimately concludes that the judgment that a particular event has occurred can only be justified "by *adding* to the omnipresent succession of mere representations a *rule* from which it can be inferred that in the circumstances at hand *one state of affairs* could *only* succeed the other."[21]

Since this added rule requires that one state *had* to follow the other, it can be inferred that the one state *did* follow the other. Thus, adding the rule enables us to justify the judgment that the event has occurred.

So, according to Guyer, Kant has argued that in order to justify the judgment that a particular event has occurred we must possess "a rule which dictates that in a given situation one state of affairs must succeed another."[22] According to Guyer, however, such a rule fits Kant's description of a causal law. So, according to Guyer, since Kant has shown that such rules are required for the justification of judgments that events occur, he has also successfully shown that causal laws are required. That is, it is possible to justify our judgment that a particular event occurred "only if there are causal laws entailing that in such circumstances the relevant sequence of states of affairs must have occurred."[23]

Since our judgments concerning the occurrence of particular events can be justified, the causal principle is true.

This fourth strategy I will call the Justification Strategy and I will represent it as follows:

1. If the causal principle is false, then it is not possible to justify (or verify or confirm) a judgment that a particular event occurred.

2. It is possible to justify (or verify or confirm) a judgment that a particular event occurred.

Therefore, the causal principle is true.[24]

---

19. Ibid., 246.
20. Ibid., 248.
21. Ibid.
22. Ibid., 249.
23. Ibid., 448–49, end note 25.

I argue, however, that none of these strategies adequately accounts for the emphasis Kant places on the notion of an "object of experience."[25]

When we turn to the Second Analogy we find that the discussion in the third paragraph in B (first paragraph in A) undeniably focuses on the requirements for something's being an object of experience. The discussion in this paragraph is strongly reminiscent of the discussion of the meaning of the phrase "an object of representations" in the subjective deduction of the first edition (A104ff). Some might argue, however, that just as the subjective deduction was expunged in the second edition Kant attempts to downplay the significance of this discussion by the changes he made in the second edition text of the Second Analogy. Fortunately, such a suggestion does not stand up to scrutiny, because the notion of an "object of experience" also plays a central role in the second paragraph added in B (B233–34).

In addition to ordinary physical objects (i.e., appearances) such as a house, Kant also holds that *events* (i.e., successions of appearances) such as a ship floating down the river or water freezing are *objects* (i.e., objects of experience). If the causal principle is false, Kant argues, then it would be possible for there to be some event (succession of appearances) that is not subject to a rule. Kant argues, however, since any event (succession of appearances) that is not subject to a rule is not a possible object of experience, there cannot be any event (succession of appearances) that is not subject to a rule. Therefore the causal principle is true.

This final strategy I call the Object of Experience Strategy and I represent it as follows:

1. If the causal principle is false, then there could be some succession of appearances (some event) that is not subject to a rule.

2. Successions of appearances (events) are objects of experience.

---

24. Among the commentators who argue that Kant adopted the Justification Strategy include the following: Guyer, Van Cleve. I should note that Van Cleve does not strictly write in terms of *justifying* our judgments that a particular event occurred. Rather he writes of *knowing* that a particular event occurred. Van Cleve makes it clear that he does not intend to equate knowing that a particular event occurred with simply being aware that a particular event occurred. So, since there is (presumably) a close connection between knowledge and justification, I have taken Van Cleve's position to fall in this category.

25. There are actually a number of more specific phrases that could replace "object of experience." For example, "object of representations," "object of cognition," "object of judgment," or "object of knowledge." Furthermore, it seems to me, the choice of phrase may have a significant effect on the expectations we have concerning the meaning of the causal principle and the results of Kant's argument. I prefer the phrase "object of representations" and this is the phrase I will use when I present the details of my view in chapter 5, but the more general "object of experience" better suits the introductory nature at this stage of the discussion. In the last section of the Conclusion I revisit this issue.

3. A succession of appearances that is not subject to a rule is not a possible object of experience.
4. So, there cannot be any succession of appearances that is not subject to a rule.

Therefore, the causal principle is true.[26]

There are two things to note about these five strategies. The first point is that I take each of these strategies to be in an important way incomplete. The important thing that is needed in order to complete each strategy is some sort of argument (or at least argument strategy) for the first premise. Most commentators do actually discuss Kant's argument strategy for the first premise and although there is a good deal of variety among the suggested strategies, all of the strategies suggested by the commentators I will be discussing have some connection with their views on Kant's Irreversibility Argument. In order to keep the evaluation manageable here, I have chosen to postpone my discussion of strategies for the first premise until chapter 4.

The second point is that although none of these argument strategies is strictly speaking principle specific (i.e., none of these general argument strategies literally requires the adoption of any particular formulation of the causal principle), the individual proponents of each of these five strategies usually have one particular formulation of the causal principle in mind. In my evaluation of these strategies I will follow the lead of the main proponent's choice concerning the formulation of the causal principle.[27]

EVALUATION OF ARGUMENT STRATEGIES

In the rest of the chapter I will turn to an examination of the problems involved with each of the first four routes to the principle of causation. Since

---

26. Other commentators who argue that Kant adopted the Object of Experience Strategy include the following: Allison, Beck, Harper, Kemp Smith. Beck is actually a little hard to pin down. In some places (e.g., "A Prussian Hume and a Scottish Kant" and in "Once More unto the Breach: Kant's answer to Hume, Again," both in *Essays on Kant and Hume*) he is most plausibly interpreted as holding the Object of Experience Strategy. In "A Non Sequitur of Numbing Grossness?" (also in *Essays on Kant and Hume*) it seems most plausible to interpret him as holding the Justification Strategy.

27. Although, as I said, technically any one of these strategies can be combined with either of the formulations of the causal principle from chapter 2, it will be interesting to note a couple of tendencies. In particular, given the emphasis on the need for causal laws to determine the temporal relations between events or to justify the judgment that a particular event has occurred, the Event/Event Strategy and the Justification Strategy respectively will fit much more easily with the SCSE formulation than they would with the EESC formulation. As far as I know no Event/Event strategist or Justification strategist has in fact adopted the EESC formulation. Also, as far as I am aware, everyone who adopts the EESC formulation also adopts the Object of Experience Strategy, but not all Object of Experience strategists adopt EESC.

I adopt the Object of Experience Strategy I will not evaluate it here, but instead I will examine it in detail in chapter 5.

The Veridical Strategy

The main problem with the Veridical Strategy is that it is not supported by the text. Nowhere in the text of the Second Analogy does Kant give us reason to believe he intends to base the proof of the causal principle on the necessity of utilizing the causal principle to ground the distinction between veridical representations and non-veridical representations.

There is only one place in the Second Analogy that could be taken to hint that Kant is even *concerned* with, as Lovejoy puts it, the distinction between "merely subjective, and objectively valid, perceptions of change, between veridical representations and 'mere dream.' "[28] This is a passage that occurs in the second half of the Second Analogy at A201–202/B246–47. It is not surprising that this is the passage that Lovejoy apparently takes to be Kant's clearest statement of the proof strategy he intends.

In this passage we find the only reference in the Second Analogy to dreams. Kant writes:

> If, therefore, my perception is to contain the cognition of an event, namely that something actually happens, then it must be an empirical judgment in which one thinks the succession as determined *(daß die Folge bestimmt sei),* i.e., that it presupposes another appearance in time on which it follows necessarily or according to a rule. Otherwise, if I were to posit that which precedes and the event did not follow upon it necessarily, then I would have to take it to be only a subjective play of my imagination, and if I still represented something objective by it, I would have to call it a mere dream. (A201–202/B246–47)

Now although this is the passage that Lovejoy takes to be the one in which Kant most clearly expresses the Veridical Strategy, it is far from clear that this passage actually supports Lovejoy's interpretation. For most of the passage Kant is reformulating what he has already presented in the Irreversibility Argument. The only thing that is new in this passage is the mention of dreams.

Lovejoy takes this mention of dreams to signify that after he has already written more than *thirteen* pages, Kant has finally gotten around to introducing his intended argument for the causal principle. That is, according to Lovejoy, this shows that the argument strategy in which the causal principle is grounded

---

28. Lovejoy, 296.

upon the supposed necessity of assuming that principle as the basis of the distinction between merely subjective, and objectively valid, perceptions of change, between veridical representations and "mere dream" . . . is precisely the line of argument to which Kant resorts when he finally reaches, in the "Second Analogy of Experience," his central problem.[29]

There are two problems with Lovejoy's assertion that I will discuss.

First of all, we should notice that the passage where we find the mention of dreams actually intimates that whatever distinction Kant is concerned with, it cannot be the distinction between waking experience and dream experience. For even here where Kant contrasts a succession that I would have to take to be "only a subjective play of my imagination" with a succession that represents something objective, Kant does not place dream experience and waking experience in opposing camps. That is, Kant does not regard dream experience as something that is "only a subjective play of my imagination" while waking experience is regarded as representing something objective. For here, even dreams are classified by Kant as "something objective." So even here Kant does not place dream experience and waking experience on opposing sides of some distinction with which he is concerned. So even Lovejoy's central text cannot lend support to the Veridical Strategy.

The second problem with Lovejoy's assertion concerns Kant's failure to even come close to addressing this problem, which is supposed to be "his central problem," until thirteen pages into the analogy.

It seems to me this lack of discussion poses a very serious problem for the Veridical Strategy interpretation. For if Kant's strategy is the Veridical Strategy, then we have strong reason for expecting Kant to devote his discussion to the distinction between veridical and non-veridical perceptions. Since Kant does not spend time on the veridical/non-veridical distinction, I take this to be a compelling reason to reject this strategy.

Although Lovejoy agrees that this lack of discussion of the veridical/non-veridical distinction poses a serious problem, he does not think it poses a problem for the Veridical Strategy. Instead, Lovejoy believes that this lack of discussion poses a serious problem *for Kant's reasoning powers*. That is, instead of taking this to provide a reason for rejecting the Veridical Strategy, Lovejoy believes this provides us with good reason to think Kant was hopelessly confused. For, claims Lovejoy, it is clearly

> the Wolffian sort of argument that he really intends to present; but with characteristic confusion of thought he allows this argument, unobserved,

---

29. Ibid., 296, 290.

by a subtle metamorphosis resulting essentially form verbal ambiguities, to transform itself into something quite incongruous with the proof that he intends.[30]

Now, it is very difficult to reply to this line of argument in terms that are likely to be accepted by Lovejoy. For if I point out that in Kant's main illustrative examples (the house and ship examples) as well as in his statements of his positive arguments for the causal principle, Kant appears to be concerned with the requirements that must be met in order for a succession of appearances to be an object of representations rather than with the problem of veridicality, Lovejoy will simply reply that all this shows is that Kant was badly confused.

There is good reason to believe, however, that Lovejoy's defense of the Veridical Strategy cannot, in the end, be maintained. For if Kant invokes the causal principle as being necessary to ground the distinction between veridical experience and dream or illusory experience, then one would expect, *if* one supposes for the sake of argument that one's representations in some instance are veridical, then there would be no need to invoke the causal principle in that particular instance. For the causal principle would be necessary for grounding the distinction between veridical and non-veridical perceptions and in this case we are supposing that there is no problem in regard to this. Kant would argue, however, that even if I know I have one veridical perception followed by another veridical perception, this will not help to solve his worries concerning the connection between the order in my perceptions of the states of objects and the order in the states of the objects themselves. For even if I know that my perceptions are veridical I am still "only conscious, that my imagination places one before, the other after, not that one state precedes the other in the object" (B233). Knowing that each of my successive perceptions of a state of an object is veridical still leaves unanswered Kant's question of how we are to determine the connection of these *objective* states in the object.

Of course, Lovejoy will try to argue that this once again points out Kant's confusion. For Lovejoy claims that this question "is a problem which exists only for Kant's imagination."[31] For Lovejoy argues that in actual perception, "so long as our attention to a given object be continuous, objects are directly *given* as moving or stationary, as altering or retaining their original sensible qualities."[32] Hence, he will argue, if my perception in this case is veridical, then the *connection* of the states in the object will be veridically *given*.

---

30. Ibid., 297.
31. Ibid.
32. Ibid., italics in original.

This position, however, cannot be the position that Kant held. For this position requires transcendental realism. Transcendentally speaking, for the transcendental idealist objects cannot be simply *given* in this way.[33] For the transcendental idealist, the understanding plays a constitutive role with regard to objects. That is, no objects are simply given through sensibility and passively received by the understanding.[34]

So the fact that Kant is apparently worried by some problem other than the veridicality problem in the Second Analogy, cannot simply be attributed to Kant's confusion. There is a problem here and it is not just something we can pass off on Kant's confusion.[35] We cannot solve this problem in Lovejoy's way because his solution requires transcendental realism.

The Event/Object Strategy

The main problem with the Event/Object Strategy concerns the interpretation of the importance of Kant's use of the irreversibility of perceptions. The irreversibility of perceptions clearly plays a crucial role in the argument of the Second Analogy and the irreversibility of perceptions is even supposed to show us something important about our perceptions of ordinary physical objects and our perceptions of events. We should not be misled, however, into thinking that Kant intends to show that we actually utilize the irreversibility of perceptions as a criterion for distinguishing between objective succession and objective coexistence as Strawson suggests.

The first three sentences in A may indeed tempt us to accept Strawson's reading. Here Kant writes that

> [t]he apprehension of the manifold of appearance is always successive. The representations of the parts follow one another. Whether they also follow in the object is a second point for reflection which is not contained in the first. (A189/B234)

---

33. It is important to remember, however, Kant would argue that it is only (what we might call) *deceptive* transcendental realism that asserts that objects are given in this way. It is an important part of Kant's argument for transcendental idealism to argue that the transcendental realist is fundamentally self-deceptive. Transcendental realism, Kant argues, does not legitimately allow the transcendental realist to reach the solid ground at which he is aiming. Although the transcendental realist claims he has reached firm ground with a clear conscience, Kant argues that this is just transcendental illusion.
34. For more on this see the discussion of objects of representations in chapter 5.
35. Now, one might argue that since transcendental idealism is ultimately confused, Kant is ultimately confused. If this claim were true, this would not show that Kant is confused about his intentions here in the Second Analogy. Rather, if it were right it would show that Kant was confused about what is true.

This may tempt us to expect that, in line with Strawson's reading, when he gets to his main illustrative examples in the Second Analogy, the house and ship, Kant will provide us with a criterion by which we can determine whether or not appearances themselves are successive. When we finally get to the house and ship examples, however, this is not what we actually find.

The problem with Strawson's suggestion with regard to the house and ship examples is that Kant does not begin by wondering how it is that I can tell whether or not my perceptions are of an event or of an ordinary physical object and then proceed to show how we make such a determination in the house and ship cases. That is, in the house example Kant does not begin by thinking about some set of perceptions, and then determine that they were reversible, and finally conclude that because the order of perceptions was reversible what he perceived was an ordinary physical object rather than an event. Kant writes:

> So e.g., the apprehension of the manifold in the appearance of a house that stands in front of me is successive. Now the question is: whether the manifold of this house is also in itself successive, which certainly no one will admit. (A190/B235)

Kant does discuss the successiveness of apprehension here, but that it is a house in front of him is never in question. Even when he momentarily poses the question about whether the manifold in the house itself is successive it is still taken for granted that his perceptions are of a house—that is, a particular ordinary object rather than an event. The house being the object of perception here is never the result of a conclusion drawn from an investigation of the order of my perceptions as we would expect to find if this were Strawson's Kant.

In the ship case things are no different. That is, Kant does not begin by thinking about some set of perceptions, and then determine that they were irreversible, and finally conclude that because the order of perceptions was irreversible what he perceived was an event rather than an ordinary physical object.

Instead, when he gets to the ship example Kant *begins* by supposing that he perceives an event. Kant tells us "I see, for example, a ship floating down the river" (A192/B237). This is not a conclusion he reaches after examining the order of his perceptions, but it is the accepted starting point in the ship example. In the ship example he begins by supposing that there is "an appearance which contains a happening" (A192/B237). Again, this is not a conclusion he draws only after he examines the order of his perceptions. As a matter of fact, the conclusion that the order of perceptions is irreversible is based on the supposition that what he perceived was an event in the first place.

Indeed, at the beginning of the paragraph that immediately follows the discussion of the house and ship examples Kant warns us against interpreting these examples in the way Strawson suggests. For Kant writes: "Thus in our case I must derive the *subjective succession* of apprehension from the *objective succession* of the appearances" (A193/B238). So it seems Strawson has things reversed. Kant makes it clear that he is not endorsing an inference in which we move from some feature of the order of our perceptions to some feature of the order of the things perceived. Indeed, he insists that things are supposed to work the other way around.

A second problem with the Event/Object Strategy is that it appears to conflict with what Kant tells us in the First Analogy. Kant's line of argument in the First Analogy should help us see why we must reject the view that the irreversibility of perceptions is the criterion by which we determine whether what we perceived was a succession of states or coexistent states. Kant's argument for the "Principle of the permanence of substance" turns on his claim that since it is only "in time, as substratum . . . that *coexistence* as well as *succession* can be represented" (B224), and since "time by itself cannot be perceived" (B225), we must find some other substratum that can serve as proxy for time.

Kant further claims that we cannot find this proxy substratum in our apprehension of appearances, because our apprehension "is always changing. Thus, through it alone we can never determine whether this manifold, *as object of experience,* is coexistent or sequential" (A182/B225; italics added). "Consequently," Kant argues,

> the substratum, which represents time in general and in which all succession *[Wechsel]* or coexistence, through the relation of appearances to it in the apprehension, can be perceived, must be met with in the objects of perception i.e., the appearances. (B225)

Kant finally concludes that "the permanent, in relation to which all temporal relations of appearances alone can be determined, is substance in the appearance, i.e., the real in it, which as substratum of all change always remains the same" (B225).

Now, I am not concerned with the soundness of Kant's argument. I am only concerned with what this argument tells us about the way in which Kant thought succession and/or coexistence would be determined. It is clear that Kant thought we would determine whether appearances are coexistent or sequential against the backdrop of some proxy substratum. It is also clear that Kant thought we would find this proxy substratum in appearances—that is, in the objects of perception. Neither the irreversibility of my perceptions nor the reversibility of my perceptions is itself an object of perceptions. Thus, neither irreversibility nor reversibility could be the proxy substratum that Kant had in mind. Therefore, Kant did not intend the irreversibility or reversibility of perceptions to be the criterion by which we determined whether appearances are coexistent or sequential. Therefore, the Event/Object Strategy cannot be what Kant intended.

A final problem for the Event/Object Strategy is that knowing the order of my perceptions is irreversible does not seem to be necessary for knowing that what I have perceived is an event rather than an ordinary physical object. For Kant an event will be "a successive being and not being of the determinations of the substance that persists there *[die da beharret]*" (B232). Kant further talks of these determinations of a substance as being opposites. That is, an event (a succession of appearances) involves "a state of things is at one time the opposite of which was in the previous state" (B233). Opposite states of a substance are pairs of states such that in the one state the substance has some particular feature while in the other state the substances lacks that same feature. So, for example, a sample of water in a liquid state and the sample of water not in a liquid state are opposite states of the water.

Given Kant's understanding of what an event is, a number of commentators have pointed out that this seems to mean that if I know that what I have perceived are opposite states of a substance, then this is sufficient for me to know that my perceptions are of an event rather than coexistent states. This is because opposite states of a substance cannot coexist. A substance cannot be in opposite states simultaneously. The sample of water cannot be in a liquid state at the very same time it is not in a liquid state. Thus, I do not need to know that the sequence of my perceptions is irreversible in order to know I have perceived an event.[36]

The Event/Event Strategy

The first problem with the Event/Event Strategy is that it runs into problems with its interpretation of the nature of the causal principle. As we saw in chapter 1, principles of understanding are supposed to be constitutive with regard to experience rather than regulative. So the causal principle of the Second Analogy, as a principle of understanding, must be understood as being constitutive rather than regulative. As Kant puts things in the Second Analogy itself, this will mean that a principle of understanding is required not to make "the representation of objects distinct, but that it makes the representation of an object possible at all" (A199/B244). This creates a problem for the Event/Event Strategy. For the Event/Event Strategy holds that

---

36. Included among these commentators are Van Cleve, Beck, and Harper and Meerbote (in their introduction).

according to Kant the causal principle is what enables us to make "inferences from features of events to the temporal ordering of events."[37] That is, it is the causal principle that makes determining the temporal positions of distinct events possible. In other words, if the causal principle were not true, then it would not be possible to date distinct events in relation to one another. The causal principle is what enables us to determine the temporal ordering of sets of events of which we are antecedently aware.

If the causal principle enables us to make the inference from features of events to the temporal ordering of events, it should be clear that the causal principle would not be something that is required to make the representation of an event *possible*. Instead it would be something that is required in order to make the representation of an event or events *distinct*. For it seems to be possible to have a representation of an event without also having determined the temporal position of the event in relation to other events. Indeed, this is a possibility that advocates of the Event/Event Strategy must acknowledge. For if it were the case that I could not have a representation of an event without also having determined the temporal position of the event in relation to other events, then there would not be any dating problem in the first place. For on this position if I represent myself as having perceived an event, then I would have already determined the temporal position of this event and so do not have any dating problem. So on the Event/Event Strategy the causal principle is required *not* for making the representation of an event possible, but for making the representation of an event distinct. So with the Event/Event Strategy we see the introduction of regulative elements into what is supposed to be a constitutive principle. So it cannot be Kant's intended strategy.

The Event/Event strategist may have some recourse here. As long as we understand the Event/Event Strategy as dealing with the ability to temporally order individual events, then the objection stands with full force. Of the two commentators I have listed under the Event/Event Strategy, Bennett straightforwardly holds that the temporal ordering in question is between individual events. Melnick, however, sometimes writes as if the problem of the determination of temporal position involves the relations between distinct events, but sometimes he writes as if it involves the relations between distinct states of a substance (or substances).[38] If the Event/Event strategist adopts the position that the causal principle (or more specifically causal laws) is (are) required for the ability to temporally order the individual states of a substance, then it looks as if he could try to argue that the causal principle (or

---

37. Melnick, 133.
38. Unfortunately, Melnick does not carefully distinguish between these. Most of the time, however, it does seem as if Melnick intends to apply his discussion to the ordering of distinct events.

more specifically causal laws) is (are) required for the representation of an event. This would then be a step in the right direction toward making sure that we do not improperly introduce any regulative functions into the causal principle. However, for two reasons, this modification has only limited success.

First of all, focusing on the requirements for representation is really foreign to the Event/Event Strategy. Melnick's view doesn't utilize the causal principle as a prerequisite for the *possibility of representation*, it utilizes the causal principle as a prerequisite for the *ability to order things temporally*. If those things are events, then on his view we must utilize causal laws to order events we are antecedently aware of. If those things are the constituent states of an event (that is, the states of a substance or substances), then on his view we must utilize causal laws to order the constitutive states that we are antecedently aware of. In either case the focus of the position is the temporal ordering of things that have already been represented. If we use the constituent states interpretation, then it would be possible to *twist* Melnick's view into one that focuses on the prerequisites for the possibility of representation, but rather than representing his view properly it would really transform it into a variant of the Object of Experience Strategy.

Secondly, even if we resist the temptation to change the focus of the Event/Event Strategy, there would still be a problem. On the constituent state interpretation of Melnick's view it would turn out that the ability to temporally order the states of a substance would require the application of causal laws between states as inference tickets. That is, to determine the temporal order of states of a substance we figure out the order that is in accordance with the appropriate causal laws (that is, the laws that apply to states of this type in the appropriate type of circumstances) and we judge that this required order is the actual order. The problem with this is that in order to utilize the causal principle in this way it will have to include some sort of repeatability requirement. However, as I have argued in chapter 2 and will further argue in chapter 5, a repeatability requirement would be a regulative function rather than a constitutive function and so the Event/Event Strategy could not escape improperly importing regulative functions into what is supposed to be a constitutive principle by adopting the constituent states interpretation.

A second problem with the Event/Event Strategy is that it does not fit well with the examples Kant selects in order to illustrate the way the causal principle works. In the Second Analogy Kant's main illustrative example is the event of the ship floating down the river. Kant contrasts the perception of the ship floating down the river with the perception of a house. When he is discussing the causal principle in a passage near the end of the second edition Transcendental Deduction, Kant selects the perception of a different event to contrast with the perception of a house. Instead of the ship floating down the river, Kant chooses to discuss a sample of water freezing (B162).

The textual problem these two examples pose for the Event/Event Strategy is clear—they cannot be taken to be examples of the dating problem. For neither the ship example nor the water example is a case in which we utilize the causal principle in order to determine the temporal position of one distinct event in relation to other distinct events. For both cases involve only *one* event. In the ship case we only have *one* event (the ship's moving from A to B) and in the water case we only have *one* event (the water changing from a liquid state to a frozen state). In both texts Kant uses the examples in order to illustrate how the requirements for the perception of an event are different than the requirements for the perception of an ordinary object, but in neither of these examples does Kant go on to illustrate how the one event can be related temporally to other events. So it is hard to see how either example could be taken to illustrate how the dating problem must be solved by the utilization of the causal principle.

An Event/Event strategist may take some encouragement from the fact that there is one example in the Second Analogy where Kant does make a connection between temporal order and cause and effect, but this encouragement will be very short lived. This example is the case of the cushion and the leaden ball. In this case Kant imagines a lead ball sitting on a cushion. When we see the ball sitting there, then how do we determine which is the cause and which is the effect? Is the lead ball the cause and the indentation the effect or vice versa? Kant says what gives us pause in this case is that the cause "is simultaneous with the effect" (A203/B248). This raises a problem, because in normal cases, Kant implies, we determine which is cause and which is effect by means of the temporal sequence (i.e., the one that occurs first is the cause and the one that occurs second is the effect). In this case since the cause and effect are simultaneous, then how can we distinguish which is which? Kant tells us that even in cases where the cause and effect are simultaneous, then

> I still distinguish the two through the temporal relation of their dynamical connection. For if I lay the ball on the cushion, then the dent follows the previously smooth shape of the cushion, but if the cushion (for whatever reason) has a dent, then a leaden ball does not follow it.
>
> Therefore the temporal sequence is indeed the sole empirical criterion of the effect in relation to the causality of the cause that precedes it. (A203/B248–49)

This example and Kant's conclusion clearly present a problem for the Event/Event strategist. For if the Event/Event strategist is right, then we are supposed to be determining the temporal ordering of events based on cause and effect, but Kant tells us here that things are just the reverse. That is, we use temporal sequence in order to determine cause and effect, not the other way around. Although this example is not as central to Kant's argument as the house and ship are, in some ways this case is much more damaging to the Event/Event Strategy. At least with the ship case, one could say it is simply a bad example and rest in the assurance that Kant does not use it to draw any conclusions that are inconsistent with the Event/Event Strategy. With the lead ball and cushion example, however, we cannot just dismiss the example as a bad one, because Kant does draw a conclusion that is in clear conflict with the Event/Event Strategy.[39]

A final problem with the Event/Event Strategy concerns the strategy's first premise. That is, the claim that determining the positions of events relative to each other would be impossible if the causal principle were false. The main problem with this claim is that it is false and unless there is some overriding reason to commit Kant to a proof strategy with a false first premise, then we should reject the Event/Event Strategy. In order to see this objection more clearly we need to recall some of the details of Melnick's account.

According to Melnick, what is required to determine the temporal position of an event relative to another event "is some way of connecting two events or states x and y . . . on the basis of what kind of events x and y are."[40] This connection between events must enable us "to order events temporally as asymmetric . . . on the basis of what kind of events they are (and the circumstances of their occurrence)."[41] According to Melnick, Kant holds that this connection between events is provided by causal laws. That is, causal laws are what enable us to determine the temporal ordering of events.

According to Melnick, *given* that we know what types of events x and y are and *given* that we know the relevant features of the circumstances in which x and y occur, a causal law is what enables us to infer either that x is prior to y or y is prior to x. Melnick says:

> Kant's claim may be put as follows: Causal laws are rules that license inferences from features of events to the temporal ordering of events

---

39. Melnick does discuss this example, but not in the context of dealing with a problem for his interpretation. He does not seem to realize the significance of it. After quoting the first two sentences of the passage I quoted from A203/B248–49, Melnick writes this: "Let us note that we are here offered an analysis of how to distinguish cause and effect when they are simultaneous. But this seems perfectly irrelevant if we take the problem to be, not how to distinguish cause and effect but, having determined what caused what, how we can infer some succession in appearances" (Melnick, 98). It seems as if he doesn't even entertain the possibility that the conclusion Kant makes explicit in the next sentence conflicts with the interpretation he has been arguing for. For immediately after this, Melnick simply proceeds to discuss what causal rule would be required in order to determine the succession of appearances in this case.
40. Melnick, 89.
41. Ibid., 90.

("inference tickets" in Ryle's terminology). When we determine the temporal order of events in terms of a causal law, we are using the law as a license.[42]

To determine the temporal order of events we figure out the order that is in accordance with the appropriate causal laws (i.e., the laws that apply to events of this type in the appropriate type of circumstances) and we judge that this required order is the actual order.

Furthermore, Melnick argues that

> if a causal law is to serve as a rule for ordering events temporally on the basis of what kind of events they are (and the circumstances of their occurrence), then causal laws must be universal and necessary in a certain sense.[43]

According to Melnick, causal laws are necessary and universal in the sense that given that we determine the temporal order of events based on which order is required by the appropriate causal law or laws, it will be impossible for us to determine that some series of events fails "to take place in accordance with that law."[44]

If, however, causal laws of this sort are what are required in order to determine the temporal position of an event relative to other events, then it seems to me that the requirement is much too stringent. The reason it is too stringent is that it seems to require a human perceiver to be cognitively aware of a great deal of information before one is able to determine the temporal position of an event relative to other events. In order to use a causal law (of the sort Melnick has in mind) to determine the temporal position of an event relative to other events it seems a person would have to be (1) cognitively aware of the causally relevant features of this event,[45] (2) cognitively aware of the causally relevant features of the other event(s),[46] (3) cognitively aware that there are causal laws connecting events of these two (or more) types in certain types of circumstances,[47] and (4) cognitively aware that the appropriate type of circumstances (for the causal laws) obtains in the present case.[48]

---

42. Ibid., 133.
43. Ibid., 90.
44. Ibid., 134.
45. If I do not know this, then a causal law that provides a connection between this type of event and some other type of event cannot be of any use to me.
46. If I do not know this, then a causal law that provides a connection between the first type of event and this type of event cannot be of any use to me.
47. Of course, if I am not aware of the appropriate causal law, I cannot make use of it to date the event in question.
48. If I do not know that the current circumstances are of the right type, then I will not be able to apply the causal law in these circumstances.

It seems to be at least possible, however, that we can know the temporal position of an event relative to other events even though we are unaware of the causally relevant features of the events involved. On what grounds could we deny even the possibility of this? Furthermore, even though I can understand how being aware of causal laws of the appropriate sort would enable us to temporally order events, ruling out the possibility of temporally ordering events relative to each other in those cases where we are unaware of and/or unable to find any such appropriate causal laws seems unwarranted. For not only does it seem to be *possible* that we can determine the temporal position of an event relative to other events even though we are unaware of any appropriate causal laws, but it seems that this is the situation *in most cases* in which we take ourselves to know the temporal position of an event. Let me be clear, I am not claiming that in most cases there are no causal laws connecting the relevant types of events. Such a claim is far stronger than necessary. Even if there are true causal laws connecting every event to every other event, this would not help. For if I am to use the causal laws that obtain in the appropriate circumstances as *inference tickets* I must be *aware of* the causal laws and *aware that* those appropriate circumstances do in fact obtain. In most cases, however, this awareness simply does not exist.

For example when I say I know the first detection of an extra-solar planet occurred after the Berlin Wall was torn down, must I be aware of some set of causal laws that connect these two events? When I say my stomach ache occurred before I sneezed, must I be aware of some set of causal laws that connect my stomach ache and my sneezing? It seems to me that I cannot plausibly be taken to be aware of causal laws connecting the events in either of these cases. Since I am not aware of the appropriate causal laws, I cannot be using the causal laws as inference tickets to determine the temporal position of one event relative to another. Yet in both of these cases I know the temporal position of one event relative to another, so it must be the case that I can determine the temporal position of an event relative to another without any appeal to a causal law. So the Event/Event strategist is wrong in thinking that we cannot determine the temporal position of an event relative to other events without utilizing the causal principle.

The Event/Event strategist might argue that in cases like these wouldn't it make sense to say that it was my awareness of some features of these two events that enabled me to temporally order the one as being before the other? Well, the Event/Event strategist argues, this means you are aware of or are utilizing a causal law, because "a causal law, in the most general (and skeletal) sense" is "a rule that enables us to order events temporally as asymmetric on the basis of features of the events (taking into consideration features of the circumstances)."⁴⁹ The problem is that even working with this skeletal notion of a causal law it is still not clear that we get the desired result.

After all, I am able to temporally order the event of the first detection of an extra-solar planet in relation to the event of the Berlin Wall being torn down. The Berlin Wall was torn down in November 1989 and the first detection of an extra-solar planet allegedly occurred six years later in October 1995. However, I am not aware of any features of the event of the Berlin Wall being torn down or any features of the event of the first detection of an extra-solar planet that would enable me to infer from those features that the tearing down of the Berlin Wall occurred before the first detection of an extra-solar planet. After all there is nothing I am aware of about the features of the tearing down of the Berlin Wall or the circumstances of its occurrence that would have prevented it from occurring only after the first detection of an extra-solar planet. Since I am not aware of any such features of these events, it is hard to see how I could be using causal laws *even in the skeletal sense* as inference tickets to determine the temporal position of the one event relative to the other.

An Event/Event strategist may object here that when he says that "causal laws are rules that license inferences from features of events to the temporal ordering of events ('inference tickets' in Ryle's terminology)"⁵⁰ this does not require that we are actually aware of the causal law in order for the law to license the appropriate inference concerning the temporal ordering of events. That is, perhaps an Event/Event strategist can be an externalist with regard to the justification of this inference concerning the ordering of events.⁵¹ That is, the existence of the appropriate causal laws and my being in the appropriate circumstances, rather than my awareness of the laws and circumstances, are what license my temporal ordering of events.⁵² On this reading of the Event/Event Strategy what we would be committed to claiming is that our ability to temporally order events in relation to each other requires that there

---

49. Melnick, 90.
50. Ibid., 133.
51. Eric Watkins (formerly Anonymous Reviewer B) suggested this possible defense.
52. I should note that although I used a quote from Melnick above, this should not be taken as an indication that Melnick himself would endorse an externalist account of the temporal ordering of events. I think it is pretty clear that for Melnick when it actually comes to determining an event's position in time by means of causal laws, then these laws would be things we are aware of. When discussing how much order or regularity our experience exhibits he makes it clear that this depends on "the stock (or range) of particular (specific) causal laws at our disposal." He writes that "*if* we knew the actual causal connections, we could actually determine the position of any event vis-à-vis every other event" (Melnick 93). What transforms temporal orderings from being determinable to actually being determined is our being aware of the particular causal laws.

are causal laws that connect events of certain types under certain circumstances whether we are at all aware of the laws and circumstances. That is to say, the externalist Event/Event strategist is committed simply to the position that if there are no causal laws connecting events of certain types under certain circumstances, then it will be impossible for us to order such events temporally in relation to each other. Since this reading of the Event/Event Strategy does not require the suspect cognitive awareness of the appropriate causal laws, it looks as if we can use it to get around this objection.

I have some misgivings about the externalist response, however. First of all, I'm not sure what evidence we have for believing even the externalist version of the first premise of the Event/Event Strategy is true. I can understand how my being aware of causal laws of the appropriate sort would enable me to temporally order events, but what about those cases where I am unable to find any such appropriate causal laws? That is, cases like my knowing that the first detection of an extra-solar planet occurred after the Berlin Wall was torn down. In this case I am unaware of and, I believe, unable to find any appropriate causal laws or connections between these two events. What evidence could we have, then, that there *is* a set of causal laws in this case and that it is nonetheless *only* because of the existence of the unknown causal laws that I was able to temporally order these two events in relation to each other? Or to use a case of a type Kant could not have known about, what about the decay of a particular Uranium$_{238}$ atom occurring before my fortieth birthday? What evidence could we have here that there is a set of causal laws and it is *only* because of the existence of the unknown causal laws that I am able to determine that the Uranium$_{238}$ atom decayed before my fortieth birthday? Since I am still able to temporally order the two events in relation to each other, a case like this shows that even on an externalist reading the first premise of the Event/Event Strategy is on shaky ground.

Now, of course, whether or not it turns out to be true that in a case like this there are no appropriate causal laws, the externalist Event/Event strategist can try to find refuge in the fact that Kant himself is committed to the existence of appropriate causal laws in all circumstances. However, Kant is committed to this only as a regulative principle. The existence of the appropriate causal laws between any two events is something we would be committed to in a system of nature, but Kant tells us it is not something that can be guaranteed by the understanding. Understanding does require "a certain order of nature in its particular rules," but these "can only be known empirically and in its view are contingent" (*CJ*, 184). If the existence of particular causal laws is something that is contingent, this will once again leave the externalist Event/Event strategist in a bad position. For the externalist Event/Event strategist's commitment to the causal principle includes a commitment to the existence of the particular causal laws.[53] Since the causal principle is supposed to be an *a priori* principle of the understanding, this would mean the externalist Event/Event strategist would be committed to having particular causal laws included under an *a priori* principle of understanding. This, however, conflicts with Kant's position that particular causal laws are to the understanding only contingent.[54]

The Justification Strategy

According to the Justification Strategy, in the Analogies, "Kant is dealing strictly with the principles that would have to be appealed to in the justification of empirical claims to knowledge."[55] On this view, Kant intends to show that the causal principle is required for the justification, verification, or confirmation of our judgment that a particular event occurred. Now, in the Second Analogy the word *judgment (Urteil)* does occur twice.[56] Both occurrences are in a paragraph that begins around two thirds of the way into the Second Analogy. In the first text Kant writes:

> If, therefore, my perception is to contain the cognition of an event, namely that something actually happens, then it must be an empirical

---

53. Remember it is the existence of the appropriate particular causal laws that would enable us to temporally order events in relation to each other.
54. One further deep misgiving we might have concerning the externalist defense of the Event/Event Strategy concerns the plausibility of interpreting Kant as an externalist with regard to the licensing of causal inferences and the temporal ordering of events in relation to each other. We might worry about the plausibility of ascribing a modern epistemological theory to Kant. Of course in the eighteenth century, philosophers did not use the word *externalism,* but this in itself does not mean Kant's position can't be an externalist position. After all, I think it is plausible to interpret Hume as developing an externalist position concerning the justification of matters of fact. For Hume, what ultimately justifies our beliefs in matters of fact are the habits produced in us by our interactions with the world. For Kant, however, when dealing with either principles of understanding or principles of reason utilizing this sort of justification would clearly be unacceptable. This is in fact one of the main shortcomings Kant finds with Hume. He tells us that Hume held "all supposed *a priori* principles of our understanding to be imaginary, and found, that they are nothing but a habit arising from experience and its laws . . ." (A765/B793). I think Kant's position here indicates that he would view an externalist position concerning the justification of either a principle of understanding or a principle of reason as tantamount to denying the existence of such principles. Of course, the particular inferences we make concerning the temporal ordering of events in relation to each other would be empirical judgments rather than principles of understanding or reason, so this doesn't settle the issue of whether Kant could be an externalist with regard to our temporal orderings of events. I think even here, however, the ascription of externalism to Kant is problematic, but a proper investigation of this issue goes beyond the scope of this project.
55. Guyer, 258–59.
56. The verb *to judge (urteilen)* does not occur at all in the text of the Second Analogy.

> judgment in which one thinks the succession as determined [*daß die Folge bestimmt sei*], i.e., that it presupposes another appearance in time on which it follows necessarily or according to a rule. (A201/B246–47)

The important thing to notice about this passage, however, is that even if Kant were now making judgment the focus of the argument, it would clearly be the judgment itself and not the *justification* of this judgment that would require the causal principle. So this passage cannot be taken be taken as support for the Justification Strategy.

A sentence after this first passage we find the second and final use of the word *judgment* in the Second Analogy. Here Kant writes that

> the relation of appearances (as possible perceptions) according to which what follows (that which happens) is determined in time through something preceding its existence necessarily and according to a rule, consequently the relation of cause to effect, is the condition of the objective validity of our empirical judgments in regard to the series of perceptions, consequently empirical truth itself, and therefore of experience. The principle of the causal relation in the succession of appearances, therefore, is also valid for all objects of experience (under the conditions of succession), because it is itself the ground of the possibility of such an experience. (A201–202/B246–47)

It is important to note, though, that even this passage does not provide unambiguous evidence for the Justification Strategy. On the one hand, it is not implausible to hold that a passage where Kant writes that "the relation of cause to effect, is the condition of the objective validity of our empirical judgments in regard to the series of perceptions" (A202/B247) leads to the Justification Strategy. On the other hand, when we examine where Kant actually ends up in this paragraph we see that it is not at the Justification Strategy. What we find in this paragraph is that the discussion has led to the conclusion that

> the principle of the causal relation in the succession of appearances, therefore, is also valid for all objects of experience (under the conditions of succession), because it is itself the ground of the possibility of such an experience. (A202/B247)

In other words, even in this paragraph, the conclusion Kant ultimately draws is not that the causal principle is necessary because it is a requirement for justification, but instead it is necessary because it is a requirement for the *possibility of experience*. In turn it is this conclusion that leads to the first main objection to the Justification Strategy.

The first problem with arguing that Kant intends to adopt the Justification Strategy is that even if the Justification Strategy were successful then, on its own terms, it would not provide adequate proof of the causal principle that Kant adopts in the Second Analogy. In order to see why this is we must again recall the distinction between constitutive principles and regulative principles. As we saw back in chapter 1, constitutive principles are ones that deal with the possibility of experience. As we also saw in chapter 1, the Principles of Understanding are supposed to be constitutive principles, so they will be dealing with the constitutive requirements for the possibility of experience. Within the Second Analogy itself Kant puts it this way: "[U]nderstanding is required by all experience and its possibility, and the first thing it does is not that it makes the representation of objects distinct, but that it makes the representation of an object possible at all" (A199/B244). The objects we will be dealing with in regard to the constitutive causal principle that we find in the Second Analogy will be events. So in the Second Analogy, the causal principle is not required for making our representation of an event distinct, but it is required for making our representation of an event possible.

If, however, I set out to justify, verify, or confirm my judgment that a particular event occurred, I am attempting to justify, verify, or confirm what I have already represented to myself—namely, that some event has occurred. Justification, verification, and confirmation are not requirements for the possibility of experience or representation, so they will not play a role in a constitutive principle of understanding. Justification may play a role in the expansion, systematization, or regulation of our beliefs or judgments, but these go beyond what is required for the possibility of experience or representation, so they also go beyond the constitutive task with which understanding is engaged in the Principles of Understanding. If we are to remain true to the constitutive nature of the Principles of Understanding, then it will not help us to argue that the causal principle is required in order to justify, verify, or confirm our judgment that an event has occurred. Kant must be able to show that the causal principle is required for the possibility of experience or representation. Otherwise, even if we were able to show that the causal principle is required for some non-constitutive task, however interesting or important it may be, this would fall short of proving that the causal principle *must apply to experience*. Proving that the causal principle is required for some non-constitutive (and hence ultimately optional) task cannot count as proof that it must apply to experience. Proving that the causal principle is required for the constitutive task is the only way to prove that the causal principle must apply to experience. Making representation or experience possible is the first step understanding takes. It is the constitutive task with which a principle of understanding is concerned. The justification, verification, or confirmation of our beliefs, however interesting and important, is a non-constitutive task. So, even if it were on its own terms successful, the Justification Strategy would fail to provide Kant with the necessary means for showing that the causal principle must apply to experience. Since this is Kant's ultimate goal, unless there are extraordinarily strong overriding reasons, the Justification Strategy should be rejected.

A second problem with the Justification Strategy is that it cannot do a very good job of explaining the house and ship examples. As we saw above in the Second Analogy Kant's main illustrative example is the event of the ship floating down the river. Kant contrasts the perception of the ship floating down the river with the perception of a house. We also saw earlier that when he is discussing the causal principle in a passage near the end of the second edition Transcendental Deduction (B162), Kant contrasts the perception of a sample of freezing water with the perception of a house. The problem these two examples pose for the Justification Strategy is that in both texts Kant uses the examples in order to illustrate how the requirements for the perception of an event are different than the requirements for the perception of an ordinary object, but in neither of these examples does Kant go on to illustrate how we would utilize the causal principle in order to justify the judgment that the ship floated down the river or that the water froze. If Kant's strategy were the Justification Strategy, then we would expect that his examples would have something to do with the justification, verification, or confirmation that a particular event has occurred, but they don't seem to involve the justification that a particular event has occurred at all.

A final problem with the Justification Strategy concerns its first premise. That is, the claim that the justification of the judgment that a particular event occurred would not be possible if the causal principle were false. The problem is that this premise doesn't appear to be true. That is, appealing to the causal principle simply does not appear to be a requirement for the justification, verification, or confirmation of the judgment that a particular event occurred. For the Justification Strategy, this problem arises because of the close connection its proponents have drawn between justification and causal laws.

As we saw above, the Justification strategist believes that it is possible to justify the judgment that a particular event occurred "only if there are causal laws entailing that in such circumstances the relevant sequence of states of affairs must have occurred."[57] So in order to justify my judgment that some event occurred, I must appeal to a causal law that dictates that in these circumstances this is the event that had to occur.

---

57. Guyer, 448–49, end note 25.

Now, it may be the case that sometimes I come to believe or to justifiably believe or to know that a particular event has occurred through appeal to a true causal generalization. So, for example, suppose I own a lamp that is plugged into a socket that is activated by sounds of a certain pitch and intensity. Suppose it is also the case that when the bell on my dresser is rung this always produces a sound of the appropriate pitch and intensity. Thus, ringing this bell always activates the plug and turns on the lamp. Now, on some occasion I hear the bell ring and come to judge that the lamp has turned on. It is plausible to think that in such a case I can, and sometimes do, justify my judgment that the lamp has turned on by appealing to the true causal generalization that whenever the bell rings the lamp turns on.

It is hard to see, however, why we would think that all cases work in an analogous way. Suppose I am a person who is unfamiliar with the bell-activated lamp. If I am in the room when the bell is rung and the lamp goes on, then I will come to judge that the lamp turned on. In this case, however, it is clear that I cannot justify my judgment that the lamp turned on by appealing to the true causal generalization that whenever the bell rings the lamp turns on, because I am unaware of the causal connection between the bell's ringing and the lamp's turning on. Does this mean my judgment that the lamp turned on is not justified? Isn't is plausible for me to justify my judgment that the lamp turned on simply by appealing to my having seen it turn on?

Of course a case like this one is not unusual. In many cases my belief in the occurrence of an event seems to work in a similar way. I am entirely unable to appeal to causal laws from which I could infer the occurrence of the Berlin Wall's being torn down—does this mean I cannot justify my belief that it was torn down? I am not in possession of a rule that dictates that in my recent circumstances I had to sneeze rather than laugh—does this mean I cannot justify my belief that I just sneezed? Cases such as these provide us with reason to believe that I can at least sometimes justifiably believe or know that a particular event has occurred without making an appeal to any true causal generalization. So, it seems that the causal principle isn't a prerequisite for justifying, verifying, or confirming the judgment that a particular event has occurred. That is to say, this gives us reason to believe that the first premise of the strategy is false, for justifiably believing or knowing that a particular event has occurred does not require appeal to the causal principle as interpreted by proponents of the Justification Strategy. So, in light of the problems with the first premise and in the absence of extenuating circumstances, this gives us reason to reject the Justification Strategy.

A Justification strategist may object here that when he says it is possible to justify our judgment that a particular event occurred "only if there are causal laws entailing that in such circumstances the relevant sequence of states of affairs must have occurred,"[58] this does not require that we consciously appeal to the causal laws in order to be justified in our judgment that a particular event has occurred. That is, perhaps a Justification strategist can be an externalist with regard to the justification of the judgment that a particular event has occurred.[59] That is, the existence of the appropriate causal laws and my being in the appropriate circumstances, rather than my awareness of the laws and circumstances, are what justify my judgment that a particular event has occurred.[60] On this reading of the Justification Strategy what we would be committed to is that in order to justify our judgment that a particular event has occurred there must be causal laws that require "that in such circumstances the relevant sequence of states of affairs must have occurred"[61] whether or not we consciously appeal to the laws and circumstances. That is to say, the externalist Justification strategist is committed simply to the position that if there are no causal laws mandating a particular sequence of states of affairs in these circumstances, then it will be impossible for us to justify our judgment that a particular event has occurred. Since an externalist reading of the Justification Strategy does not require any cognitive appeal to causal laws, it looks as if it could be used in order to avoid this objection.

Since, as opposed to the Event/Event Strategy, on the Justification Strategy it is clear that we are restricted to successive states of a substance (that is, a single event), as opposed to dealing with the relationships of more than one distinct event, the externalist defense of the Justification Strategy might seem more promising than the externalist defense of the Event/Event Strategy. However, this promise doesn't actually materialize. Since an externalist Justification strategist would insist on the existence of the causal laws as the basis of justification that a particular event occurred, then the

---

58. Ibid.
59. As in the previous section, Eric Watkins suggested this possible defense.
60. I should note that although I use quotes from Guyer in discussing this externalist defense of the Justification Strategy, this should not be taken as an indication that Guyer himself would endorse an externalist account of the justification that a particular event has occurred. To the contrary, it is clear that he is not an externalist. According to Guyer, when we attempt to justify the judgment that a particular event has occurred we "invoke a rule from which it follows that one objective state can only succeed and not coexist with the other..." (Guyer, 248). He tells us that we can justify our judgment "only if we are in possession of causal laws which dictate that..." (Guyer, 252). Finally, he writes according to Kant " in order to determine that perceptions of two states of affairs represent the occurrence of an event, ... all that is required is a rule from which it can be deduced that, *of the two states comprising the event at issue*, the later of them can only have obtained after the earlier, or the earlier can only have preceded the later" (Guyer, 260). *Invoking, possessing,* and *deducing* are hallmarks of internalist accounts of justification.
61. Guyer, 448–49, end note 25.

externalist defense will run into the same sort of problems that the externalist defense of the Event/Event Strategy ran into.[62] That is, on the one hand, it is not clear that there are appropriate causal laws covering all circumstances. Are there causal laws covering my judgment that some particular Uranium$_{238}$ atom decayed rather than some other Uranium$_{238}$ atom? On the other hand, we may again try to find reassurance in the fact that Kant himself is committed to the existence of the appropriate causal laws in all circumstances. Once again, however, we must remember that Kant is committed to them as a requirement of a system of nature, not as a requirement of the possibility of experience. To the understanding these laws are contingent, so they won't play a part in an *a priori* principle of understanding. So ultimately the externalist defense of the Justification Strategy will not be successful.[63]

---

62. See p. 65ff above for more detail.
63. Once again we may also have deeper misgivings about ascribing an externalist position to Kant in the first place. See footnote 54 above in this chapter.

Chapter Four

The Irreversibility Argument

With a general evaluation of four of the five routes to the principle of causation behind us we must now turn our attention to the completion of this task. Remember that each of the argument strategies is in a sense incomplete. The main thing missing is an interpretation of the argument Kant is supposed to use in order to justify the first premise of the argument strategy. There is general agreement that this argument is supposed to be found in what I will call the Irreversibility Argument. The heart of the argument can be found in the following passage:

> I see, for example, a ship floating down the river. My perception of its position downstream follows the perception of its position higher up in the course of the river, and it is impossible that in the apprehension of this appearance the ship should first be perceived downstream and afterwards higher up in the river. The order in the succession of perceptions in the apprehension is thus here determined, and to this order apprehension is bound down. In the previous example of a house, my perceptions in the apprehension could begin at the top and end at the ground but could also begin below and end above; similarly I could apprehend the manifold of empirical intuition from the right or from the left. In the series of these perceptions there was thus no determinate order which made it necessary where in the apprehension I would have to begin in order to connect the manifold empirically. (A192–93/B237–38)

Some have thought, for various reasons, that the Irreversibility Argument provides Kant with a sound basis in his argument for the causal principle.

Others have thought, for various reasons, that the Irreversibility Argument is, as it stands, unsound. Some of these, however, have suggested ways in which it can be successfully modified. Some others have thought, for various reasons, that the Irreversibility Argument as it stands is invalid. Some of these, however, believe it can be successfully modified so that it is valid. Still others have thought, for various reasons, that the Irreversibility Argument is as it stands simply laughable.

These positions above are basically the ones I will examine in the first part of this chapter. For each view I examine I will be concerned with two things: First, I will examine a commentator's exposition of the Irreversibility Argument. Second, I will examine his discussion of the suitability of the Irreversibility Argument as an argument for the first premise of Kant's argument for the causal principle. In the last part of the chapter I will finally turn to an exposition and defense of the Irreversibility Argument itself and I will there deal with a few loose objections that could not be dealt with earlier.

LOVEJOY'S POSITION: SCSE, THE VERIDICAL STRATEGY[1]

Lovejoy argues that Kant brings the irreversibility argument into his attempted proof of the causal principle in order to solve a particular problem—namely, the problem of how it is "that we can distinguish—and, indeed, can conceive of—a moving or changing object, in contrast with the stationary or unchanging."[2] Lovejoy notes, however, that there is a serious objection to this "supposed" problem. Lovejoy's objection is that this problem "is a problem which exists only for Kant's imagination."[3] That is, there is no problem. In actual cases of perception, "so long as our attention to a given object be continuous, objects are directly *given* as moving or stationary, as altering or retaining their original sensible qualities."[4]

Setting aside his objection (as being the least of Kant's problems) Lovejoy argues that Kant goes on to solve this problem in the Irreversibility Argument by showing that when we observe an event the sequence of our perceptions is irreversible. That is, an event must "be observed by us, if it is observed at all, in one single order, which is independent of the action of our will, of any shifting of our attention."[5] When we observe ordinary physical

---

1. At the heading for each commentator I discuss I list which formulation of the causal principle he attributes to Kant (see chapter 2 above) as well as which general argument strategy for the causal principle he attributes to Kant (see chapter 3 above).
2. Lovejoy, 296.
3. Ibid., 297.
4. Ibid.
5. Ibid., 299.

objects, however, the sequence of our perceptions can be altered. That is, when we observe ordinary physical objects the order of our perceptions is subject to the voluntary shifting of our attention. Thus, the Irreversibility Argument gives us a way to make the distinction that Kant confusedly thought was problematic.

The Irreversibility Argument, according to Lovejoy, fares even worse when we consider how well it supports the first premise of Kant's general argument strategy. In order to show that the Irreversibility Argument fails to support the first premise, Lovejoy develops two distinct arguments.

Lovejoy first argues that showing in the case of an event that the order of our perceptions is irreversible while in the case of an ordinary physical object the order of our perceptions is reversible cannot be sufficient ground for the first premise of Kant's general argument. Although the Irreversibility Argument *may* ground the distinction between perceptions of events and perceptions of physical objects it cannot ground the distinction between perceptions that are objectively grounded and perceptions that are merely subjective.[6] We can see this, says Lovejoy, when we realize that

> in the "subjective play of my imagination," I do not ordinarily find any difficulty in discriminating those sequences of images that "contain an event" from those that—though themselves successive—image only objects that are thought as permanent and stable. Throughout the whole range of our perceptual experience—true or false, objective or subjective, waking or dreaming—we have perceptions alike of motion and of rest, of change and of fixity.[7]

That is, if the Irreversibility Argument grounds some distinction that is made *both* in veridical and non-veridical experiences, then the Irreversibility Argument will be of no help in grounding the distinction between veridical and non-veridical perceptions. Since the distinction between perceptions of events and perceptions of physical objects is such a distinction, the Irreversibility Argument cannot ground the distinction between veridical and non-veridical perceptions.

According to Lovejoy, since it is the distinction between veridical and non-veridical perceptions that Kant invokes in his general argument strategy for the causal principle, the Irreversibility Argument does not provide any support at all for the first premise in Kant's argument for the causal principle.

---

6. As a proponent of the Veridical Strategy it is this distinction between perceptions that are objectively grounded and perceptions that are merely subjective that Kant is supposed to use as the ground for the proof in the Second Analogy.
7. Lovejoy, 296.

Kant, however, can accept most of Lovejoy's claims while also rejecting his conclusion. There is no reason to suppose either that Kant simply failed to realize that the distinction between perceptions of events and perceptions of ordinary physical objects can be made regardless of the veridicality of the perceptions or that Kant believed that whenever the perceptions are not veridical, the distinction between perceptions of events and perceptions of ordinary physical objects actually is not (or cannot be) made. I see no reason to think Kant would reject Lovejoy's claim that "[t]hroughout the whole range of our perceptual experience—true or false, objective or subjective, waking or dreaming—we have perceptions alike of motion and of rest, of change and of fixity."[8] Kant does not even discuss this claim, so why would we suppose he rejects it. Of course, Kant's lack of discussion of this claim cannot provide us with a reason for supposing that he failed to realize the claim is true—after all, if we accept such grounds we could equally well suppose Kant failed to realize that he owned a left-handed glove.

If we were sympathetic to Lovejoy's position, then this resolution would present the Kant interpreter with a dilemma. Either Kant accepted the supposition that whenever perceptions are not veridical, the distinction between perceptions of events and perceptions of ordinary physical objects actually is not (or cannot be) made or he did not. If he accepted this supposition, then we would be able to explain why it is that Kant confusedly thought that the Irreversibility Argument had anything to do with showing that the causal principle is required for grounding the distinction between veridical and nonveridical perceptions. If, however, Kant did not accept this supposition, then it becomes very difficult to explain why it is that Kant confusedly thought that the Irreversibility Argument had anything to do with showing that the causal principle is required for grounding the distinction between veridical and non-veridical perceptions. So, if we believe Kant intended to adopt the Veridical Strategy, we might feel compelled to think Kant confusedly accepted this (clearly false) supposition—for this would make our job of explaining another of Kant's confusions easier.

However, as we saw in chapter 3, the Veridical Strategy is not Kant's intended strategy. So, the dilemma of the last paragraph does not present us with any real problem, because it rests on the false assumption that Kant thought the Irreversibility Argument could help to show that the causal principle is required for grounding the distinction between veridical and non-veridical perceptions. So Lovejoy's criticism of the Irreversibility Argument on this score simply misses the target.

Lovejoy's second criticism of the Irreversibility Argument stems from his examination of the possibility of taking the Irreversibility Argument and

---

8. Ibid.

what it "actually" proves as an argument for the causal principle. What Kant has proven, says Lovejoy, is that an event must "be observed by us, if it is observed at all, in one single order, which is independent of the action of our will, of any shifting of our attention."[9] That is to say, when we observe an event the sequence of our perceptions is irreversible. From this irreversibility of sequence in this one case, according to Lovejoy, Kant infers either "the necessary *uniformity* of the sequence of my perceptions in *repeated instances* of a given *kind* of phenomenon"[10] or "the necessary *uniformity* of the sequence in all cases in which the same kind of event appears as antecedent"[11] or both.[12]

In regard to the uniformity of the sequence of perceptions, Lovejoy correctly points out

> that a proof of the *irreversibility* of the sequence of my perceptions in a *single instance* of a phenomenon is not equivalent to a proof of the necessary *uniformity* of the sequence of my perceptions in *repeated instances* of a given *kind* of phenomenon.[13]

Thus, it is clear that the Irreversibility Argument cannot establish the uniformity of perceptions in repeated instances.

In regard to the uniformity of the sequences of events, Lovejoy points out (again correctly) that a proof of the irreversibility of the series of perceptions in the case of an event "is by no means equivalent to a proof that similar changes in objects must at all times follow one another in a fixed and invariable order."[14] Thus, it is clear that the Irreversibility Argument cannot establish the necessary uniformity of the sequence of events. Lovejoy's criticisms, however, have no force against Kant's argument, because Lovejoy has not correctly represented that argument.

First of all, I see no reason to think Kant would disagree with Lovejoy's judgment about the inference from the irreversibility of perceptions in the single case to the irreversibility of perceptions in all similar cases. Kant never endorses such an inference and it is hard to see *why* he would even be interested in entertaining such an inference. In order for Kant to show that the concept of causation must have application to experience he must prove

---

9. Ibid., 299.
10. Ibid., 300–301.
11. Ibid., 303. It is Kant's supposed inference to the uniformity of the sequence of events that Lovejoy has famously called "one of the most spectacular examples of the *non-sequitur* which are to be found in the history of philosophy" (Lovejoy, 303).
12. In fact, Lovejoy seems to think Kant made both of these inferences.
13. Lovejoy, 300–301.
14. Ibid., 304.

something concerning the *objects* that are perceived. Showing something about the uniformity of sequences of perceptions does not help us get any closer to showing that causation is at work in the world than we already are when we represent the sequence of perceptions in a single case as irreversible. So the point of the Irreversibility Argument cannot be to move from a single sequence of perceptions to repeated sequences of perceptions. In order for the Irreversibility Argument to help Kant attain his goal it must enable him to make some connection not between perceptions and more perceptions, but between perceptions and objects. As we will see in chapter 5 the point of the Irreversibility Argument is to show that in order to be able to represent the succession of my perceptions as irreversible, that which I perceive must meet the requirements for being an *object of representations*. How this helps Kant establish the causal principle I will make clear in chapter 5, but what should already be clear is that this is a conclusion about the object that is perceived and not simply a conclusion about sequences of perceptions.

Secondly, I also see no reason to think Kant would disagree with Lovejoy's judgment about the inference from the irreversibility of the *sequence of perceptions* in a single case to the uniformity of the *sequence of events* in all similar cases. On the one hand, it is very difficult to find any text that supports attributing this inference to Kant. There is no problem in suggesting that Kant believes the order of my perceptions of an event are irreversible. Some commentators think we should also interpret Kant as holding that the sequence of events in similar cases must be the same. The text, however, does not in any way support the claim that Kant infers the uniformity in the sequence of events *from* the irreversibility of perceptions in a single case. *Even if* it were the case that Kant ultimately argues for the uniformity of the sequence of events of the same type in the Second Analogy, the irreversibility of perceptions in a single case would stand only as a single premise *not the complete argument*.[15] When I spell out the details of Kant's argument in chapter 5, however, it will become clear that Kant does not make the inference from the irreversibility of perceptions in a single case to the uniformity of the sequence of events. So the details of Kant's argument will not provide us with any reason to think Kant endorses the claim Lovejoy rejects.

On the other hand, another reason to reject the claim that in the Second Analogy Kant made the inference from the irreversibility of perceptions in a single case to the conclusion that the sequence of events in similar cases is uniform, is that in the Second Analogy Kant does not have any motivation

---

15. Melnick is one commentator who supports the SCSE reading of the causal principle who is careful to emphasize that the irreversibility of perceptions is only a single part of Kant's argument. See the discussion of Melnick's position later in this chapter. Also see Melnick, 82–84.

for drawing this conclusion. For as I argued in chapter 2 and I will show in full detail in chapter 5, Kant does not intend to prove the SCSE formulation of the causal principle. The causal principle of the Second Analogy does not include a requirement for the repeatability of sequence. So, since this conclusion is not part of what he wants to prove in the Second Analogy, there is no reason to think Kant would want to endorse an inference from the irreversibility of perceptions in a single case to the uniformity of sequence of events.

Now, Lovejoy does have a rejoinder to my attempt to get Kant out of his purported troubles. Kant must, says Lovejoy, argue for one of these conclusions, because he intends to provide an answer to Hume and answering Hume requires one of these conclusions. Lovejoy claims that if Kant's proof

> is meant to have *any relevancy* to Hume's problem, it should mean that every event has some determinate antecedent and that it can be certainly known *a priori* that the same kind of antecedent will in all instances be followed by the same kind of consequent.[16]

This claim, however, is clearly false. We only need to recall Hume's problem to see this. In what is traditionally called Hume's problem, he formulates it as two questions:

> First, for what reason we pronounce it *necessary,* that every thing whose existence has a beginning, should also have a cause?
>
> Secondly, why we conclude, that such particular causes must *necessarily* have such particular effects; and what is the nature of that *inference* we draw from the one to the other and of the *belief* we repose in it?[17]

Hume's problem has (at least) two parts. Lovejoy writes as if nothing less than answering *both* of these questions would "have any relevancy to Hume's problem." But why should we think this? Clearly, if Kant can provide an answer to the first question, even if he does not attempt to provide an answer to the second question, he has proved something relevant to Hume's problem.

STRAWSON'S POSITION: SCSE, THE EVENT/OBJECT STRATEGY

Although Strawson agrees with Lovejoy's assessment of the success of the argument of the Second Analogy, his reasons for this assessment differ from Lovejoy's reasons. Unlike Lovejoy, Strawson does think the Irreversibility

---

16. Lovejoy, 301; italics added.
17. *Treatise*, 78.

Argument is relevant to Kant's intended strategy in the Second Analogy, but he also believes that the Irreversibility Argument conjoined with Kant's intended argument strategy cannot provide a sound basis for Kant's intended conclusion (i.e., the causal principle).

Strawson argues that Kant hopes to establish, through the Irreversibility Argument, a criterion for distinguishing between perceptions of events and perceptions of coexistent objects. Kant is supposed to establish this criterion by showing that

> any use we may make in experience of the concept of an objective event depends upon our implicit use of the notion of a necessary order of the relevant perceptions. Similarly, our knowledge, through perception, of the co-existence of things depends upon our implicit recognition of the order-indifference of the relevant perceptions.[18]

Strawson then proceeds to consider whether or not this is correct. Strawson sees no real problems with the claim that in the perception of coexistent objects the order of the perceptions is not a necessary order—that is, it is reversible. He also concludes that given a certain qualification it is true that in the perception of an event the order of perceptions is a necessary order—that is, it is irreversible.

The qualification Strawson has in mind has to do with the causal dependence of perceptions on the object (or state) perceived. Strawson believes as long as we require that the causal process that begins with one object (or state) and ends with one perception is isomorphic with the causal process that begins with the second object (or state) and ends with the second perception, then Kant's claims are true.[19] Letting A and B be two states of affairs that constitute some one event and letting *a* equal the perception of A and *b* equal the perception of B, then the qualification can be stated as follows:

> there is no relevant difference in the modes of causal dependence of *a* on A and *b* on B (a relevant difference being any which affects the time taken by the causal process whereby the object (A or B) produces its effect (*a* or *b*) to complete itself)[20]

---

18. Strawson, 134.
19. Strawson argues that such a qualification is needed in order to handle some special cases. Among those included in this category of special cases are those involving more than one sense modality or those in which some but not all of my perceptions are in some way obstructed. Basically, he thinks this qualification is needed in order to handle the sort of objections that Bennett and Wolff would later raise. See Strawson, 135–36 for his discussion of this. I will discuss both Bennett's and Wolff's objections later in this chapter.
20. Strawson, 136.

With this qualification Strawson believes he can show that in the case of perception of an event the order of perceptions is a necessary order, while in the case of the perception of coexistent objects the order of perceptions is not necessary. More specifically, he thinks he can show that the order of perceptions, in the case of event perception, is a *logically* necessary order, but that with perceptions of coexistent objects the order is not *logically* necessary. Strawson argues that if we suppose "(1) That A and B are objective states of affairs of which A precedes B in time, this succession constituting a single event (the event of A's being succeeded by B), (2) *a* is a perception of A and *b* is a perception of B,"[21] and we add to these suppositions our qualification above, "then there follows, with *logical* necessity, the consequence that *a* precedes *b*."[22] If, however, we substitute for (1) "the supposition that A and B are co-existent objects," then it is "a logically open question which, of *a* and *b*, comes first."[23]

Given the necessity of supposing that in event perception the order of perceptions must be a necessary order, Strawson next examines Kant's success in transforming this necessity into the necessity of supposing, in event perception, that the states of the event themselves have a necessary order. If Kant succeeds, then he would have a successful argument for the first premise of the general strategy that Strawson attributes to him. Unfortunately, Strawson argues, Kant is not successful. Strawson represents Kant's argument as follows:

> To conceive the sequence of perceptions as the perception of an objective change is implicitly to conceive the order of the perceptions as, in this sense,[24] necessary. But, . . . to conceive this order of perceptions as necessary is equivalent to conceiving . . . the event of change or transition as preceded by some condition such that an event of that type invariably and necessarily follows upon a condition of that type.[25]

Strawson believes there are two main errors in this argument. The first lies in the fact that with the succession of perceptions we are only dealing with *one* instance of succession, but when we make the transition to the event perceived we are no longer dealing with a single case. In the second part of the equivalence statement cited above we are not only conceiving something about the particular event perceived, but we are conceiving something about it as well as *all* other events of the same type. Even if we are justified in

---

21. Ibid.
22. Ibid.
23. Ibid.
24. As we saw in the last few paragraphs, the *sense* to which Strawson refers is *logical* necessity.
25. Strawson, 137–38.

asserting that the order of perceptions is necessary in the single case, this does not enable us to assert the existence of any sort of necessity in more than one case. So in moving from the premise to the conclusion, Strawson argues, Kant has illegitimately moved from applying this necessity in one case to applying this necessity in more than one case.[26] There is, however, no reason to think Kant himself believed that this inference is justified.

Just as with Lovejoy's second criticism the plausibility of Strawson's first objection rests on the acceptance of the SCSE formulation of the causal principle. If Kant's causal principle invokes repeatability, then this would clearly give him reason to accept a conclusion that involves more than a single case because this would commit him to holding that what happens in the single case must also hold for all cases in which the same type of event is involved. If Kant rejects SCSE and accepts EESC, however, then he has no motivation to accept a conclusion that involves all events of a given type. Since, as I argued in chapter 2 and will conclude in chapter 5, Kant rejects the SCSE formulation, he has no motivation to accept a conclusion that requires an expansion of the scope of application from a single case to all cases that involve an event of the same type. Without this motivation, unless there is overwhelming textual evidence to the contrary,[27] there is no reason to saddle Kant with this inference. So the first of Strawson's objections does not succeed.

Strawson believes Kant's second error lies in the fact that his argument involves two different types of necessity. In connection with the order of perceptions, the type of necessity involved is *conceptual* necessity, but in connection with the order of the states of an event the necessity involved is not conceptual, but *causal* necessity. Strawson argues that the order of perceptions of an event is conceptually necessary "given that what is observed is in fact a change from A to B, and that there is no such difference in the causal conditions of the perception of these two states as to introduce a differential time-lag into the perception of A."[28] The event itself is causally necessary, according to Strawson, if it is "preceded by some condition such that an event of that type invariably and necessarily follows upon a condition of that type."[29] Since these two types of necessity are clearly not equivalent, Strawson argues, the transition from the necessary order of the perceptions of an event to the necessity of the event itself is illegitimate.

---

26. Strawson notes that he does not think Kant notices this shift in the number of cases involved. According to Strawson, "Kant is under the impression that he is dealing with a single application of a single notion of necessity." See p. 138.
27. And in chapter 5 I will argue that this is not the case.
28. Strawson, 138.
29. Ibid., 137–38.

So when Kant argues that "to conceive this order of perceptions as necessary is equivalent to conceiving the transition or change from A to B as *itself* necessary, . . . it is a very curious contortion indeed whereby a conceptual necessity based on the fact of a change is equated with the causal necessity of that very change."[30] The problem with this second objection, however, is that the contortion that is found in Strawson's reconstruction of Kant's argument is not in Kant's argument.

It is difficult to find the basis for Strawson's reconstruction in the text of the Second Analogy. First of all, Strawson's reconstruction is couched in the terminology of conceptual analysis. Strawson's Kant gets things started by analyzing the concept of a necessary order of the perceptions of an event. Strawson's Kant argues that our analysis will lead to the conclusion that conceiving the order of the perceptions of an event to be a necessary order is equivalent to conceiving the event itself to be necessary. Conceptual analysis, however, cannot be what Kant himself intends to be doing. Kant is committed to holding that through conceptual analysis alone it is not possible to prove the causal principle. According to Kant, the causal principle although *a priori* is synthetic not analytic. Something more than the analysis of concepts is required for the proof of a synthetic judgment. In order for Strawson's reconstruction to have any plausibility, there would have to be very strong textual evidence that in the case of the proof of the causal principle Kant makes an exception to his fundamental position on the proof of a synthetic principle.

Secondly, even if Kant were doing conceptual analysis in the Second Analogy, I see no reason to think he would endorse the claim Strawson's Kant endorses. The assertion that conceiving the order of the perceptions of an event to be a necessary order is equivalent to conceiving the event itself to be necessary is nowhere to be found. Unfortunately, when Strawson writes that Kant asserted this equivalence in the Second Analogy he did not provide us with any textual references. Strawson does, however, regard the assertion of this equivalence as laughable—indeed, it is this very assertion that according to Strawson turns Kant's argument into "a *non sequitur* of numbing grossness."[31] In order to plausibly saddle Kant with such a laughable assertion there must be compelling textual evidence, but unlike Strawson, I find no place in which Kant asserts this equivalence between conceiving the order of perceptions to be necessary and conceiving the order in events to be necessary.

Perhaps we can salvage some of the force of Strawson's objection by reformulating it as an objection to an assertion of a logical equivalence that

---

30. Ibid., 138. It is this "contortion" that Strawson famously calls "a *non sequitur* of numbing grossness" (137).
31. Ibid.

holds between the two necessary orders themselves rather than an equivalence that holds between the conceiving of these two necessary orders. That is, perhaps we should see Strawson as objecting to the claim that the order of perceptions of an event is a necessary order if and only if the event itself is necessary. Strawson's argument against this would be that we can have a necessary order of perceptions without having to assume a necessary order of the states that make up the event perceived. For "given that what is observed is in fact a change from A to B, and that there is no such difference in the causal conditions of the perception of these two states as to introduce a differential time-lag into the perception of A,"[32] it follows as a logical consequence that "the observer's perceptions should have the order: perception of A, perception of B—and not the reverse order."[33] Yet the fact that in this particular case we have a change from A to B in no way requires the order of the change to be necessary. Therefore, we can have a necessary order of perceptions without also having a necessary order in the event. So, Strawson might argue, there is no equivalence between the necessary order of perceptions and the necessity of the event itself.

It is difficult, however, either to see Kant's motivation for asserting this equivalence or to find textual evidence that Kant actually asserted this equivalence. The difficulty does not lie in the assertion that if the event is necessary, then there is a necessary order in the perceptions. This is not controversial, because if the event perceived is necessary, then there *is* an event that is perceived. Since there is an event that is perceived and since Kant clearly asserts that in the perception of an event a "rule is always to be found . . . and it makes the order of the perceptions that follow one another (in the apprehension of the appearance) *necessary*"(A193/B238), it follows that if the event perceived is necessary, the order of perceptions is also necessary.[34]

When, on the other hand, we consider the claim that if the order of perceptions is necessary, then the event perceived is necessary, we run into difficulties. It is extremely difficult to see what textual evidence for this claim Strawson has in mind. Strawson simply does not tell us what texts he has in mind and I can't find any text in which Kant endorses this claim.

When we turn to the possible *motivation* for claiming that if the order of perceptions is necessary, then the event perceived is necessary, things are a little clearer. For if Strawson's version of the Event/Object Strategy were Kant's intended proof strategy, then it would make sense for Kant to endorse

---

32. Ibid., 138.
33. Ibid.
34. Notice this is not a special claim that attaches only to events that are necessary. It is not the necessity that is important. The only thing required for the necessary order in perception is the occurrence of an event whether that event be necessary or contingent.

this claim. For on this strategy Kant held that the necessary order of perceptions was the criterion we use in order to determine that what we have perceived was an event rather than an ordinary physical object. In addition, according to this strategy, Kant thought the concept of a necessary order of perceptions "could have no application unless the relevant causal principles applied to the objects of the perceptions."[35] Since this last claim entails the claim that if the concept of a necessary order of perceptions has application then the relevant causal principle has application to the object of perception, it would make sense for someone who endorses Strawson's Event/Object Strategy to accept this claim. As we saw in chapter 3, however, the Event/Object Strategy is not a correct interpretation of Kant's arguments in the Second Analogy. So, this possible motivation would not have motivated Kant.

So, there is neither textual nor motivational support for the claim that Kant is committed to holding that the order of perceptions of an event is a necessary order if and only if the event itself is necessary. Thus, Strawson's second objection (even in this weaker form) is unsuccessful.

BENNETT'S POSITION: SCSE, THE EVENT/EVENT STRATEGY

Jonathan Bennett agrees with Strawson that Kant introduces the Irreversibility Argument in order to ground the distinction between perceptions of coexistent objects and perceptions of an event. According to Bennett, Kant's "distinction turns on whether the order in which my sensory states occur can be re-arranged."[36] Kant's claim is that in the case of coexistent objects the order of my sensory states can be rearranged, but in the case of an event the order of my sensory states cannot be rearranged. Bennett thinks there are three different ways in which this claim can be read and he believes it is false on each of the three readings. So according to Bennett there is no reading of the claims of the Irreversibility Argument in which those claims turn out to be true. Since the claims of the Irreversibility Argument are held to be false, these claims cannot provide any support for the first premise of Kant's general argument strategy for the causal principle. I will deal with Bennett's first two readings here, but I will postpone my discussion of his third reading until after I have examined the details of the Irreversibility Argument for myself.

The first reading is a strictly temporal reading. Saying that a sequence of perceptions cannot be rearranged amounts to saying that those very same perceptions cannot now be had in some sequence other than the original sequence. Saying that a sequence of perceptions can be rearranged amounts to saying that those very same perceptions can now be had in a sequence that

---

35. Strawson, 137.
36. Bennett, *Kant's Analytic*, 220.

is not the same as the original.[37] Although Bennett agrees that the perceptions of an event cannot be rearranged in this sense, he argues that the same thing is true of perceptions of coexistent objects. For it is not possible to *re-have* past perceptions at all. Once I have them "they are all over and done with."[38] So, since I cannot re-have them, I certainly cannot re-have them in a different order than before.

It is very difficult, however, to see why we would want to saddle Kant with a view that is tantamount to affirming our ability to travel backward in time. Bennett acknowledges that Kant does not express this reading in the Second Analogy, but he does interpret A211/B258 in the Third Analogy as being Kant's assertion of this reading. Kant writes there:

> Things are coexistent in so far as they exist at one and the same time. But how does one cognize that they exist at one and that same time? When the order in the synthesis of apprehension of this manifold is indifferent, i.e., it can go from A through B, C , D to E, or also the reverse from E to A. Because if it were sequential in time (in the order that begins with A and ends in E), then it is impossible to begin the apprehension in the perception of E and to advance backwards to A, because A belongs to a past time and thus can no longer be the object of apprehension. (A211/B258)

The thing about this passage that makes Bennett's reading a logically possible reading is the ambiguity of "A, B, C, D, and E." Do they refer to the things in the world that are the contents of the apprehension or do they refer to the apprehensions themselves. If they refer to the *things* that are being apprehended, then it wouldn't make sense to read this passage in Bennett's first sense. In this case it would just be making the same point that was unambiguously made in the passage from the Second Analogy. If, on the other hand, "A, B, C, D, and E" refer to the apprehensions themselves, then Bennett's first reading becomes logically possible. Unless there is compelling independent evidence to accept this rendering of the text's ambiguity, however, we should not accept it. If there is an acceptable rendering of the passage that does not attribute to humans the ability to travel backward in time (an ability we know Kant did not think humans have), then it does not make sense to interpret it otherwise.

On Bennett's second reading the claim that my perceptions of an event cannot be rearranged means that my perceptions of an event could not have (at the time of their occurrence) occurred in any other order. Once again

---

37. Ibid., 221.
38. Ibid.

Bennett has no qualms with this first part, for he agrees that "my sensory states when I saw the ship leave the harbor *could not have* occurred in any other order."[39] Yet once again he thinks that the same thing goes for my perceptions of coexistent objects. For "given that I walked and looked where I did, my visual states as I surveyed the house *could not have* occurred in any other order."[40]

As I read Kant's claims, however, they are not incompatible with this. We need to understand Kant's claim about the house as saying that in the house example I must be able to represent the situation as being such that *if* the series of my perceptions had been ordered differently, then I still would have perceived the house. As I have construed the claim, then, it is not that I must represent the situation as being such that it is physically possible for me to have had my perceptions in a different order. All this reading requires is that I must be able to represent the situation as being such that I would still have perceived the house *if* it had been the case that my perceptions were ordered differently than they actually were.

MELNICK'S POSITION: SCSE, THE EVENT/EVENT STRATEGY

Arthur Melnick argues that according to Kant "it must be possible for a subject who judges about what is given temporally to determine the position in time of what is given."[41] In the Second Analogy, since we are dealing with objective succession, this means it must be possible for us (since we do make judgments about these temporally given items) to determine the position in time of a given succession. As we saw in chapter 3, according to the general strategy that Melnick attributes to Kant the position in time of a given succession can be determined only through the utilization of the causal principle. Melnick argues that the Irreversibility Argument plays an important role in Kant's intended proof of this important premise.

On Melnick's account, Kant's argument for this premise is an eliminative argument. Melnick claims there are three possible ways in which the temporal order of a succession could be determined. First, we could relate the states of the succession to absolute time. Second, we could determine the temporal order simply by appealing to the order of our apprehension of the succession. Third, we could determine the temporal order by appeal to some feature of appearances (ultimately, Melnick will argue that the operative feature of appearances will be their causal relations). Melnick then claims Kant argues

---

39. Ibid.
40. Ibid., 222.
41. Melnick, 85.

that the first two methods for determining temporal order will not be sufficient. Thus, we must determine temporal order by the third method.

Melnick argues that the Irreversibility Argument comes into play when Kant is attempting to show that the second possible method of determining the temporal order of a succession is not adequate for actually determining the temporal order. Furthermore, Melnick argues that this is the *only* role that the Irreversibility Argument plays in Kant's argument. Melnick writes: "Bringing in the irreversibility in the apprehension of a succession . . . is meant merely to refute the idea that I can determine appearances as successive merely on the basis of my apprehensions."[42] That is, Kant did not intend for the Irreversibility Argument to provide *all by itself* an adequate argument for the first premise of his general argument strategy for the causal principle. The Irreversibility Argument is only one stage in Kant's eliminative argument for this first premise.

According to Melnick, we must keep this realization about the intended role of the Irreversibility Argument in mind when we consider whether or not the argument is successful. Given its intended role the Irreversibility Argument should be considered successful if it provides adequate support for Kant's provisional conclusion that the order of a succession cannot be determined solely on the basis of perception.

According to Melnick, however, the Irreversibility Argument only problematically succeeds in proving this conclusion. For this argument depends on the claim that "no succession can be apprehended in the specious present of a perception."[43] That is, the conclusion of the Irreversibility Argument can be reached only by supposing that it is impossible to have a single perception in which, for example I "just see" the ship move.[44] Melnick grants the possibility that a "succession can be apprehended in the specious present of a perception."[45] That is, according to Melnick it is possible "that I (nonsuccessively) perceive α preceding β."[46] Melnick also grants that Kant would deny this possibility, because according to Kant "the apprehension of the manifold of appearance is always successive" (A189/B234). Melnick, however, does not want the argument of the Second Analogy to rest on "this highly problematic thesis."[47] For he does not think it wise to let the claim that "perception is never sufficient for determining time-order," rest on "this highly problematic thesis."[48]

The problem with Melnick's position on the specious present is, as he has noted, that Kant would deny the possibility of apprehending a succession

---

42. Ibid., 82–83.
43. Ibid., 85.
44. Notice that this is one of the complaints that Lovejoy aimed at Kant.
45. Melnick, 85.
46. Ibid., 84.
47. Ibid., 85.
48. Ibid.

in the specious present. Of course, this does not automatically invalidate an interpretation in which it is argued that Kant accepts the possibility of apprehending a succession in the specious present. It may be that all things considered it will be best to interpret Kant's denial of the possibility of apprehending a succession in the specious present as a slip. It might be that the Second Analogy is the only place Kant makes this denial and in the end it may be that his denial does not fit very well with other things he says. It might also be the case that Kant's denial is not really very clearly stated and so someone might argue that since the assertion that it is impossible to apprehend a succession in the specious present is false, then we should find another way to interpret the passage that is supposed to contain Kant's denial. I do not see, however, how we can go in either of these directions.

First of all, Kant's denial in the Second Analogy is formulated in no uncertain terms. This is one case in which we do not have the luxury of explaining away a false claim (if it is false) on the basis of a problematic text. In the Second Analogy Kant's denial is clear, so unless his denial conflicts with what he writes elsewhere, we are stuck with interpreting Kant as holding something false (if it is false).

Furthermore, Kant's denial is not limited to his statement in the Second Analogy. Kant just as clearly makes the same denial in the First Analogy.[49] So, it is hard to see how we would be able to argue that Kant's denial is limited to the Second Analogy and it does not fit well with what he says elsewhere.

Now, regardless of whether the specious present is a real problem for Kant, Melnick believes he can formulate an argument that supports the conclusion of the irreversibility argument, but nonetheless does not rest on this problematic assumption that Kant makes in the Irreversibility Argument. His argument begins with the claim, which he attributes to Kant, that "it must be possible for a subject who judges about what is given temporally to determine the position in time of what is given."[50] In regard to perception of a succession, this means that it must be possible to determine the temporal position of that succession. In order to determine the temporal location of a succession, say A-B, it is not enough to say that B follows A. "For we have not thus determined at all when the succession A-B as a whole took place."[51] To do this we must be able to specify A-B's location in a series of events— that is, determine A-B's temporal relation to other events. To locate the temporal position of this whole series of events, we would have to determine the whole series' temporal relation to still other events.

---

49. "Our *apprehension* of the manifold of appearance is always successive" (A182/B226).
50. Melnick, 85.
51. Ibid., 86.

Ultimately, the relative position of all events or states of affairs to all other events or states of affairs must be determinable. It is only against the background of this thoroughgoing determinability of any two states or events *vis-a-vis* one another that the position of any event can be determinable.[52]

Once we realize just what is involved in determining the temporal location of a succession we will realize that the possibility of perceiving a succession all at once in the specious present poses no real problem for Kant. For perceiving that B follows A in the specious present is not equivalent to perceiving the temporal position of A-B.

The problem with this interpretation of the Irreversibility Argument is that it introduces foreign elements into Kant's argument. It cannot be Kant's point to argue that the irreversibility of apprehension in the ship example (with or without specious present worries) shows that we cannot perceive the temporal relation of the ship floating downstream to other events. For in the ship example there is mention of only one event—the ship floating downstream. There are no other events mentioned. It is hard to take Kant to be pointing out that we cannot determine its temporal relation to other events through perception alone when he does not even talk about any other events.

GUYER'S POSITION: SCSE, THE JUSTIFICATION STRATEGY

Paul Guyer argues that in the Irreversibility Argument Kant's aim is to show how it is possible to justify a judgment that a particular event has occurred. The judgment that a particular event has occurred cannot be justified by any direct appeal to the temporal positions of the states that make up the event, "for the temporal positions of the objective states themselves are not directly given."[53] So, my judgment that an event occurred must be justified on some other basis.

According to Guyer, at the beginning of the Irreversibility Argument Kant introduces and rejects the most straightforward way in which such judgments might be justified. One might think that the occurrence of a particular event can be justified by appeal to the actual order of perceptions. That is, one might think that from the fact that my perception of A preceded my perception of B it can be inferred that objective state A actually precedes objective state B. This inference, however, is unacceptable. For

---

52. Ibid.
53. Guyer, 248.

The Irreversibility Argument 93

> the mere occurrence of such a sequence of representations is not incompatible with the possibility of the occurrence of precisely the opposite sequence of representations ... and this possibility is presumably to be explained by the *simultaneous existence* of the objects of both representations.[54]

Thus, the actual order of perceptions cannot serve as the basis for the justification of the judgment that an event has occurred.

Kant then notices, according to Guyer, that "if there were an actual event, thus if one state of affairs did succeed the other, then the *perception* of the one would not only succeed that of the other, but would *have to* succeed it."[55] That is, as a consequence of actually perceiving an event, the order of my perceptions is a necessary order. Their order is irreversible—the one perception must follow the other and not the reverse. What follows from this, according to Guyer, is that if I know the order of my perceptions of two states is irreversible, then "the temporal positions of the objective states themselves ... *could* be inferred from the *necessary* sequence or irreversibility of the representations of them."[56] So, according to Guyer, this leads Kant to conclude that *if* I can justify the judgment that a sequence of my perceptions is irreversible, then I can justify my judgment that a particular event has occurred. Unfortunately, this is not as simple as one might think.

I might think I can justify my judgment that the order of a sequence of perceptions is necessary or irreversible by direct appeal to some fact about my representations, but according to Guyer this thought would be incorrect. For Kant holds, Guyer argues, that the irreversibility or necessity of a sequence of representations is no more directly given to consciousness than is the temporal location of the objective states themselves. That is, just like the temporal location of objective states, the necessary order of perceptions is not directly given, but is something that must be inferred. This is

> of course nothing but a consequence of Kant's most fundamental assumption that experience "to be sure tells us what is, but not that it must necessarily be so and not otherwise" (A1). No necessities of any kind, whether in the objective realm or even in the subjective arena of representations themselves, are ever given by uninterpreted apprehension.[57]

With the failure of this last possible way to justify the judgment that a particular event has occurred, Guyer argues that there is only one alternative

---

54. Ibid., 247.
55. Ibid.
56. Ibid., 248.
57. Ibid.

left. On this alternative the judgment that a particular event has occurred can be justified only "by *adding* to the omnipresent succession of mere representations a *rule* from which it can be inferred that in the circumstances at hand *one state of affairs* could *only* succeed the other."[58] Since this added rule requires that one state *had* to follow the other, it can be inferred that the one state *did* follow the other. Thus, adding the rule enables us to justify the judgment that the event has occurred.[59]

We can see more concretely how such rules work using Kant's ship example. In the ship example, Guyer argues, Kant's conclusion is that we can justify the claim that what we have perceived is the event of the ship sailing downstream "only if we are in possession of" a rule according to which "in the particular circumstances of wind, tide, setting of the sails, and so forth, which are assumed to obtain—the ship could *only* sail downstream."[60]

So at the conclusion of the Irreversibility Argument Kant has argued that in order to justify the judgment that a particular event has occurred we must possess "a rule which dictates that in a given situation one state of affairs must succeed another."[61] It still remains to be seen, however, whether or not this conclusion successfully provides any support for the first premise of Kant's general argument for the causal principle.

Guyer believes it is only a short step from the conclusion of the Irreversibility Argument to the first premise of Kant's general argument. For Guyer argues that the sort of rule that is required for the justification of the judgment that a particular event has occurred simply is a causal law. "A rule which dictates that in a given situation one state of affairs must succeed another is just what Kant means by a causal law."[62] So, according to Guyer, since Kant has shown that such rules are required for the justification of judgments that events occur, then he has also successfully shown that causal laws are required.

Of all the commentators I have discussed in this section, Guyer is the only one who strictly speaking regards the Irreversibility Argument as being a successful argument for the first premise of Kant's general argument strategy for the causal principle. As far as I can tell, Guyer is the only commentator who attributes to Kant the SCSE formulation of the causal principle and

---

58. Ibid.
59. It is also interesting to note that according to Guyer, adding this rule is also precisely what enables us to justify the judgment that our perceptions are irreversible. Since the addition of such a rule would allow us to infer that a particular event did occur, and since as we saw above, if we perceive an event, the order of our perceptions is a necessary one, then we can conclude that the order of our perceptions is a necessary order.
60. Guyer, 252.
61. Ibid., 249.
62. Ibid.

who also regards the Irreversibility Argument as providing a successful argument for the first premise of Kant's general argument strategy.

In order to clearly formulate my worries about Guyer's position it is important to focus on his characterization of how things work in the case of the ship. Guyer writes that

> Kant's theory is precisely that it is only if we are in possession of causal laws which dictate that in the relevant circumstances—that is, not in general, but in the particular circumstances of wind, tide, setting of the sails, and so forth, which are assumed to obtain—the ship could *only* sail downstream that we actually have sufficient evidence to interpret our representations of it to mean that it *is* sailing downstream.[63]

As I see it, there are two main problems with the interpretation presented in this passage. The first problem concerns how Guyer's interpretation fares as an interpretation of Kant. The second problem concerns the truth of the conclusion that Guyer here attributes to Kant.

First, once again it is difficult to make this interpretation mesh with the examples that it is supposed to fit—that is, Kant's main illustrative examples. When we examine the ship example we find no discussion of the "particular circumstances of wind, tide, setting of the sails, and so forth." We do not find Kant citing such particular circumstances as evidence that the event perceived was the ship floating downstream at all. Instead, what we find is a discussion of what is required in order to be able to represent the occurrence of the event. This same situation is true when we examine the example of the water freezing at B162.

What these examples should tell us is that in the Second Analogy Kant is not concerned with the justification of our empirical judgments that a particular event has occurred, but rather he is concerned with what is required in order for the representation of the occurrence of an event to be possible. In chapter 5 I show that this concern with the possibility of representation of the occurrence of an event is not limited to Kant's discussion of his illustrative examples. Instead, it is the central focus of the whole discussion in the Second Analogy. Thus, Guyer's interpretation of the Irreversibility Argument must be rejected.

The second problem with Guyer's interpretation of the Irreversibility Argument involves the truth of the conclusion he attributes to Kant. As interpreted, the conclusion of the Irreversibility Argument is that I am justified in judging that my representation is of the ship floating downstream *only if*

---

63. Ibid., 252.

I am in possession of causal laws that dictate that "in the particular circumstances of wind, tide, setting of the sails, and so forth," the ship *must* sail downstream and not upstream. If we generalize, then we get the claim that I am justified in judging that my representation is of the occurrence of a particular event only if I am in possession of causal laws that dictate that in the particular circumstances that obtain this event (and no other) *must* occur.

By making the possession of causal laws a requirement for *justification* Guyer has staked out a position that is much stronger than Melnick's position above. Melnick makes the possession of causal laws a requirement for knowledge, and in chapter 3, I have argued that such a requirement on the knowledge of the temporal position of one event in relation to other events should be rejected. Accepting such a requirement for knowledge, however, leaves open the possibility that we can attain justification without being in possession of the appropriate causal laws that would be required in order to have knowledge.

So in chapter 3, when I argued against Melnick that it seems to be the case that sometimes I actually and/or possibly know the temporal position of an event in relation to other events without making appeal to the appropriate causal laws, Melnick might have tried to soften the blow by saying that although I do not have *knowledge* in those cases he is willing to admit that I do have *justification*. To make the transition to Guyer's view, we could say the same thing in terms of the occurrence of particular events. That is, although we cannot *know* that a particular event has occurred without possessing the appropriate causal laws, we can at least *justifiably believe* that a particular event has occurred without possessing the appropriate causal laws. On Guyer's interpretation, however, we must deny even the possibility of justifiably believing that a particular event has occurred without possessing the appropriate causal laws.

What was implausible in weaker form is even less plausible when made stronger. If in order to be justified in interpreting my representation as being of a ship floating downstream I am required to be in possession of causal laws that dictate that "in the particular circumstances of wind, tide, setting of the sails, and so forth," the ship *must* float downstream and not upstream, then I must confess that as far as I know I have never been justified in interpreting my representations as being of a ship floating downstream. Furthermore, I do not believe my position is unique. For it seems that human cognizers are hardly ever in possession of such causal laws. This makes clear a serious problem with attributing such a view of justification to Kant. For if we accept this view of justification it seems we will also have to accept justification skepticism with regard to our judgments that a particular event has occurred. Now, it may be that we are willing to commit *ourselves* to such justification skepticism, but it is not at all plausible to attribute such skepticism to *Kant*.

We might, however, try to avoid this conclusion by modifying Guyer's actual position. Guyer, as we have seen above in chapter 3, is an internalist concerning the justification of our judgments that particular events have occurred, and this is what really causes the trouble here. If instead we adopt an externalist position with regard to the justification of the judgment that a particular event has occurred, then this objection can be largely mitigated. An externalist account of justification will not require a cognizer to possess the implausible quantity of information that is required on Guyer's account. Instead, the judgment that the ship floated downstream would be justified by a cognizer's standing in the appropriate relationship to the world rather than by a cognizer's appealing to the set of causal laws that apply in these particular circumstances.

We should note two things, however. First, any worries we may have about the plausibility of attributing an externalist theory of justification to Kant apply here just as they did when considering general argument strategies.[64] On the other hand, when considering the Irreversibility Argument in isolation from the general argument strategies introduced in chapter 3, an externalist theory of justification doesn't immediately face the problems concerning the existence of appropriate causal laws in all circumstances and the contingency of these laws if they do exist. This is because these problems arose in connection with adopting an externalist reading of the first premise of the general argument strategy attributed to Kant and that posed special problems that don't arise here in isolation. If, however, we adopt an externalist theory of justification here in the Irreversibility Argument, then we would have to make sure that when we fit the Irreversibility Argument into its place in one of the general argument strategies we have a way to prevent these problems from recurring.

THE HOUSE, THE SHIP, AND IRREVERSIBILITY

At last it is time to finally turn to an exposition of the basic details of the Irreversibility Argument itself. In lots of ways the Irreversibility Argument is quite simple. The real problems begin with what we claim Kant is going to do with this simple argument. In other words, it is the significance of the Irreversibility Argument that causes the controversy. I can't deal with the significance of this argument yet, because in order to see that we must see how the Irreversibility Argument fits into the correct understanding of Kant's argument strategy in the Second Analogy and that is the topic for chapter 5. What we will find here are the simple details of the argument, but investigating the real significance of the argument must wait until chapter 5.

---

64. See footnote 54 in chapter 3.

Suppose "I see a ship floating down the river" (A192/B237). Do I represent myself as having perceived a succession of appearances (the event of the ship floating down the river), simply because I represent "my perception of its position downstream" as following "the perception of its position higher up in the course of the river" (A192/B237)? Kant says his house example shows us that the answer to this question is "no." Suppose, in a series of perceptions, I see a house. Now, Kant would say I must represent my perceptions as having some order—that is, one perception follows another perception. So perhaps I represent my perception of the east wing of the house as following my perception of the south wing which in turn follows my perception of the west wing. Although I represent my perceptions as following each other in this way, I do not also represent the east wing itself as following the south wing which in turn follows the west wing. On the contrary, I represent the east wing, the south wing, and the west wing as coexistent parts of the one house.

Although in both cases my perceptions follow one another, there is, according to Kant, a characteristic that the series of my perceptions of the ship floating downstream has that the series of my perceptions of the house lacks. This feature is the irreversibility of the perceptions involved. That is, not only do I represent my perception of the ship downstream as following my perception of the ship upstream, but I also represent it as being "impossible that in the apprehension of this appearance the ship should first be perceived downstream and afterwards higher up in the river" (A192/B237). My perception of the house, however, is subject to no such constraint. For

> my perceptions in the apprehension could begin at the top and end at the ground, but could also begin below and end above; similarly I could apprehend the manifold of empirical intuition from the right or from the left. (A192/B237–38)

I take the following two claims to capture Kant's position concerning the reversibility or irreversibility of perceptions in the two cases. In the case of the perception of the house I must be able to represent the situation as being such that while keeping the perceptual conditions and the membership of the series of my perceptions constant *if* the series of my perceptions had been ordered differently, then I would have still perceived the house. In the case of the perception of the ship floating down the river, however, I must represent the situation as being such that while keeping the perceptual conditions and the membership of the series of my perceptions constant *if* the series of my perceptions had been ordered differently, then I would *not* have still perceived the ship floating downstream. That is to say in the case of the perception of the ship floating down the river I must represent the situation as being such that while keeping the perceptual conditions and the membership of my series of perceptions constant, *if* I also keep the event constant, then I could not have had my series of perceptions in any other order.[65]

Suppose I represent my perception of the house in the following way: First I looked at the front door, then I looked at the chimney, then I looked at the bay window in the living room, then I looked at the easternmost window on the second floor, and finally I looked at the garage door. Now suppose I had started my perusal by first looking at the bay window in the living room, then I looked at the chimney, then I looked at the front door, then I looked at the garage, and then finally I looked at the easternmost window on the second floor. If this had been the order of my series of perceptions would the house still have been the object of my perceptions, as it was in the first case? Yes it would. So it seems in the case of the house, while allowing the ordering of the series of my perceptions to vary in the two cases I am able to keep the membership of that series, the perceptual conditions, and the object of my perceptions constant between the two cases.

Suppose I represent my perception of the ship floating down the river in the following way: First I looked at the ship in front of the dock, which is at the highest navigable part of the river, then I looked at the ship in front of the castle, which is two hundred meters downstream from the dock, then I looked at the ship in front of the village, which is three hundred meters downstream from the castle, then I looked at the ship in front of the farm, which is two hundred meters downstream from the village, and finally I looked at the ship at the point where the river joins the ocean, which is four hundred meters downstream from the farm. Now, suppose I had started my perusal of the ship floating down the river by looking at the ship in front of the village. Could I have then gone on to look at the ship in front of the dock, then in front of the castle, then in front of the farm, and finally at the point the river joins the ocean? The answer is "no." In its floating down the river the ship arrives in front of the village only after it has already passed in front of the dock and castle. So if when I had first looked at the ship it was in front of the village, this means I would have already missed my chance to look at the ship while it was in front of the dock or in front of the castle. In fact, any ordering of this series other than the original ordering would face this same problem. So it seems I could only have had all five of these perceptions if I first looked at the ship at the dock, then at the castle, then at the village,

---

65. I have spelled these out being careful to speak of the situation as I represent it and the order of my perceptions as I represent it, and so on. I have done this in order to make it clear that I do not interpret Kant as taking any of these things as some sort of uninterpreted given—even the order of my perceptions is something that I must *represent* to myself. Guyer's treatment of the Second Analogy includes a interesting discussion of this. See Guyer, 237ff.

then at the farm, and finally at the ocean. That is, I can have all five perceptions only in the original order.

There remain, however, a few objections to Kant's claims about the reversibility or irreversibility, which I have not dealt with above. I want to look at these objections now that the Irreversibility Argument has been spelled out properly. One such objection is made by Robert Paul Wolff. Wolff's objection involves the use of mirrors.[66] Wolff says that we might set mirrors up in such a way that the light from the ship's position upstream gets reflected from mirror to mirror in such a way that it only reaches my eye after the light from the ship's position downstream reaches my eye. In such a case, I would perceive the ship downstream before I perceive it upstream. So, argues Wolff, Kant's claim that I must represent the situation such that I could not have had my perceptions of the ship downstream before my perceptions of the ship upstream is false.

As I have construed Kant's claim, however, Wolff's objection fails. For in Wolff's mirror case the perceptual conditions have not been kept constant. In fact Wolff's objection *requires* the perceptual conditions in the mirror case to be different than the conditions in the original case. So in the mirror case Wolff does not succeed in reordering the series of perceptions while keeping the object and perceptual conditions constant. Wolff's case could only have any force if we read Kant as claiming that we must represent the series of our perceptions of the ship floating down the river as being such that we could not have had them in any other order *even when* we take into consideration cases in which *the perceptual conditions differ radically from the original perceptual conditions*. Now, it may in fact be that such a claim is false, and it may even be that its falsity is something that even, as Wolff puts it, "the least reflection will show,"[67] but there is no reason to stick Kant with such a claim.

Wolff also proposes another case that is supposed to show Kant's claim that I must represent the situation such that I could not have had my perceptions of the ship downstream before my perceptions of the ship upstream is false. Letting A be one of the ship's positions upstream and B be one of its positions downstream, Wolff says "We might hear its whistle at A after we see its smoke from B."[68] So, says Wolff, I could have perceived the ship downstream before I perceived it upstream.

This objection, however, is also unsuccessful. It may be that we can suppose we have kept the perceptual conditions constant and *perhaps* we can suppose that we have kept the event constant, but this case does nothing to

---

66. Wolff, *Kant's Theory of Mental Activity*, 268.
67. Ibid.
68. Ibid.

show that in the situation as represented I could have had my series of perceptions in any order other than the original order. For the set of perceptions involved in this possible series of perceptions is a *different* set of perceptions than the set involved in the original series. In this case Wolff asserts that in the situation as represented I could have seen smoke that the ship produced while it was downstream before I heard the sound that the whistle produced while the ship was upstream. This, however, does not show that I can represent the situation as being such that I could have *looked* at the ship downstream before I *looked* at the ship upstream.[69] Yet this is exactly what must be shown in order to show that I could represent the situation as being such that I could have had my series of perceptions in a different order—for these alone are the perceptions I represent myself as having had. This objection could only have any force if claiming that I must represent the situation as being such that I could not have looked at the ship downstream before I looked at it upstream requires that I also claim that I could not have seen the smoke produced downstream before I heard the sound that the ship's whistle produced while it was upstream. There is, however, no reason to think this is the case.

A third objection to Kant's claims about the reversibility or irreversibility in the house and ship examples is lodged by Jonathan Bennett. Bennett claims that in the ship example it is false that I must represent the situation such that I could not have had my perceptions of the ship downstream before my perceptions of the ship upstream. Bennett argues, on the contrary,

> since the coxswain of the boat was under orders from me, I *could have* secured for myself the spectacle of the boat being back-paddled, stern foremost, into the harbor.[70]

So, I could have had the coxswain float the boat up the river, and thus I could have perceived the boat downstream before I perceived it upstream.

As I have construed Kant's claims, however, Bennett's objection also fails. For in Bennett's case we have not kept the object constant. In the first case the object of my series of perceptions is the event of the ship floating down the river (or, in Bennett's terms, it is the ship leaving the harbor), but in the case that "I *could have* secured for myself" the object of my series of perceptions would be the event of the ship floating up the river (or into the

---

69. It is easy to imagine a case like this that involves the house as well. Suppose I represent myself as looking at the door of the house before I looked at the chimney of the house. The possibility that I could represent the situation as being such that I could have seen the smoke from the chimney before I heard the doorbell ring does not tell me anything about whether or not I could have first looked at the chimney and only then looked at the door.
70. *Kant's Analytic*, 222.

harbor). The ship's floating down the river is not the same event as the ship's floating up the river. It would only be possible for Bennett's objection to have any force if Kant were claiming that I must represent the situation as being such that I could not perceive the ship downstream before I perceive it upstream *even when* we take into consideration cases in which *the event perceived is different than the event in the original case.* In considering whether or not the series of perceptions is reversible in the house example Kant only discusses a case in which the object remains constant. Indeed, what would be the point in saying that when I perceived one house I began with the top and ended at the bottom, but when I perceived some other house I began at the bottom and ended at the top? So, what reason could we have for thinking that when he turns to the ship example, he will suddenly be considering whether or not the order of the perceptions of one event could be the reverse of the order of the perceptions of some other event.

A final objection focuses not on Kant's claims in the ship example, but on his claims in the house example. It is claimed that it will not always be the case that my perceptions of the house are reversible.[71] That is, it can be the case that the perceptual circumstances involved in the house example will make it physically impossible for me to have had my perceptions in any other order. If I am in such perceptual circumstances when I look at the top of the house and then look at the bottom of the house, then it would not be true that I could have had my perceptions in any other order. That is, I could not have looked at the bottom of the house before I looked at the top of the house. So, it is claimed, Kant's claim about the house example is wrong.

As I have construed Kant's claims, however, they are not incompatible with such a situation. I claim that we should read Kant's claim about the house as saying that in the house example I must be able to represent the situation as being such that *if* the series of my perceptions had been ordered differently, then I still would have perceived the house. As I have construed the claim, then, it is not that I must represent the situation as being such that it is physically possible for me to have had my perceptions in a different order. All this reading requires is that I must be able to represent the situation as being such that I would still have perceived the house *if* it had been the case that my perceptions were ordered differently than they actually were.

---

71. Wolff makes this claim on p. 268. Bennett comes close to making this claim on p. 220ff.

Chapter Five

Objects of Representations

In the last two chapters we have seen that proponents of each of the first four possible interpretations of the strategy utilized by Kant in his proof for the causal principle have run into serious problems. In addition to the textual and/or internal problems each of these first four strategies runs into, none of these strategies adequately accounts for the emphasis Kant places on the notion of an "object of representations." Both ordinary physical objects, such as a house or a rock, and successions of appearances (events), such as a ship floating down a river or water freezing, are objects of representations. The truth of the causal principle hinges not on the requirements for our being able to distinguish between veridical and non-veridical perceptions, nor on the requirements for our being able to apply the concepts of an objective change and an objective coexistence, nor on the requirements for our being able to temporally order events in relation to each other, nor on the requirements for our being able to justify the judgment that a particular event has occurred. Instead, the truth of the causal principle hinges on the requirements for an event's being an object of representations. Kant argues that the causal principle must be true (that is, the causal principle must apply to all events), because no event that fails to meet the specifications of the causal principle would be a possible object of representations. This is the basic position of the Object of Experience Strategy interpretation of Kant's argument in the Second Analogy. Once again I will represent this strategy schematically this way:

1. If the causal principle is false, then there could be some succession of appearances (some event) that is not subject to a rule.

2. Successions of appearances (events) are objects of experience.

3. A succession of appearances that is not subject to a rule is not a possible object of experience.

4. So, there cannot be any succession of appearances that is not subject to a rule.

Therefore, the causal principle is true.

In this chapter I will turn to a detailed exposition and defense of the Object of Experience Strategy. This exposition and defense must begin with a closer look at the causal principle itself.

THE PRINCIPLE OF THE SECOND ANALOGY

In the second edition Kant states the principle he will prove this way: "*All alterations [Veränderungen] take place in accordance with the law of the connection of cause and effect*" (B232). In the first edition the principle is stated as follows: "Everything that happens (begins to be) presupposes something upon which it follows *according to a rule*" (A189). There are two differences between the A and B formulations of the principle. The first change Kant made in the B formulation was to replace the phrase "everything that happens (begins to be)" with the phrase "all alterations." The second change is the replacement of the phrase "presupposes something upon which it follows according to a rule," with the phrase "take place in accordance with the law of the connection of cause and effect."

Although, as I argued above in chapter 2, the two versions have the same meaning, it may be that the expectations created by the second edition version are different than the expectations created by the first edition version. The changes made in the second edition allow the B version of the principle to have the advantage of expressing more clearly the connection between the Second Analogy and the First Analogy as well as between the Second Analogy and the Transcendental Deduction. Using the word *alterations* clearly alludes to Kant's discussion of alterations in the last section of the First Analogy (A187ff./B230ff.). Using the unanalyzed phrase "the law of the connection of cause and effect'" has the advantage of reminding the reader that there is supposed to be a connection between the principle of the Second Analogy and the pure concept of cause and effect. These two advantages, however, come at a price. The price is that, in the B formulation of the principle, the connection between the Second Analogy and the Schematism is not clearly expressed.

The A version of the principle neither alludes to the discussion of the First Analogy nor does it leave any reminder that the Second Analogy is somehow connected with the pure concept of cause and effect. The A version does, however, have the advantage of reminding us of the connection between the Second Analogy and the Schematism. The wording of the A version clearly alludes to the schema of cause and effect. The schema of cause and effect "consists, therefore, in the succession of the manifold, in so far as it is subject to a rule" (A144/B183).

The lack, in the B version, of a clear expression of the connection between the Second Analogy and the Schematism combined with the B version's reminder that there is a connection between the principle of the Second Analogy and the pure concept of cause and effect might encourage the reader to have false expectations. The B version might leave the reader with the impression that in the proof of the causal principle Kant is going to be concerned with the pure concept *simpliciter*. That is, one might be tempted, by the second edition formulation, to think Kant will be concerned with the *category* of causality and dependence (cause and effect), but not with the *schema* of that category. Such an expectation, however, cannot be correct.

There are two reasons for holding that in the Second Analogy Kant is not dealing with the pure concept *simpliciter*, but rather he is dealing with the pure concept *combined with* its schema—that is, he is dealing with the so-called *schematized* category of causality and dependence.

The first reason is that if Kant's treatment of causation in the Second Analogy dealt with the pure concept *simpliciter*, then it would be inconsistent with his theory of concepts. As we saw in chapter 1, according to Kant's theory of concepts, concepts can be applied to intuitions only through the utilization of schemata. A concept, according to Kant, is a discursive and general representation while the sensible intuitions to which it applies are pictorial and concrete. Yet if concepts are to apply to sensible intuitions, there must be some way to specify to which sensible intuitions a concept applies. It is the schema of a concept that provides the method for linking the concept and the sensible intuitions (and ultimately objects) to which the concept applies. (Or conversely, the schema of a concept provides the method for linking sensible intuitions and the concepts under which they are subsumed.) The schema does this by providing, in imagination, "an image for a concept" (A140/B179–80).

As we saw in chapter 1 there are two kinds of images that schemata produce. The schema of an empirical or mathematical concept produces a spatial image, but the schema of a pure concept produces a transcendental time determination (that is, a distinct temporal structure or pattern). With the image provided by the schema in hand, we have a guide in the search for the sensible intuition(s) (if any) that is (are) correlated with the concept. That is, it is the schema that tells us what pattern(s) of sensible intuition(s) is (are) correlated with a concept. Without the image or pattern formulated through the schema we are left without any guide in the search for the sensible intuitions that are correlated with the concept.

So, if in the Second Analogy Kant were attempting to prove that the category of causality and dependence must have application to experience and if in attempting to prove this he utilized only the pure concept, then he would have to carry on his search without the guide (the schema of cause and effect) that his theory of concepts requires. So in order to remain consistent with Kant's theory of concepts we need to realize that in the Second Analogy it is not the pure concept *simpliciter* with which we are dealing, but it is the pure concept conjoined with its schema. That is, the so-called *schematized* category.

The second reason for holding that in the Second Analogy Kant is not dealing with the pure concept *simpliciter* is that if Kant's treatment of causation in the Second Analogy dealt with the pure concept *simpliciter*, then it would be inconsistent with his reasons for giving the third set of three principles the name *Analogies of Experience*. As we saw in chapter 1 there are two reasons for calling the third set of principles "Analogies." One of these reasons is a feature the Analogies share in common with all of the other principles, and this is what is important here. As we saw above, Kant tells us the Analogies and all of the other principles are "analogous" to their respective pure concepts. "The category," Kant says, "contains the function restricted by no sensible condition" (A181/B224). Such a concept can only be employed as "the unity of the thought of a manifold in general. Now through a pure category . . . no object is determined, but rather only the thought of an object in general, according to various modes, is expressed" (A247/B304). In the principles, however, we are concerned not with thought in general, but with the contents of human sensibility. What Kant thinks we need from the principles is a function that is, unlike a pure concept, restricted by sensible conditions, but that nevertheless remains analogous to the pure concept. In order to get both of these, the principle must provide a formula for the unity of a given sensible manifold. "This however, is alone thought in the *schema* of the pure concepts of understanding" (A181/B224; italics added).

If, however, Kant is utilizing only the pure concepts in the principles, he will be unable to achieve this goal. So, in order to remain consistent with his general statements about the relation between principles and categories, we must realize, in the principles, Kant is trying to prove that "appearances must be subsumed *not* under the categories *per se,* but rather under their schemata" (A181/B223; italics added). So, given these two reasons, when we examine Kant's attempted proof that the concept of cause and effect must have application to appearances, we must keep in mind that it is the schematized category that is at stake.

So what exactly is this schematized category of cause and effect? It is the concept of "succession of the manifold, in so far as it is subject to a rule" (A144/B183). So it will turn out, then, that the schematized category of cause and effect has application to experience just in case there is some succession of the manifold of appearances that is subject to a rule. Of course, Kant is not simply concerned with showing that as a matter of fact the schematized category of cause and effect *does* have application to experience, but instead, with the causal principle, he will try to show that it *must* have application to experience. It will turn out that the schematized category of cause and effect must have application to experience just in case the succession of the manifold of appearances must be subject to a rule.

In the Second Analogy Kant shows us that we do in fact find successions of appearances. For we clearly perceive that "appearances follow one another, i.e., that a state of things is at one time the opposite of which was in the previous state" (B233). There are, however, two important questions that must be asked about these successions of appearances. On the one hand, we will want to know whether any of these successions of appearances are in fact successions that are subject to a rule. If any are, then this of course will show us that the concept of cause and effect does have application to experience. On the other hand, and most importantly, we need to know whether these successions of appearances must be successions that are subject to a rule. Of course, if Kant can show that successions of appearances must be subject to a rule, then this will count as a successful proof of the causal principle. Understanding Kant's proof is the main objective in this chapter, but given the crucial role that being subject to a rule plays in the causal principle, then in order to understand this principle and Kant's attempted proof of it we must first examine what Kant takes to be involved in being subject to a rule.

SUBJECT TO A RULE

In at least three passages of immediate concern for the Second Analogy, Kant discusses the notion of being subject to a rule. As we have seen above, in the Schematism Kant says the schema of cause and effect "consists in the succession of the manifold, in so far as it is subject to a rule" (A144/B183). Once again in the statement of the principle of the Second Analogy in the first edition Kant states that "everything that happens (begins to be) presupposes something upon which it follows *according to a rule*" (A189). Finally in a passage that may be the most important for the Second Analogy, just after raising the house example and before presenting the ship example Kant writes that "appearance, in contradistinction with the representations of apprehension, can only be represented as an object distinct from them if it stands under a rule" (A191/B236).

In order to see what being subject to a rule will amount to in the Second Analogy, we will need to briefly explore the connection between rules, unity, and the object of representations.

Oftentimes when Kant discusses rules, he writes of them as being the means by which unity is produced in something. For example, when Kant is comparing reason *(Vernunft)* with understanding *(Verstand)* he states that

> the understanding may be a faculty *[Vermögen]* of the unity of appearances by means of rules, so reason is the faculty *[Vermögen]* of the unity of the rules of understanding under principles. (A302/B359)

It will be the unity of appearances that will be important for Kant's proof in the Second Analogy. Of course, the unity of appearances and the possibility of such unity will be of great importance for all of the Transcendental Analytic. Kant reminds us of this in a passage from the second section of the introduction to the system of principles where he writes:

> The *possibility of experience* is thus that which gives all our cognitions *a priori* objective reality. Now experience is founded on the synthetic unity of appearances, i.e., on a synthesis according to concepts of the object of appearances in general, without which it would not even be cognition, but only a rhapsody of perceptions that would not fit together in any context according to rules of a thoroughly connected (possible) consciousness, consequently it would also not fit into the transcendental and necessary unity of apperception. Experience thus has principles of its form *a priori* lying at the foundation, namely, general rules of the unity in the synthesis of appearances. (A156–57/B195–96)

Still of even more importance for the Second Analogy is Kant's discussion of the unity that is required for the possibility of an *object of representations*.

OBJECTS OF REPRESENTATIONS AND BEING SUBJECT TO A RULE

Right from the start of the Second Analogy Kant makes it clear that the notion of an object of representations has a central role to play in the proof of the causal principle. In the third paragraph of the Second Analogy Kant writes:

> The apprehension of the manifold of appearance is always successive. The representations of the parts follow one another. Whether they also follow in the object is a second point for reflection that is not contained in the first. Now admittedly one can call everything, and even every representation, in so far as one is conscious of it, an object, but what meaning this word has with regard to appearances, not in so far as they (as representations) are objects, but rather only in so far as they signify an object, is a matter for deeper investigation. (A189–90/B234–35)

Kant, of course, regards himself as having already made significant progress in this "deeper investigation." For it was back in the Transcendental Deduction (in A) that Kant writes: "And here then it is necessary to make clear what is meant by the expression 'an object of representations' " (A104). What we find, writes Kant, is that "the object is viewed as that which ensures that our cognitions are not haphazardly or arbitrarily determined" (A104).

Kant's point is straightforward. The object is that which grounds the objectivity of cognition. If I take some set of my representations to have an object, then I represent my cognition in this case as having been constrained by the features of the object.[1]

On the other hand, if I regard some set of my representations as having no object, then I represent myself as having been constrained only by my imagination. If I had imagined a green sphere resting on top of a green cube, then I represent the situation as being such that it had been up to me whether to imagine the sphere being on top of the cube or the cube being on top of the sphere. In this case, I represent my desire as being responsible for the content of my representations.

Now, it may be easy enough to see how objects in the ordinary sense (i.e., tables, chairs, lions, tigers, and bears, etc.) can ground the objectivity of cognition, but how will this work when, as Kant puts it, we "raise the concept of an object to the transcendental meaning" (A190/B235–36)? For better or worse, when we consider the meaning of the phrase "object of representations" in the transcendental sense we will have to focus on representations. For transcendentally speaking an object "is no thing in itself, but rather only an appearance, i.e., representation" (A191/B236).

If this is true, then how can objects, which are themselves representations, *be* "that which ensures that our cognitions are not haphazardly or arbitrarily determined" (A104). Kant's answer is that in order for representations to be objects in this sense they themselves must not be associated in a haphazard or arbitrary way. That is, the representations must themselves be connected *according to rules*. In other words, representations,

> in so far as they are in these relations (in space and time) connected and determinable according to the rules of the unity of experience are called *objects*. (A494/522)

---

1. Now, it may be that psychological studies show that a person's desires actually do have an effect on what the person perceives, but this should not pose any problem for Kant. It is not Kant's point to argue that when I take my representations to have an object I actually do not have control over the content of my perceptions. Rather, his point concerns how I *represent* the situation. In order to make this point it does not have to be the case that the way I represent things is the way things really are.

We can see more specifically the nature of these rules from the passage in the Second Analogy quoted earlier. These rules specify one determinate connection of representations and thereby make this connection of representations distinguishable from all others. For

> appearance, in contradistinction with the representations of apprehension, can only be represented as an object distinct from them if it stands under a rule, which distinguishes it from every other apprehension, and makes necessary one manner of connection of the manifold. (A191/B236)

According to Kant, then, this is a general requirement for all objects of experience or representations.

The precise nature of such rules may still not be clear, but it is important that we get a better understanding of these rules. Using Kant's example of a house, I want to explain, more concretely, what I take to be involved in being subject to a rule in the appropriate sense—that is, a rule that distinguishes an appearance from every other and that mandates one determinate connection of the manifold. The house's being subject to a rule in this sense will involve three requirements.[2]

The first requirement is that the house must have one particular spatial temporal location. At a given time throughout the duration of its existence the house must be located in one spatial region. This of course does not rule out the possibility of the house being located in different spatial regions at different times (for example, a house that is at one time located at 3 Bagshot Row may at some other time be located at 221B Baker street), but what it does rule out is the possibility that the house has more than one spatial location at any given time or that the house has no spatial location at all.

Secondly, at any given time in which it exists the house must be composed of some one determinate set of parts. Here the definition of part will include the material it is composed of. So for example the house might be composed of a bedroom with walls made out of brick and the floor made out of oak, a bathroom with brick walls and a tile floor, etc. It may be that the house is composed of different sets of parts at different times (for example, a house that has only two bedrooms on one occasion may on another occa-

---

2. In what follows I will discuss being subject to a rule that mandates one determinate connection of the manifold in empirical terms. Ultimately I think we would have to carry out the discussion in transcendental terms and so these rules would have to be spelled out strictly in terms of representations and their connections. I think, however, it will be easier to understand the nature of these rules if we stick with empirical terms.

sion have three bedrooms, or at one time the walls may be made of stone but at some other time they may be made of brick), but what this does rule out is that at any given time the house is composed of more than one set of parts or that at some time the house is composed of the empty set of parts. It should also be clear that this rules out the possibility that at any given time a part of the house has more than one determinate composition or that it is not made of anything at all. Finally, it should be noted this requirement will entail that the members of the set of parts that make up the house at any given time must *at that time* coexist with one another.

Thirdly, within the spatial region in which the house is located, the various parts of the house must be connected with each other in some one determinate way. This of course does not rule out the possibility of the parts of the house being arranged in different ways at different times (for example, at one time the kitchen may be located on the south side of the second floor, but at some other time it may be located on the east side of the first floor), but what it does rule out is the possibility of the parts of the house being arranged in more than one way at any given time or that at some time in which the house exists the parts of the house are not connected in any determinate way at all.

There are two things that should be noted with regard to being subject to a rule in this sense. First, just as the unity of apperception does not require (to *mis*quote Kant) that the *I think* must accompany all my representations, being subject to a rule in this sense does not require any cognizer to actually know the determinate manner in which the manifold is connected. That is, using the three requirements above, being subject to a rule does not require that any cognizer actually knows the spatial temporal location of the object or the parts that make up the object at a time or the arrangement of those parts. Once again, in line with the unity of apperception, which requires (to accurately quote Kant) that "the *I think* must *be able* to accompany all my representations" (B131), being subject to a rule requires that the connection of the manifold is determin*able*. That is, the object must have a determin*able* location, a determin*able* set of parts, and a determin*able* arrangement of parts.

Second, in listing the above three requirements for being subject to a rule I did so predominately with ordinary physical objects in mind. In the Second Analogy we will also be concerned with what is required in order for a succession of appearances (i.e., an event) to be subject to a rule. Although the general outline will be the same as it is with ordinary physical objects, what we want to see is whether these requirements also adequately capture the requirements for an event's (that is, a succession of appearances') being subject to a rule in the manner appropriate for its being an object of representations. Through his example of a ship floating down a river, Kant will show that these requirements do not adequately capture the requirements for an event's being an object of representations. There is an important difference between ordinary objects and events that these requirements do not capture.

IRREVERSIBILITY REVISITED: ARE SUCCESSIONS OF APPEARANCES SUBJECT TO A RULE?

Are successions of appearances subject to a rule? Must successions of appearances be subject to a rule? According to Kant, if there is a succession of appearances that is subject to a rule, then the concept of cause and effect has application to experience.[3] If *all* successions of appearances are subject to a rule, then according to Kant the concept of cause and effect must have application to experience.[4]

Kant will show us an example of a succession of appearances that is subject to a rule—the example of the ship floating downstream. Thus, the concept of cause and effect does have application to experience. Then Kant will show that all successions of appearances are subject to a rule, hence cause and effect must have application to experience. He will do this by showing that a succession of appearances that is not subject to a rule is not a possible object of representations. The Irreversibility Argument will play a central role in Kant's proof that successions of appearances must be subject to a rule.

In chapter 4 I explained and defended Kant's Irreversibility Argument, but now we must investigate the importance of the conclusions of this argument. Of what importance is it that, as opposed to the house example, in the ship example we must represent our perceptions as being irreversible? Or (to put the question in the terms Kant uses at the end of the paragraph in which the ship example is introduced), of what importance is it that, as opposed to the house example, in cases like the ship example a "rule is always to be found and it makes the order of the perceptions that follow one another (in the apprehension of the appearance) *necessary*" (A193/B238)?

The irreversibility of my perceptions of the ship floating down the river is important because this is supposed to show that in this case I represent myself as not having had control over the order of my series of perceptions. Instead, in this case, I represent the order of my series of perceptions as being controlled *by the succession of appearances that was perceived* (i.e., the ship floating downstream). That is, I represent this succession of appearances as being responsible for the order of the series of my perceptions. This is what Kant means when he says that "in our case I must derive the *subjective*

---

3. According to Kant the converse of this claim is also true.
4. Once again Kant also holds the converse of this claim as well.

succession of apprehension from the *objective succession* of the appearances" (A193/B238).

Again, this is in contrast to the way things work in the house case. For in the house case I do represent myself as having control over the order of my series of perceptions. I do not represent any succession in the appearance as being responsible for the order of the series of my perceptions.

Now, when we put together the irreversibility of our perceptions with what we have just said about the source or ground of this order we can see the most important result from the ship example—namely, that we are treating this succession of appearances (the ship floating downstream) as an *object of representations*. For "that in the appearance which contains the condition of this necessary rule of apprehension is the object" (A191/B236). Since the order of my perceptions is represented as a necessary order and the succession of appearances is represented as being that which mandates this order, the succession of appearances is being represented as an object. So in the case of the ship floating down the river I represent the succession in my perceptions *as having an object* and its object is this succession of appearances.

Once again this is in contrast to the way things work in the house example. In the house case I have control over the succession of apprehension, and thus I represent the succession in my perceptions as *not having* any succession of appearances as its object.

When we recall that in his discussion of an object of representations Kant said "the object is viewed as that which ensures that our cognitions are not haphazardly or arbitrarily determined" (A104), the conclusion drawn from the case of the ship should not be too surprising. For in the case of the ship floating down the river I represent the succession in my perceptions as having a succession of appearances as its object and this object is represented as being that which prevented me from having had my perceptions in just any order I might have chosen. Instead, I represent the succession of appearances as being such that I could have had my perceptions of it in one order only.

Now, we must also remember that in order for an appearance to be an object in this sense (i.e., in the sense of being "that which ensures that our cognitions are not haphazardly or arbitrarily determined") the appearance itself must not be connected haphazardly or arbitrarily, but instead it must be connected according to rules. In other words, as we have already seen, in order for an appearance to be an object of representations it must be subject to "a rule which distinguishes it from every other apprehension, and makes necessary one manner of connection of the manifold" (A191/B236). Now, in the ship case we have a succession of appearances (namely, the ship floating down the river) that is an object of representations. It can only be an object of representations if it is subject to a rule. So, the ship floating downstream is a succession of appearances that is subject to a rule. More importantly since the ship floating down the river is a succession of appearances that is subject to a rule, this also shows that the concept of cause and effect *has application to experience* in at least one case.

I have already used Kant's house example to explain concretely what is involved in being subject to a rule that distinguishes an appearance from every other and that mandates one determinate connection of the manifold in the case of an ordinary object. With the ship example now in hand, however, we are in a better position to use it to investigate what being subject to a rule in the appropriate sense will amount to when dealing with a succession of appearances (that is, an event) rather than an ordinary physical object. The ship's floating down the river being subject to a rule in this sense will involve three requirements.[5]

The first requirement is that the succession of the ship floating down the river must occur in a determinate spatial region and during a particular temporal period. What this rules out is the possibility that it occurs either in more than one determinate spatial region or during two or more noncontinuous temporal periods or that it actually occurs, but either it does not occur in any spatial region or it does not occur during any temporal period.

The second requirement is that the event of the ship floating down the river must be composed of some one determinate set of parts. Here a part of the succession would be defined as the ship floating in a particular determinate spatial position. So, for example, the succession might be composed of the ship floating in front of the dock, the ship floating in front of the village, and the ship floating at the ocean. What this rules out is the possibility that the event of the ship floating down the river is composed of more than one determinate set of parts or that it is composed of the empty set of parts.

Thirdly, the parts of the succession of the ship floating down the river must be connected with each other in one determinate manner. So, given that this is a succession, this will mean that the parts must be connected with each other in some determinate temporal order. This rules out the possibility that they are connected in more than one determinate temporal order or that they are not connected in any determinate temporal order at all.

There are three things that should be noted with regard to this characterization of the requirements for being subject to a rule in the case of a succession of appearances. First, just as in the house case, being subject to a rule in this sense does not require any cognizer to actually know the determinate manner in which the manifold is connected. That is, using the three requirements above, being subject to a rule does not require that any cognizer actually knows the spatial temporal location of the succession of appearances or the

---

5. In what follows I will again keep my discussion on empirical rather than transcendental terms.

membership of the set of parts of that succession, or the temporal ordering of those parts. Once again in line with what was said in the house case, being subject to a rule requires that the connection of the manifold is determin*able*. That is, the object must have a determin*able* location, a determin*able* set of parts, and a determin*able* temporal ordering of parts.

Second, Kant's choice of the ship example as an example of a succession of appearances makes things a little interesting. This is because Kant's "official" definition of a succession of appearances seems to be one state of a substance following another state of a substance,[6] but here in the ship example (the first example he introduces in the Second Analogy) we have a succession of appearances, but it does not seem that we have one state of an object followed by a different state of the object. Instead, we have an object changing not states but spatial positions. So the conclusions about the requirements for a succession of appearances' being subject to a rule will need some revision after the examination, in the next section, of what can be concluded about successions of appearances in general as opposed to this specific case. As we will see, however, the required revisions will not force us to go in any significantly new direction, but they will be needed in order to make clear how what was said in the ship case can be formulated for successions of appearances that fit Kant's "official" definition.

Third, up to this point in my explication of what is involved in an appearance's (the house) or more importantly a succession of appearances' (the ship floating down the river) being subject to a rule I have not made any use of the notion of repeatability based on the type of object or succession we have. On my reading of Kant the sense of being subject to a rule that is appropriate here has nothing to do with repeatability. Being subject to a rule is what is required for an appearance to be an object of representations. This rule "distinguishes it from every other apprehension, and makes necessary one manner of connection of the manifold" (A191/B236). So in the case of the house I represent it as having a certain location, and a certain set of parts arranged in a certain manner. But, whether or not all other objects of this type (i.e., all houses) have parts of the same type arranged in that same manner, does not have any bearing on whether or not *in this case* appearances are connected in some one determinate manner. So repeatability does not have any bearing on whether or not the appearance in the house case meets the requirements for being an object of representations. Similarly, in the case of the ship floating down the river I represent it as having a certain location and a certain set of parts arranged in a particular temporal order. But, whether or

---

6. At B233 Kant says that "appearances follow one another, i.e., that a state of things is at one time the opposite of which was in the previous state," and at A187/B231 he says "some determinations [of a substance] cease and others begin."

not all other events of this same type (i.e., all ships floating downstream) have parts of the same type arranged in that same order, does not have any bearing on whether or not *in this case* appearances are connected in some one determinate manner. So repeatability does not have any bearing on whether or not the succession of appearances in the ship case meets the requirements for being an object of representations.

Since repeatability has no bearing, in these cases, as to whether or not the appearance or the succession of appearances meets the requirements for being an object of representations, the appropriate sense of being subject to a rule will not involve any repeatability requirement. Since a succession of appearances that is subject to a rule gets subsumed under the concept of cause and effect, the concept of cause and effect at work here does not include a repeatability requirement. So at this stage, based on the features of the succession of appearances in the ship case, there is reason to hold that EESC is the correct formulation of the causal principle in the Second Analogy. For the SCSE formulation of the causal principle incorporates a repeatability requirement. However, since, as I noted above, the requirements for a succession of appearances' being subject to a rule will be subject to review in the next section, I will postpone a complete argument and defense of EESC until later in this chapter.

AN EXAMPLE FOR THE OFFICIAL DEFINITION

Through the ship case Kant has shown that in at least one case the concept of cause and effect has application to experience. For in the ship example Kant has shown that the ship floating down the river is a succession of appearances that is subject to a rule. Since the schema of cause and effect is the manifold of appearances insofar as it is subject to a rule, Kant has shown that the ship floating down the river gets subsumed under the schematized category of cause and effect. Thus, the concept of cause and effect has application to experience. In order to show that the concept of cause and effect *must* have application to experience Kant must show that all successions of appearances are subject to a rule.

As I noted in the last section, the succession of appearances in the ship example (i.e., the ship floating down the river) is not the sort of example we would expect given Kant's official definition. A succession of appearances, according to the official definition, is one state of a substance following another state of a substance. It is "a successive being and not being of the determinations of the substance that persists there *[die da beharret]*" (B233). Again, as noted in the last section the ship floating down the river seems to involve an object changing place not states. So the conclusions from the last section concerning the requirements for a succession of appearances being subject to a rule were formulated without the aid of an example of a succession of appearances that clearly fits the official definition. So in this section I will reexamine the requirements for a succession of appearances' being subject to a rule, while keeping the official definition of a succession of appearances in focus.

Near the end of the second edition Transcendental Deduction Kant discusses first the apprehension of an ordinary physical object and then discusses the apprehension of a succession of appearances. The example he chooses for an ordinary physical object is the same as it is in the Second Analogy—a house. His example of a succession of appearances, however, is not a ship floating down the river, but instead it is the freezing of water. Kant writes: "[W]hen I (in another example) perceive the freezing of the water, I apprehend two states (that of fluidity and solidity) as ones that stand in a relation of time to one another" (B162). This example does fit the official definition. The succession consists in one state (fluidity) of an object (the water) followed by another state (solidity) of the object. This is the example I will use in my reexamination of the requirements for a succession of appearances' being subject to a rule that mandates one determinate connection of the manifold. Once again, the water's freezing being subject to a rule in this sense will involve three requirements.[7]

The first requirement is that this freezing of the water must occur in a determinate spatial region and during a determinate temporal period. This does not rule out the possibility that the water changes spatial position while it is freezing. For example, a half cup of water in a canteen might freeze while it is being carried on a ten mile hike in sub-zero temperatures. In such a case, since this freezing is not instantaneous, the spatial region in which this freezing occurs will consist in a spatial *path* rather than a fixed spatial position. This also does not rule out the possibility that this same quantity of water freezes again during some other temporal period. For example, this half cup of water that froze in the canteen might melt when it is set in front of a fire, but then re-freeze on the next day's hike. In such a case the water freezes twice.

What this requirement does rule out, however, is the possibility that this particular freezing of the water occurs *either* in more than one determinate spatial region *or* during two or more noncontinuous temporal periods. It also rules out the possibility that this freezing of the water actually occurs, but *either* it does not occur in any spatial region at all *or* it does not occur during any temporal period whatsoever.

---

7. In what follows I will once again keep my discussion on empirical rather than transcendental terms.

Secondly, the event of the freezing of the water must be composed of some one determinate set of parts. Here a part of the succession would be defined as the water being in some particular determinate state in some particular determinate spatial position. So, for example, the event might be composed of the water being in a liquid state at the trail head, the water being in a semisolid state one mile from the top of the mountain, and the water being in a solid state at the top of the mountain. What this rules out is the possibility that the event of the water freezing is composed of more than one determinate set of parts or that it is composed of the empty set of parts.

Thirdly, the parts of the succession of the water freezing must be connected with each other in one determinate manner. Given that this is a succession of one state following another, this will mean that the parts of the succession of the water freezing must be connected with each other in some determinate temporal order. So, for example, the water being in a liquid state at the trail head comes before the water being in a semisolid state one mile from the top of the mountain, which comes before the water being in a solid state at the top of the mountain. This rules out the possibility that they are connected in more than one determinate temporal order or that they are not connected in any determinate temporal order at all.

SUCCESSIONS OF APPEARANCES MUST BE SUBJECT TO A RULE

In both the case of the ship floating down the river and the water freezing we have found that we represent the succession of appearances as being subject to a rule. That is, in both cases we represent the succession of appearances as being subsumed under the concept of cause and effect. Yet it still remains to be seen whether or not this is true for *all* successions of appearances. Kant will argue for this claim by arguing that no succession of appearances can be succession that is *not* subject to a rule. The most important thing to keep in mind is that on Kant's account a succession of appearances is an object of representations.

Kant begins his argument by supposing that a succession of appearances is not subject to a rule. He continues by arguing that if we accept this supposition, then

> all succession of perception would be determined only merely in the apprehension, i.e., only subjectively, but then it would not be objec-

tively determined which of the perceptions must actually be the preceding and which the following. We would in this way have only a play of representations that would not be related to any object whatsoever, i.e., through our perception no appearance would be distinguished at all from any other with regard to temporal relations, because the succession in apprehension is always the same, and thus there is nothing in the appearance that determines it so that a certain sequence is rendered objectively necessary. Therefore I would not say that in the appearance two states follow one another, but rather only that one apprehension follows the other, which is merely something *subjective* and determines no object, consequently cannot even count as cognition of any object (not even in the appearance). (A194–95/B239–40)

The point of Kant's argument is straightforward. The supposition that some succession of appearances is not subject to a rule requires that we suppose there is a succession of appearances that fails to meet one or more of the requirements for being subject to a rule. As we saw above, this would mean that we must suppose there is some succession of appearances that *either* fails to have a determinate spatial temporal location, *or* it fails to have some determinate set of parts (stages), *or* the parts (stages) of the succession fail to be connected to one another in any determinate temporal order.

Now, as we saw above, these requirements for being subject to a rule are supposed to "make necessary one manner of connection of the manifold" (A191/B236) and to make an appearance distinguishable from all other appearances. For this is what is required in order for an appearance to be an object of representations. If a succession of appearances either does not have any determinate spatial temporal location, or if it does not have any determinate set of parts, or if its stages are not arranged in any determinate temporal order, then since it would not be distinguishable from all other appearances it will fail to meet the requirements for being an object of representations. That is, a succession of appearances that is not subject to a rule is not a possible object of representations—it is not a possible object of experience. With a succession of appearances, "as soon as I perceive or assume that in this succession there is a relation to the preceding state from which the representation follows according to a rule, I represent something as an event or something that happens, i.e. I cognize *[erkenne]* an object" (A198/B243). So, since a succession of appearances that is not subject to a rule would fail to be an object of representations, a succession of appearances must be subject to a rule. That is to say, all successions of appearances are subject to a rule—this, in turn, is what Kant needed to show in order to prove that the causal principle must have application to experience.[8]

PROBLEMS AND DEFENSE

There are two sorts of problems I now want to discuss. The first problem concerns the requirements I have spelled out for a succession of appearances' being subject to a rule. The second concerns certain textual problems with the interpretation I have adopted. I will deal with these two problems in turn.

The requirements for a succession of appearances' being subject to a rule

As we saw earlier, in order for an appearance to be an object of representations it must be subject to a rule that mandates one determinate connection of the manifold and distinguishes the appearance from all others. So being an object of representations requires that the appearance be subject to a rule. So a succession of appearances must be subject to a rule that mandates one determinate connection of the manifold and distinguishes the appearance from all others.

One might concede, however, that a succession of appearances must be subject to a rule and yet still disagree with what being subject to a rule amounts to. There are two ways in which someone might disagree. The first way is to argue that the requirements for a succession of appearances' being subject to a rule cannot be as strong as I have construed them. So they must be weakened and once they are weakened it will be seen that Kant's main conclusion cannot be supported by these requirements. The second way is to argue that the requirements for a succession of appearances' being subject to a rule, as I have construed them, are too weak. So they must be strengthened and once they are it will be seen that they must include a repeatability requirement. I will discuss each of these in order.

---

8. It may be worth noting here that when we are dealing with successions of appearances, objects of representations, the possibility of experience, etc., we are not concerned with the logical connections between the members of this set. So, for example, when we are discussing the requirements for the possibility of experience we need to be clear that we are not concerned with the requirements for the *concept* of the possibility of experience. Instead we are concerned with the synthetic and *a priori* requirements for the possibility of experience itself. If we were dealing with just the logical connections between concepts, then the best we could end up with is a demonstration of an analytic principle through the law of contradiction rather than a transcendental proof of a synthetic and *a priori* principle. For more on this issue see my discussion of transcendental proofs in chapters 1 and 6.

Are my requirements too strong?
It might be argued that successions of appearances must be subject to a rule, but this requires *only* that successions of appearances are subject to a rule in *exactly the same way* as appearances such as the house. As I have spelled things out, Kant holds that the requirements for being subject to a rule are different in the case of an ordinary appearance and a succession of appearances. The main difference between these sets of requirements is that in the case of a succession of appearances it is required that the set of parts of the succession be ordered in some determinate temporal order. In the case of the ordinary appearance, however, there is no requirement on the temporal ordering of the parts of the appearance.

It is this difference between the requirements of these two types of object that enables Kant to draw the conclusions he does. If this difference is denied, then it could be claimed that a succession of appearances is indeed subject to a rule and so can be an object of representations, but nevertheless there would be no requirement on the temporal ordering of the parts of a succession. That is, the temporal ordering of the parts of a succession would not have to be fixed and determinate. That is, the *order* would not have to be subject to a rule. So there could be a succession of appearances that is not in this crucial sense subject to a rule.

Kant would argue, however, that this is not correct. Through the house, ship, and water examples we have already seen that Kant is committed to the existence of these two distinct types of objects of representations. If, however, we hold that the only sense of being subject to a rule that is required for these two types of object is the sense spelled out in the case of the house, then we will be undermining the distinction between these two types of object.

If "there is nothing in the appearance which determines it so that a certain sequence is rendered objectively necessary" (A194/B239–40), then it becomes difficult to see the difference between an ordinary appearance and a succession of appearances. If the succession in the appearance is not subject to a rule then "there is nothing in the appearance which determines it so that a certain sequence is rendered objectively necessary" (A194/B239–40). So in the case of an ordinary appearance (e.g., the house) *as well as* in the case of a succession of appearances "the succession of perceptions would be determined only merely in the apprehension, i.e., only subjectively" (A194/B239). The problem with this is that it seems to leave successions of appearances and ordinary appearances on too equal footing.

If we are to preserve any differences between these—that is, if we are going to maintain that these are two different types of object of representations, then on Kant's terms we must be able to distinguish one appearance from another. It is hard to see, however, how this would work if being subject to a rule in the case of a succession of appearances does not require that the stages of the succession are related to one another in a determinate temporal order. With ordinary objects we do not have any provision for the determinate temporal connection of the parts, but this is essential for an event. In the case of an ordinary object there is nothing in the object that constrains our subjective succession of apprehension. That is, with an ordinary object there is nothing that prevents our cognition from being haphazard or arbitrary with regard to temporal succession. Clearly, our cognition is constrained in terms of *spatial* connections, but in terms of *temporal* connection this is not true, for no spatial part must be cognized in a particular temporal order. For in an ordinary object there is no particular temporal succession that *is the object* of our cognition.

If we try to reduce the requirements for an event's being an object of representations to the same requirements for an ordinary physical object, then we leave off what is essential for something's being an event. For an event, what is essential is that *the object* of our cognition *is a particular temporal succession*. If we drop the temporal requirement, then it is difficult to see how we will be able to distinguish between these two types of objects.

For example, consider the succession of appearances of a house being constructed and the completed house itself. If there is no determinate order in the succession of the construction, then what is to distinguish the object of representations in a case where the object is supposed to be the construction of the house and the object in a case in which the completed house is supposed to be the object. It can be supposed that in both cases I saw the same set of parts in the same order. Yet since there is no requirement that the stages of a succession be connected in a determinate temporal order, I would be unable to claim that the two cases are distinguishable because in watching the house being constructed I had to observe the parts in a certain order, but in looking at the completed house I could have observed the parts in a different order. So without the crucial temporal requirement, how could these two types of objects be distinguished?

One typical response to this question is to claim that these two types of object of representations can be distinguished by the fact that in a succession of appearances the stages involve opposite states of an object while in an ordinary appearance the parts do not involve any opposite states of an object. Since an object cannot be in opposite states at the same time, any object involving such opposite states must be a succession of appearances rather than an ordinary appearance.[9] If this answer is sufficient for distinguishing between a succession of appearances and an ordinary appearance, then an appropriate requirement could be added to the requirements for an appearance's being subject to a rule. Now, although adding an appropriate requirement would make the requirements for a succession of appearances different than the requirements for an ordinary appearance, the main objec-

---

9. A number of commentators make this point or similar points. Included among these are Van Cleve, Beck, and Harper and Meerbote (in their introduction).

tive in claiming that the requirements for these two types of objects are the same (i.e., having a succession of appearances be an object of representations while the *order* of the succession is not subject to a rule) would still be met.

Now, although this modified set of requirements would perhaps be sufficient to distinguish between a succession of appearances and an ordinary appearance, without requiring the order of the succession to be subject to a rule, it will not be sufficient to avoid a second problem with allowing the order of the succession not to be subject to a rule. That is, unless being subject to a rule requires in the case of a succession of appearances that the stages of the succession have a determinate temporal order, it will not be possible to distinguish between different successions of appearances that have the same set of parts connected in two different orders. So, for example, what distinguishes the water freezing (a sample of water in a liquid state followed by the water in a solid state) from the ice melting (the sample of water in a solid state followed by the water in a liquid state)? Simply adding the requirement that a succession of appearances (as opposed to an ordinary appearance) will involve opposite states of an object will not help us here, because both candidates involve opposite states of an object.

In order to be able to maintain the distinction between the one succession of appearances and the other the one must have a determinate order of succession that can be specified. That is, in order to be able to maintain the distinction between the one succession and the other, the *order* of the succession must be subject to a rule. If the order of the succession is not subject to a rule, then the succession cannot be distinguished from all other appearances—for it could not be distinguished from a succession with the same stages in a different order. Consequently, the succession would fail to meet the requirements for being an object of representations in the first place.

Are my requirements too weak?
The most interesting way to disagree with the requirements as I have stated them is to argue that these requirements are too weak. There are two ways someone could do this. I will discuss both of these in turn.

Repeatability. First, someone might argue that since the requirements for a succession of appearances' being subject to a rule as I have represented them do not include any repeatability requirement, they are too weak. One might argue that this conclusion is supported by passages such as the following:

> According to such a rule, therefore, there must be in that which in general precedes an event the condition of a rule according to which this event always and necessarily follows. Conversely, however, I cannot go back from the event and determine (through apprehension) what precedes. (A193–94/B238–39)

Someone might argue the phrase "this event always and necessarily follows" implies that Kant intends to include a repeatability requirement along with the other requirements for a succession of appearances' being subject to a rule. That is, someone might argue that Kant intends for the notion of being subject to a rule to include the sort of requirement that makes up the second part of the SCSE formulation of the casual principle. So on this interpretation if a succession of appearances is subject to a rule, this would require that all events that are of the same causally relevant type as the one that (in this particular succession) precedes are followed by an event that is of the same causally relevant type as the one that (in this particular succession) follows. Now, although such a requirement on being subject to a rule would have the advantage of allowing the causal principle in the Second Analogy to incorporate a feature that is often thought to be an important part of a full-fledged theory of causation, it cannot be something for which Kant argued in the Second Analogy.

As I have argued above, in the context of the Second Analogy, being subject to a rule is what is required if an appearance or a succession of appearances is to be an object of representations. The rule that is required for this is a rule that will mandate one determinate connection of the manifold of appearances and that will distinguish one appearance from all others. So if we want to hold that the requirements for being subject to a rule in the case of a succession of appearances include a repeatability clause, then it would have to be the case that a repeatability clause is required in order for a succession of appearances to be an object of representations. That is, a repeatability requirement would have to be such that if a succession of appearances fails to meet it, then either there would not be any determinate connection of appearances in this case or it would not be possible to distinguish this succession of appearances from all other appearances.

How would such a requirement be formulated? Using the example of the water freezing (that is, the succession of appearances in which a sample of water in a liquid state is followed by the sample of water in a solid state), a repeatability requirement would require something like the following: In order for this succession of appearances (the freezing of the water) to be an object of representations it would have to be the case that there is some state type of which this water being in a liquid state is an instance and some state type of which this water being in a solid state is an instance and whenever a sample of water is in a state that is an instance of the first type this is always followed by the water being in a state that is an instance of the second type. I do not see, however, why we would want to hold such a requirement.

Even if we suppose it is true that the repeatability requirement is met in the case of the water freezing, it is still difficult to see how this has any bearing on whether or not in this case the water freezing meets the requirements for being an object of representations. What is it about the fact of repeatability that would introduce some essential feature of a succession of appearances' being an object of representations? It seems to me that our answer to this question should be that repeatability *does not* introduce some essential feature. For, as Hume says, "there is nothing in a number of instances, different from every single instance."[10]

Let us suppose we have a succession of appearances that consists in object x in state A followed by x in state B. Let us also suppose that no other succession that has, as one of its parts, *either* a part that is the same type as A or a part that is the same type as B has or will ever occur. So there is no other succession that either has as one of its parts an object in a state of the same type as state A *or* has as one of its parts an object in a state of the same type as state B. Now, it seems that such a succession would meet the repeatability requirement as formulated above.[11] So supposing it also meets the other requirements for being subject to a rule, this succession would qualify as an object of representations. This case, however, shows us that insofar as being subject to a rule aims at ensuring that an appearance is suitable for being an object of representations, a repeatability requirement does not do any work.

For if repeatability introduces some essential feature, then in this case, whatever feature it introduces must be something that can be found within this particular succession of appearances. For there are no other successions that are of this same type and there are not even any other successions that have any parts that are of the same type as the parts in this succession. So, if repeatability does introduce some essential feature required for being an object of representations it must be something that this particular succession of appearances has—but what could this feature be?

Clearly, in normal cases, a repeatability requirement would introduce a feature that would have relevance for our knowledge concerning other successions of the same type. For example, if we learn something about one particular succession, this would enable us to apply some of the information to all successions of the same type. Or more importantly perhaps, if we have a repeatability requirement, then we would be able to apply what we have learned about successions of a particular type to some particular succession under investigation. Note, however, that in both cases what a repeatability requirement contributes to is making our representations of successions clearer

---

10. *Enquiry*, Section VII, part II, 50.
11. In this case every time x is in state A this is followed by x being in state B and every time x is in state B it was preceded by x in state A. Clearly this meets the requirements for repeatability.

or more intelligible. It does not contribute to making our representations possible in the first place. *Before* we can apply what we have learned about this particular succession to all other similar successions or *before* we can apply what we already know about other similar successions to this particular one, this particular succession *must already be an object of representations*. There is a time and place for both the constitutive task and the regulative task, but as we saw back in chapter 1, principles of understanding are supposed to be constitutive principles not regulative principles. The only kind of feature repeatability alone can account for is some kind of connection to all other successions of the same type. So, if we were to claim that repeatability plays a role in a constitutive principle of understanding, then we would have to hold that such features[12] are essential properties of the particular succession and would thus be required in order for it to be an object of representations in the first place. It is hard to see, however, why we would believe this. So I see no reason to strengthen the requirements for a succession of appearances' being an object of representations.

Necessary Order. Secondly, someone might argue that since the requirements for a succession of appearances' being subject to a rule as I have represented them do not appear to require that the particular order of the succession of states of an object that actually obtains be necessary, then they are too weak. That is, someone might argue that Kant intends for the notion of being subject to a rule to include a requirement that the order of the succession of states of an object is in some way necessary. So on this interpretation if a succession of appearances is subject to a rule, this would require the state that precedes in this particular succession *necessarily* precedes and the state that follows in this particular succession *necessarily* follows.

Now, although such a requirement on being subject to a rule would have the advantage of allowing the causal principle in the Second Analogy to incorporate a feature that is often thought to be an important part of a full-fledged theory of causation, it cannot be something for which Kant argued in the Second Analogy.

As I have argued above, in the context of the Second Analogy, being subject to a rule is what is required if an appearance or a succession of appearances is to be an object of representations. The rule that is required for this is a rule that will mandate one determinate connection of the manifold of appearances and that will distinguish one appearance from all others. So if we want to hold that the requirements for being subject to a rule include a necessary order clause, then it must be the case that a necessary order

---

12. That is, features that would account for some kind of connection to all other successions of the same type.

clause is required in order for an appearance or a succession of appearances to be an object of representations. That is, a necessary order requirement would have to be such that if an appearance or succession of appearances fails to meet it, then either there would not be any determinate connection of appearances in this case or it would not be possible to distinguish this appearances from all other appearances.

So in the case of an appearance (e.g., the house) I represent it as having a certain location, and a certain set of parts arranged in a certain manner. So, for example, if it is a five room house, the five rooms must be connected in some determinate order—suppose the order is: bedroom, bathroom, kitchen, dining room, living room. But, whether or not this order is a necessary order (i.e., bedroom necessarily to the left of the bathroom, the bathroom necessarily to the left of the kitchen, and the kitchen necessarily left of the dining room, and the dining room necessarily left of the living room) does not have any bearing on whether or not appearances are connected in some one determinate manner. So necessary order does not have any bearing on whether or not the appearance in the house case meets the requirements for being an object of representations.

Similarly, in the case of the ship floating downstream I represent it as having a certain location, and a certain set of parts arranged in a particular order. Suppose the order is: first the ship floats by the dock, then the castle, then the village, then the farm, then into the ocean. Whether or not, however, this order is a necessary order (i.e., the ship floating by the dock is necessarily followed by its floating by the castle, its floating by the castle is necessarily followed by its floating by the village, its floating by the village is necessarily followed by its floating by the farm, its floating by the farm is necessarily followed by its floating into the ocean) does not have any bearing on whether or not appearances in the ship case are connected in some one determinate manner. So necessary order does not have any bearing on whether or not the appearance in the ship case meets the requirements for being an object of representations.

Of course it *could* be the case that as a result of scientific investigation we come to hold that in some cases the particular order in which the parts of an appearance or succession of appearances are connected is as a matter of fact a necessary order. Or it may be that we adopt as a regulative principle for our investigation of nature, the principle that in all connection there is a necessary order to be found. Nonetheless, as we saw back in chapter 1, the type of principle we are dealing with in the Second Analogy is a constitutive principle of understanding. Only those features required for the possibility of an object of experience or representation may be included in this constitutive principle of understanding. On the one hand, it is clear that an appearance or a succession of appearances that fails to have a determinate spatial temporal location, *or* that fails to have some determinate set of parts, *or* that fails to have a set of parts that are connected to one another in some determinate order could not even be an object of representations. Yet, on the other hand, it is not at all clear what would prevent an appearance or a succession of appearances that has a determinate spatial temporal location and some determinate set of parts and that has a set of parts that are connected to one another in some determinate, but non-necessary, order from even being an object of representations in the first place. This, however, is precisely what would be required in order to justify the inclusion of a necessary order clause in the principle of the Second Analogy.

Textual Worries

Now, although I reject a repeatability and/or a necessary order requirement because of the problems with such requirements, such a rejection is not problem-free. First I will examine the texts that are of concern for my rejection of a repeatability clause and then I will discuss textual problems associated with rejecting a necessary order clause.

Repeatability

First, we may find a problem concerning the passage cited above (A193–94/B238–39) that may be thought to support a repeatability requirement. There are in addition to this passage two other very similar passages in the Second Analogy. First, at A198/B243–44 Kant writes that

> first, I cannot reverse the series and place that which happens before that upon which it follows and second, that if the state that precedes is posited, this determinate event inevitably *[unausbleiblich]* and necessarily follows.

Then, at A200/B245–46 he writes:

> Thus, that something happens is a perception that belongs to a possible experience, which becomes actual when I regard the appearance as determined in regard to its position in time, consequently as an object that according to a rule can always be found in the connection of the perceptions. This rule for determining something according to the temporal order, however, is: that the condition under which the event always (that is, necessarily) follows is to be found in that which precedes.

The line of argument in these three passages, however, is at best inconclusive. These passages cannot be taken as presenting any straightforward evidence that Kant intended to include some sort of repeatability requirement. For in each of these three passages, although there may be some hint at something like repeatability, Kant clearly keeps his discussion focused on the particular case at hand. In each of these three passages Kant always writes about a *particular* event. In the first passage he writes of "a rule according to which *this*[13] event *[diese Begebenheit]* always and necessarily follows." In the second passage Kant writes of "*this determinate*[14] event *[diese bestimmte Begebenheit]*," and in the third passage he writes of an appearance that I regard "as an object that according to a rule can always be found in the connection of the perceptions." In none of these passages does Kant mention event *types*.

In a passage in the Second Analogy in which Kant states that his view contradicts the view according to which we first come to have the concept of cause by observing the regularity with which similar events follow certain appearances, he does appear to write about event types as opposed to particular events. On this theory, Kant writes, by observing like events regularly following like appearances we

> are led to discover a rule according to which certain events *[gewisse Begebenheiten]* always follow certain appearances *[gewisse Erscheinungen]*, and in this way we are first led to form the concept of cause. (A195/B240–41)

We must be clear, however, about two differences between this passage and the three other passages. First, in the passage at A195/B240–41 Kant is discussing a theory that is not his own. This is not a statement of Kant's view, but rather it is a statement of what he will reject. Perhaps it is important to keep in mind (as theoretical background) that a theory Kant rejects, involves not just particular events but also event types. This, however, cannot be taken as substantial evidence that event types will play a substantial role Kant's discussion in the Second Analogy.

Second, and more importantly, Kant's wording in this passage is clearly distinct from that found in the other three passages. In this passage where he is more than likely discussing event types he utilizes the *plural forms* "certain events" *(gewisse Begebenheiten)* and "certain appearances" *(gewisse Erscheinungen)*. Yet in each of the other three passages Kant is careful to utilize *only the singular forms* "this event" *(diese Begebenheit)*, "this determinate event" *(diese bestimmte Begebenheit)* and "the appearance" *(die Erscheinung)*. Given this clear distinction, then, there is no clear evidence to

---

13. My italics.
14. My italics.

suggest that in these three passages Kant is concerned with anything other than particular events.

Given that the evidence of these three passages is at best inconclusive, when we weigh this against the considerations opposed to a repeatability requirement, which were developed through the examination of the connection Kant draws between being subject to a rule and being an object of representations, and with the considerations concerning the constitutive (as opposed to regulative) nature of principles of understanding, we must finally reject the inclusion of any repeatability requirement in the proper explication of being subject to a rule.

Necessary Order and Necessity

The rejection of a necessary order requirement, however well grounded it is in the constitutive nature of the causal principle, makes a number of people squeamish—both textually and otherwise. With the rejection of a necessary order requirement people want to know where all the necessity has gone. Necessity cannot be avoided here in the Second Analogy, let alone anywhere else in Kant's writings. Necessary order is *one way* in which necessity may be at work here, but it is not the only way. Well, where exactly is necessity supposed to come into the picture?

First of all, clearly the causal principle itself is supposed to be in some sense necessary, because it is the conclusion of a transcendental proof. Does this mean the causal principle is a necessary truth? Well, probably not, because it is not absolutely necessary. That is, it is not a law of logic. It is a requirement for the possibility of experience. In other words, the causal principle is a requirement for the possibility of objects of experience, but it is not a requirement for the possibility of all objects. It is a requirement for being an object of experience, but it is not required for being any sort of object at all.

Well, what about within the causal principle itself? In what sense is the relationship between the ship upstream and the ship downstream necessary? In what sense is the connection between the water in a liquid state and the water in a solid state necessary? More generally, then, in what sense is the relationship between the parts of a succession of appearances necessary? The answer is a complicated one.

There are three straightforward things we might mean by necessary in this context. In many[15] and various texts Kant has utilized each of these three meanings, but unfortunately he is not always very good at making clear which of the three he has in mind.[16]

---

15. In just the first *Critique* Kant utilizes some form of *notwendig* alone more than six hundred times.
16. Whether this is caused by lack of clarity in his writing style or by Kant's not clearly distinguishing in his own mind which sense of necessity he means or by some other cause entirely must remain a topic for another occasion.

The first meaning of necessity is the sense we find in a repeatability requirement. In this sense to say the succession *ab* is necessary is to say it *must* occur in the order *a* followed by *b,* because all successions whose constitutive parts are of the same type as *a* and *b* occur in this order. In other words for every particular succession there is a true universal generalization that applies to this case. We have already seen above in this chapter as well as in chapter 2 the problems associated with including a repeatability requirement in the causal principle, so I won't repeat that discussion here. We have also seen above that the immediate textual evidence in the Second Analogy itself is at best ambiguous with regard to a repeatability requirement, so I won't repeat that here either. The thing that must be investigated here is the source of the necessity with this formulation. That is, given that there is a true universal generalization that covers the succession *ab* (i.e., all successions whose constitutive parts are of the same type as *a* and *b* occur in this order), what grounds or explains this true universal generalization?

One answer to this question is nothing. That is, it is just a matter of fact that the regularity, *a* is always followed by *b,* holds. Of course, a second answer is to say what grounds or explains this true universal generalization is transcendental proof. That is, if there were a repeatability clause included in the causal principle, then we would be able to say this generalization is grounded in the principle that in all cases there must be a true causal generalization and this principle is grounded by transcendental proof. Notice that even with this second answer we don't get an explanation for this particular causal generalization. That is, even with a transcendental proof of a causal principle that includes a repeatability clause, we would still be able to ask why the true causal generalization in this particular case is *a* is always followed by *b* rather than *b* is always followed by *a?* The trouble with necessity in the sense of regularity is that it is not the sort of necessity we would be looking for here. In this case we would be looking for what we might call *particular* necessity. That is, necessity that is grounded in or explained by some features intrinsic to the particular succession we are investigating. Unless we ground regularity in some sort of particular necessity, then it won't be a satisfactory sense of necessity here, because it would not be a type of necessity that could be part of a constitutive rather than regulative principle. If we do, however, ground regularity in some type of particular necessity, then we have reduced it to one of the next two types of necessity, in which case it doesn't stand on its own.

The second meaning of necessity is necessary in the sense that *a* absolutely requires that *b* follows. In this sense, to say the succession *ab* is necessary is to say it *must* occur in the order *a* followed by *b,* because there is some intrinsic feature of *a* that necessitates that *b* follows. That is, given *a* it couldn't possibly be the case that *b* does not follow. It is best to think of this sense of necessity as being just the good old fashioned "necessary connection" that the rationalists accept and Hume rejects. Again, we have already seen above in this chapter the problems associated with including a necessary order requirement in the causal principle, so I won't repeat that discussion here. We can see the main problem with this type of necessity by trying to get a better understanding of this sort of necessity by thinking about the ship example in a little more detail.

Suppose we take *ab* to be the ship upstream followed by the ship downstream. Let's even throw in wind, current, temperature, condition of the sails, etc., so that it is not just the ship upstream it is the ship upstream with a 30 mph tail wind, an ambient temperature of 50 degrees Fahrenheit, the sails unfurled, etc., followed by the ship downstream with a 30 mph tail wind, an ambient temperature of 50 degrees Fahrenheit, the sails unfurled, etc. The question is just this: even in this case does this mean that the ship's being upstream *necessitates* the ship's being downstream? That is, is it absolutely necessary that once the ship's being upstream occurs, then the ship's being downstream occurs? What if at the exact moment *a* occurs, the Mir space station falls out of the sky and annihilates the ship and so *b* does not happen? If we are committed to this type of necessity we will say: well, we should have included the proximity of Mir in the specification of *a*. Once we include the proximity of Mir in our specification what we realize is that what we get is not *a*, but some other state of the ship *m* and what this necessitates is not *b*, but some other state of the ship *n*. Where does this specificity end? If we specify the details of the situation and the event does not occur, then we say we did not get the necessity because we really did not get all of the specific details. In order to avoid all cases like the Mir crashing case won't we end up having to specify every case so specifically that we will end up with each case being unique? And if we break things down this far, do we really get the required necessary connection? Kant himself discusses this question and his answer is no and yes. He tells us that

> the objects of empirical cognition, aside from the formal time condition, are still determined, or, so far as one can judge *a priori*, determinable, in a number of ways, so that specific different natures, outside of what they have in common as belonging to nature in general, can still be causes in infinitely many ways; and each one of these ways must (according to the concept of a cause in general) have its rule, which is a law, consequently follows with necessity, although according to the constitution and limits of our cognitive abilities we do not have any insight into this necessity. (*CJ*, 183)

So, insofar as we are dealing with particular objects of nature, human understanding has no insight into this necessity. So how do we account for it then?

Kant goes on to tell us that we do this in terms of supposing "the unity of nature according to empirical laws" (*CJ*, 183). This unity, however, is, to the understanding, itself contingent. So where do we finally get necessity?

> Judgment assumes for its own use as an *a priori* principle, that what is for human insight contingent in the particular (empirical) laws of nature nonetheless contains a, for us unfathomable but still thinkable, law like unity, in the combination of its diversity into an experience possible in itself. (*CJ*, 183–84)

Then Kant tells us that in order to complete this task judgment "must think of nature ... according to a *principle of purposiveness* for our cognitive abilities" (*CJ*, 184). We need to keep in mind, however, that this

> transcendental concept of a purposiveness of nature is now neither a concept of nature nor a concept of freedom, because it ascribes nothing to the object (nature), but only the unique way in which we must proceed in the reflection about the objects of nature with the intention of representing a thoroughgoing connected experience, consequently it is a subjective principle (maxim) of judgment. (*CJ*, 184)

So what this ultimately means is that we do finally get the necessary connection we were looking for, *but not from the causal principle in the Second Analogy*. For this necessary connection, which we first looked for in the objects themselves, is ultimately only accounted for by the regulative function of judgment—not the constitutive function of understanding as we would find when dealing with the causal principle of the Second Analogy.

The final meaning of necessity we find, and (for better or worse) the only one we can ultimately justify in the Second Analogy, is simply necessary in the sense of something's being *objective* rather than *subjective*. In this sense, to say the succession *ab* is necessary is to say that it does not matter who you are, where you came from, or what your subjective perspective is, objectively speaking *a* comes before *b*. That is to say, *ab* is not a subjective representation. It is not just a matter of opinion—I *must* represent things as *ab* because that is the way they are objectively (or in the object) connected. When we are dealing with things that are objective it is necessary that our judgments agree. That is, with objective occurrences we require universal agreement. Kant himself uses necessity in this way more frequently than a skeptical reader might think. In the second edition Transcendental Deduction when he is discussing the possibility of some justification for the categories other than a transcendental deduction or experience Kant tells us the argument

> against the imaginary middle way is decisive: that in such a case the categories would lack the *necessity* that essentially belongs to their concepts. Then e.g., the concept of cause, which asserts the necessity of a succession under a presupposed condition, would be false if it were only based on a subjective necessity, arbitrarily implanted in us, to combine certain empirical representations according to such a rule of relations. I would not be able to say: *the effect is combined with the cause in the object (i.e., necessarily)*, but rather I am only so arranged that I cannot think this representation other than as so connected, which is just what the skeptic most wishes, because then all of our insight through the supposed objective validity of our judgments is nothing but sheer illusion, and there would also be no lack of people who would not concede this subjective necessity (which must be felt); at the least one could not quarrel with anyone over that which is founded merely on the way in which his subject is organized. (B167–68; second italics added)

Then in the Doctrine of Method when he is discussing Hume's skepticism and in particular his views on causation Kant writes that Hume

> thus falsely inferred, from the contingency of our determination *according to laws,* the contingency of the *laws* themselves, and he mistook the going beyond the concept of a thing to possible experience (which happens *a priori* and makes up the objective reality of the concept) with the synthesis of the objects of actual experience, which admittedly is always empirical. Because of this, he turned a principle of affinity, which has its seat in the understanding and asserts *necessary connection,* into a rule of association, which is only found in the reproductive *[nachbildenden]* imagination and can only exhibit contingent, not *objective connections* at all. (A766–67/B794–95; last two italics added)

In this case, when Kant contrasts a principle of understanding with a rule of the reproductive imagination he initially tells us that a principle of understanding, as opposed to a rule of association, "asserts necessary connection." Then, in the same sentence, he turns around and tells us the contrast is between the contingent connections of laws of association and the objective connections—presumably of principles of understanding. Finally Kant makes a similar connection when he tells us,

> That is why objective validity and necessary universal validity (for everyone) are interchangeable concepts, and even though we do not know *[kennen]* the object in itself, still if we regard a judgment as universal and consequently necessary, that's exactly what we under-

stand by objective validity. We cognize the object through this judgment, (even if it also otherwise, remains unknown as it is in itself) through the universal and necessary connection of the given perceptions. (*Prolegomena*, 298–99)

Now, it should not be surprising that Kant would use necessity in this way and in particular it should not be surprising that he would use it in this way with regard to causation. Remember *one* of the objectives Kant has in the Second Analogy is to provide a way around turning causal connections into *sheer illusions* as they would be if the causal connection were ultimately grounded in a person's habits, as they are according to Hume. Kant wants to be able to show that causal connections are *not subjective,* but that they are *objective*—that is necessary.

Is this really a causal theory?
Finally, given that on my interpretation the principle of the Second Analogy does not include a repeatability clause or a necessary order clause, someone may wonder where this leaves Kant's theory of causation. The problem is that these two features are often thought to be two important parts of a full-fledged theory of causation, but according to my interpretation they are left out of the principle of the Second Analogy. Given this, someone might think my interpretation leaves Kant's full-fledged theory of causation in a bad position. If both of these features were in fact left out of Kant's full-fledged theory of causation, then his full-fledged theory of causation would be lacking. The Second Analogy, however, is not the appropriate place for Kant to present his full-fledged theory of causation.

As we saw back in chapter 1 Kant argues that principles of understanding are constitutive principles—they are requirements for the possibility of experience. Neither a repeatability requirement nor a necessary order requirement is necessary to this end, so neither one can be proven in the Second Analogy. These two requirements according to Kant, do have a role to play, but this role is only regulative. That is, they are to be utilized as principles of *reason,* not *understanding.* That is, these are not required for making experience possible, but they are required in order to provide unity for the understanding. This, according to Kant, is the role for which principles of reason are required.

Given this, we should not expect these two features to show up in the Second Analogy. As we have seen, the proper place for these is in the Transcendental Dialectic and the Transcendental Doctrine of Method of the first *Critique* as well as in the third *Critique*. So, the absence of a repeatability requirement and a necessary order requirement in the Second Analogy should not be taken to point out a defect in Kant's full-fledged theory of causation, for we should not expect to find Kant's full-fledged theory of causation here. Rather, all we can expect to find in the Second Analogy is what we could call Kant's minimal theory of causation. Lest we worry about calling a theory that includes neither a repeatability requirement nor a necessary order requirement a *theory of causation,* I should note that I take my cue from Kant's discussion about what is required in order for appearances to be subsumed under the category of causality and dependence (cause and effect). Kant writes:

> [T]he understanding says: all alteration has its cause (universal law of nature). Transcendental judgment now has nothing more to do, than to give *a priori* the condition of subsumption under the submitted concept of the understanding, and that condition is the succession of determinations of one and the same thing. (*CJ*, 183)

Notice that Kant lists neither repeatability nor necessary order among the conditions for subsumption under the category of cause and effect. In the passages that follow this text, Kant goes on to explain the regulative use of reason and it is only here that he includes these two features into his theory of causation. This minimal theory of causation may not include all the features that we would like to see in a full-fledged theory of causation, but this is by design. For this minimal theory of causation is only permitted to include those features that are subject to transcendental proof.

Chapter Six

Hume Revisited

Recall that the last time Kant's answer to Hume's skepticism concerning the causal principle was up for discussion, back in chapter 1, we had just seen that Kant's answer would involve a transcendental proof. Now that we have the details of that proof we are in a position to examine it in order to see how it stands as an answer to Hume, and after a brief review we will turn to this examination.

A BRIEF REVIEW

In the Second Analogy Kant makes it clear that the notion of an object of representations[1] has a central role to play in the proof of the causal principle. Both ordinary physical objects, such as a house or a rock, and beginnings of existence (events), such as a ship floating down a river or water freezing, are objects of representations. What exactly does it mean to say something is an object of representations? According to Kant an object of representations is "that which ensures that our cognitions are not haphazardly or arbitrarily determined" (A104). Kant's point is straightforward. The object is that which grounds the objectivity of cognition. If I take some set of my representations to have an object, then I represent my cognition in this case as having been constrained by the features of the object.

Now, it may be easy enough to see how objects in the ordinary sense (that is, tables, chairs, lions, tigers, and bears etc.) can ground the objectivity of cognition, but how will this work when we are dealing with Kant's objects

---

1. See chapter 5.

of representations? For we need to remember that, according to Kant an object "is no thing in itself, but rather only an appearance, that is, representation" (A191/B236). If this is true, then how can objects, which are themselves representations, *be* "that which ensures that our cognitions are not haphazardly or arbitrarily determined"? Kant's answer is that in order for representations to be objects in this sense they themselves must not be associated in a haphazard or arbitrary way. That is, the representations must be connected *according to rules*. In other words, representations, "as perceptions only signify a real object . . . in so far as they are, in relation to space and time, connected and determinable . . . according to the rules of the unity of experience" (A494–95/522–23) These rules specify one determinate connection of representations and thereby distinguish this connection of representations from all others. For

> appearance, in contradistinction with the representations of apprehension, can only be represented as an object distinct from them if it stands under a rule, which distinguishes it from every other apprehension, and makes necessary one manner of connection of the manifold. (A191/B236)

When proving the causal principle Kant will be concerned with determining whether an uncaused beginning of existence is a possible object of representations. The conclusion Kant draws is that an uncaused beginning of existence would not be a possible object of representations.

For Kant an uncaused beginning of existence would be a beginning of existence that does not presuppose "something upon which it follows according to a rule" (A189). That is, an uncaused beginning of existence is one that is not subject to a rule. A beginning of existence that is not subject to a rule would be a beginning of existence that either fails to have a determinate spatial temporal location, or it fails to have some determinate set of parts (stages), or the parts (stages) fail to be connected to one another in any determinate temporal order.[2]

Now, as we saw above, these requirements for being subject to a rule are supposed to "make necessary one manner of connection of the manifold" (A191/B236), and to make an appearance distinguishable from all other appearances. For this is what is required in order for an appearance to be an object of representations. If a beginning of existence either does not have any determinate spatial temporal location, or it does not have any determinate set of parts (stages), or its parts (stages) are not arranged in any determinate temporal order, then since it would not be distinguishable from all other

---

2. See chapter 5.

appearances it will fail to meet the requirements for being an object of representations. That is, a beginning of existence that is not subject to a rule is not a possible object of representations—it is not a possible object of experience. For I only

> represent something as an event *[Begebenheit]* or something that happens, i.e., I cognize an object, . . . [if] I perceive or assume that in this succession there is a relation to the preceding state from which the representation follows according to a rule. (A198/B243)

So, since a beginning of existence that is not subject to a rule cannot be an object of experience, every beginning of existence must presuppose "something upon which it follows according to a rule" (A189). That is, "whatever begins to exist, must have a cause of existence."[3] This is the basic outline of Kant's transcendental proof for the causal principle.

TRANSCENDENTAL PROOF AND THE MISTAKE STRATEGY

The problem with this line of argument is that in terms of its being an answer to Hume, then it just seems to miss the point. In terms of Kant's own reasons for thinking we can avoid proving the causal principle through observation and experience this line of argument is on target. If Kant wants to introduce a third type of proof and use this type of proof to prove the causal principle, that is his business. If, however, Kant wants to give a proof for the causal principle that is acceptable to Hume, then introducing transcendental proofs is a risky strategy.[4] Clearly, if Hume rejects the methodology of the proof, then what reason would we have for thinking he will accept the results of the proof? Neither of the two types of proof Hume recognizes[5] are transcendental proofs, so Kant's proof for the causal principle utilizes a methodology that Hume does not recognize as legitimate. So any such proof appears to be one that fails to be an answer to Hume in terms he would have to accept.

Someone might argue, however, that Hume cannot get himself off the hook so easily here. The fact that on his system, Hume *does* recognizes only two types of proof does not mean that he *should* recognize demonstrations and proofs from experience as being the only types of proof. It might be

---

3. *Treatise*, Bk. I, pt. III, § III, 78.
4. Recall from chapter 1 that we can give an answer to a person in two senses: the first is just to give a sound refutation of the person's position while the second provides a refutation which that person does or should (if that person wants to maintain a logically consistent position) accept. I will once again focus mainly on Kant's answer to Hume in the second sense.
5. As we saw back in chapter 1 these are demonstrations and proofs from experience.

suggested that since transcendental proofs simply show that something is a necessary condition for a particular type of experience, then this is a perfectly legitimate kind of proof. Furthermore, since transcendental proofs are legitimate, then shouldn't a properly instructed Hume simply accept them as a type of demonstrative reasoning?[6] First we need to be clear about an inaccurate characterization of transcendental proof that this might mistakenly suggest.

There is a sense in which spelling out the necessary conditions for something should and would be recognized by Hume as a type of demonstrative proof. This would be the case as long as we are dealing with the necessary conditions for what Kant calls concepts and Hume calls ideas. Suppose, for example, I give the following sort of argument: being unmarried is a necessary requirement for being a bachelor. If Mike is a bachelor, then, as a necessary prerequisite, he must be unmarried. This easily fits what Hume would call a demonstration. Or again: being made of gold is a requirement for the possibility of a mountain being a golden mountain. If Mount Oro is a golden mountain, as a requirement of the possibility of this, Mount Oro must be made of gold. This again easily fits what Hume would call a demonstration. The problem with such a characterization of transcendental proof should be obvious. Kant would simply reject any characterization of transcendental proof that revolves around the necessary conditions for some particular concept. The conclusion of a transcendental proof is supposed to be a synthetic *a priori* claim. The conclusions of the above demonstrations may turn out to be *a priori*, but they will be analytic rather than synthetic. Ultimately, as with all other demonstrations they can be proven through (or by) the law of contradiction. For Kant, transcendental proofs do not rely on the law of contradiction, but instead rely on the necessary conditions for experience.

Of course, when we are dealing with transcendental proofs and we talk about the necessary conditions for experience we don't mean the necessary conditions for some particular experience like the experience of a tree or the experience of a sunrise.[7] Instead, with transcendental proof we will be concerned with the necessary conditions for the possibility of experience.[8] Once

---

6. This line of argument was suggested by Eric Watkins (formerly Anonymous Reviewer B).
7. If instead of dealing with the conditions for the experience of particular objects we discuss the conditions for the objects themselves, then we are getting much closer to the right idea. The necessary requirements for the possibility of a certain type of object of experience will be a basis for transcendental proof. We do not need to treat these as a separate case from those involving the necessary conditions for the possibility of experience, however, because these conditions are necessarily connected together. For as Kant tells us: "The conditions of the *possibility of experience* in general are at the same time conditions of the *possibility of objects of experience*" (A158/B197).
8. Back in chapter 1 when I first discussed transcendental proof I mentioned two types. In addition to those whose synthetic *a priori* conclusions rely on the possibility of experience there are those whose synthetic *a priori* conclusions rely on the pure *a priori* intuitions of space and time (i.e., mathematics). It is interesting to note that in the Second Section of the Principles of Pure Understanding: On the Highest Principle of all Synthetic Judgments, Kant suggests that

we are clear that transcendental proofs deal neither with the necessary conditions for some concept(s)[9] nor with the necessary conditions for some particular experience, but with the necessary conditions for the possibility of experience, then before we can see whether or not such a proof is one that either Hume does or should accept, we must first find out just what sort of thing this *possibility of experience* is.

On the one hand, as the basis of transcendental proof, it is clear that the possibility of experience will have to be something *a priori*. Kant tells us that the possibility of experience is

> the only type of cognition, which gives all other synthesis reality, as *a priori* cognition it also has truth (agreement with the object), only because it contains nothing more than what is necessary for the synthetic unity of experience in general. (A157–58/B196–97)

It becomes clear here that with the possibility of experience we are also dealing with something synthetic, and Kant tells us what we are dealing with is "the necessary conditions of the synthetic unity of the manifold of intuition in a possible experience" (A158/B197). Furthermore, we see that we will somehow be dealing with intuition. It will not, of course, be empirical intuition, but instead Kant tells us that

> synthetic *a priori* judgments are possible, if we relate the formal conditions of *a priori* intuition, the synthesis of imagination, and the necessary unity of the same in a transcendental apperception to a possible empirical cognition *[Erfahrungserkenntnis]* in general. (A158/B197)

So the possibility of experience will involve *a priori* intuition. A last piece of the puzzle we find in this passage is the relationship to the unity of imagination in transcendental apperception. Kant tells us that

---

even the synthetic *a priori* truths of mathematics ultimately depend on the possibility of experience for their objective validity. There Kant writes: "[A]lthough we cognize so much *a priori* in synthetic judgments about space in general or the shapes which the productive imagination registers *[verzeichnet]* in it so that we really require no experience at all for this, . . . those pure synthetic judgments relate, although only mediately, to possible experience, or rather to the possibility of experience itself, and on it alone is the objective validity of their synthesis founded" (A156/B195).

9. We should be clear that this means that in transcendental proofs Kant is not utilizing either the *concepts* of space and time or the *concept* of the possibility of experience. Transcendental proofs involve either the pure *a priori* intuition of space and time or the possibility of experience itself, not the concepts of either of these. If they did utilize the concepts of these, then we would once again be turning them into proofs of something analytic—something that could be proven through (or by) the law of contradiction.

> experience is founded on the synthetic unity of appearances . . . without which it would not even be cognition but only a rhapsody of perceptions that would not fit together in any context according to rules of a thoroughly connected (possible) consciousness, consequently also not into the transcendental and necessary unity of apperception. (A156/B195–96)

So the possibility of experience will involve the transcendental unity of apperception. When we put all of this together we find the possibility of experience is a synthetic *a priori* cognition that is connected both to *a priori* intuition and the transcendental unity of apperception.

Now, given what we have learned about the possibility of experience, I think we can see that transcendental proof's road to legitimacy is not an easy one. If Hume either recognizes or should recognize (on pains of inconsistency) the legitimacy of the possibility of experience as a base of proof, then I think the path to his acceptance of transcendental proof would be clear. The problem, however, is that accepting the possibility of experience as a legitimate basis for demonstrative reasoning would in turn require Hume to acknowledge the existence of a synthetic *a priori* cognition. This Hume does not acknowledge and it is difficult to see what would force him, on pains of inconsistency, to accept the existence of a synthetic *a priori* cognition. So in the end it appears that any proof of the causal principle that utilizes a transcendental proof would be one that fails to be an answer to Hume in terms he would have to accept. Kant, however, is not ready to give up so easily.

Kant adopts what we might call the mistake strategy. He believes that if it were not for a single mistake, Hume himself would have come to realize how unsatisfactory the results are when the empiricist framework is applied to the study of metaphysics. This in turn, Kant argues, would have enabled him to see the need for using something like transcendental proof in metaphysics. In the particular case at hand, Kant believes, Hume himself would have come to realize the need to ground the causal principle on something other than observation and experience. Thus, but for this one mistake, Hume himself would have come to see the necessity of giving something like a transcendental proof for the causal principle. This one mistake concerns the status of mathematical propositions.

Kant believes that although he correctly understood that "metaphysics [contains] synthetic *a priori* [propositions]" (*Prolegomena*, 272), Hume, along with every other philosopher before him, failed to make a particular "and seemingly unimportant observation" (*Prolegomena*, 272). Namely, the observation that mathematics as well as metaphysics contains synthetic *a priori* propositions. Instead, Hume believed that "pure mathematics contains purely analytic propositions" (*Prolegomena*, 272). Since Hume failed to realize that the principles of metaphysics and the axioms of mathematics are equally synthetic, he also failed to realize that consistency would require that his conclusions concerning the justification of metaphysical principles (such as the causal principle) also be applied to the justification of the axioms of mathematics. So since, according to Hume, metaphysical principles are based on observation and experience, this would require that he "subject the axioms of pure mathematics to experience as well" (*Prolegomena*, 272–73). According to Kant, however, subjecting the axioms of mathematics to observation and experience was something Hume would not have been willing to do. So if Hume had only realized that mathematics as well as metaphysics was synthetic, then

> the good company in which metaphysics would come to stand would thus have protected it against the danger of a despicable mistreatment, because the blow that was meant for the latter must also strike the former, which was not and could not have been his intention. (*Prolegomena*, 273)

So, if Hume had only realized that mathematics was synthetic, then he would also have recognized the need to ground metaphysics on something other than observation and experience. If only this need had been recognized, Kant believes, Hume himself would have seen beyond his empiricist framework and would have developed something like transcendental proof. Kant tells us that in this case "the sharp witted man would have been drawn into considerations that would have to be similar to those with which we are now occupied" (*Prolegomena*, 273). So, according to Kant, a properly instructed Hume would as a matter of fact accept the legitimacy of transcendental proof. There is, however, a problem with Kant's description of Hume's mistake.

A PROBLEM WITH KANT'S TRANSCENDENTAL PROOF AND MISTAKE STRATEGY

This problem has to do with Kant's view of Hume's beliefs about mathematics. Kant's description of Hume's position is accurate when considering his position in the *Enquiry,* but it is not accurate when considering his position in the *Treatise.*[10]

---

10. Kant's mistake here should not be considered egregious. The *Enquiry* was available in a German translation in 1755—the year Kant was first permitted to teach at the university. In 1771 a translation of the conclusion of Book I of the *Treatise* appeared in the *Königsberger Zeitung,* but of course this section does not contain Hume's exposition of his position on mathematics. It is not until 1790–1792 that there was a first translation of the *Treatise.* See Manfred Kuehn, "Kant's Conception of 'Hume's Problem,' " *Journal of the History of Philosophy* XXI, no. 2, (1983).

In the *Enquiry* Hume lists geometry, algebra, and arithmetic as sciences that deal with relations of ideas.[11] These sciences deal with propositions such as "that the square of the hypothenuse is equal to the square of the two sides" and "that three times five is equal to the half of thirty."[12] Such propositions are "discoverable by the mere operation of thought, without dependence on what is any where existent in the universe."[13] Hume characterizes such propositions as being "either intuitively or demonstratively certain."[14] Hume implies that the contrary of such propositions would imply a contradiction. This makes Kant's claim that for Hume "pure mathematics was founded . . . merely on the principle of contradiction" (A 35) look accurate.

In the *Treatise*, however, algebra, arithmetic, and geometry do not all have the same status. Algebra and arithmetic appear to have the same status as they do later in the *Enquiry*. Hume writes that they are "the only sciences, in which we can carry on a chain of reasoning to any degree of intricacy, and yet preserve a perfect exactness and certainty."[15] Geometry, however, "falls short of that perfect precision and certainty, which are peculiar to arithmetic and algebra."[16] The reason Hume cites for this difference in status concerns the ground of geometry. Hume writes that geometry's "first principles are still drawn from the general appearance of the objects" and "the reason why I impute any defect to geometry, is, because its original and fundamental principles are deriv'd merely from appearances."[17] What this shows is that in the *Treatise* Hume classified geometry as falling into a category that Kant would call synthetic. Hume also appears to realize that this means that the principles of geometry cannot be justified by the "mere operations of thought." Instead the principles of geometry must be justified by experience. Furthermore, it appears, at least in the *Treatise,* rather than moving beyond his empiricist framework in order to save geometry from "a despicable mistreatment," Hume was perfectly happy to subject geometry to experience. This, of course, is what Kant believed Hume too acute to do.

THE IMPLICATIONS OF THIS PROBLEM

What are the implications of this problem for the acceptability of Kant's answer to Hume? Ultimately, I believe, it shows that there is no easy way to turn the proof for the causal principle, as Kant has formulated it, into a proof that

---

11. See *Enquiry*, §IV, pt. I, p. 15.
12. Ibid. There are italics in the original text.
13. Ibid. There are italics in the original text.
14. Ibid.
15. *Treatise,* Bk I, pt. III, § I, 71.
16. Ibid.
17. Ibid.

would be acceptable to Hume. On the one hand, the change Hume made in his position on mathematics suggests that Kant's use of the mistake strategy cannot succeed. In giving an answer to Hume, Kant relies on his being able to account for his differences with Hume by making reference to a simple mistake concerning the nature of mathematics—the mistake of taking mathematics to be analytic rather than synthetic. It is supposed to be a simple mistake because it is supposed to be the result of the "*neglect* of an otherwise easy and seemingly unimportant observation" (*Prolegomena,* 272; italics added). It looks, however, as if Hume was aware of the possibility of taking mathematics to be what Kant would call synthetic rather than what Kant would call analytic. Whatever Hume's motivation for changing his position on the status of (at least a part of) mathematics, Kant cannot simply write off Hume's position as the result of his neglecting to consider the possibility that mathematics is synthetic not analytic. At least for geometry, Hume was aware of this possibility and he accepted it in the *Treatise*, but rejected it by the time of the *Enquiry*. So it appears that Hume's position on mathematics was one he consciously chose.

On the other hand, Hume's position in the *Treatise* indicates that even if he agreed with Kant that mathematics is synthetic, this in no way would guarantee that he would accept the need for something like transcendental proof. Again, in the *Treatise* Hume considers geometry to be what Kant would call synthetic. Again, Hume appears perfectly satisfied with holding, as a result of the status of geometry, that it is grounded solely by observation and experience. If Hume is satisfied with grounding geometry on observation and experience, then the synthetic nature of geometry would not force him to recognize any special need for transcendental proof. If Hume concedes that mathematics is in fact synthetic rather than analytic, this would not clearly force him to look for a ground of justification other than demonstrations and observation and experience. He could adopt the strategy he adopted for part of mathematics in the *Treatise*—mathematics is synthetic and it is grounded solely on observation and experience.

These two possibilities show that the ultimate implication of the problem with Kant's position is that the path to giving a proof for the causal principle that Hume should accept on pain of inconsistency is not nearly as clear as Kant hints. For Kant's path clearly leads to the goal by way of a transcendental proof. It is clear that Kant believed that if Hume could have been made to realize mathematics was synthetic, this would have opened the door to his accepting the need for something like transcendental proof. Unfortunately, given Hume's account of the status of mathematics in both the *Treatise* and the *Enquiry,* Kant's belief is overly optimistic. For even given this "seemingly unimportant observation" about the synthetic nature of mathematics it is clear that Hume has left himself with room to consistently reject any proof of the causal principle that depends on transcendental proof.

Perhaps this shows that giving an answer that proceeds from premises that Hume does or should (if he is to remain consistent with himself) accept is too much to ask. Kant believed the simple realization that mathematics was synthetic would have provided Hume with a straightforward and decisive way to go beyond the empiricist framework, but given his view of geometry in the *Treatise* it is not clear that Hume would have found it either straightforward or decisive. In light of this there seem to be two main options. On the one hand, we might simply give up any hope of any such answer to Hume. Perhaps the gulf between Hume and Kant is simply too great. On the other hand, we might try to find some answer to Hume other than the mistake strategy. In particular, since on the mistake strategy the crucial problem has to do with whether Hume must accept the legitimacy of transcendental proof, it would be interesting if Kant had an available argument against Hume that does not rely on a transcendental proof. This is the possibility I will investigate in the next section.

TURNING THE COPY THESIS ON ITS HEAD

From the start of the Second Analogy Kant makes it clear that the notion of an object of representations has a central role to play in the proof of the causal principle. Kant's proof of the causal principle is rooted in the requirements for being an object of representations. It will also be the requirements for being an object of representations that may have enabled Kant to turn Hume's copy thesis on its head.

Hume uses the copy thesis as the driving force behind his derivability thesis. Hume tells us if we have

> any suspicion, that a philosophical term is employed without any meaning or idea (as is but too frequent), we need but enquire, *from what impression is that supposed idea derived?* And if it be impossible to assign any, this will serve to confirm our suspicion.[18]

According to the Object of Experience Strategy, Kant would be able to turn the copy thesis against Hume in precisely this way.[19] That is, Kant would run

---

18. *Enquiry*, § II, 13.
19. Of course, Kant does not actually accept the copy thesis. It is also clear that according to Kant the only sound proof of the causal principle must be a transcendental proof. However, the copy thesis does not have to be true and this argument does not have to utilize a transcendental proof in order for this argument against Hume to be successful. All that is required for this argument to be a successful answer to Hume in the second sense is that *Hume* accepts the copy thesis and that *Hume* would have to accept the argument as legitimate.

the derivability thesis against Hume's arguments concerning the causal principle. The suspicious philosophical term is "an uncaused beginning of existence." Following Hume, it is agreed that "we need but enquire, from what impression is the supposed idea" of "an uncaused beginning of existence" "derived?" According to Kant, the answer is: there is and can be no such impression. In order to see how this works we must see exactly what it would mean to have an uncaused beginning of existence.

As we saw above, for Kant an uncaused beginning of existence would be a beginning of existence that is not subject to a rule. A beginning of existence that is not subject to a rule would be a beginning of existence that either fails to have a determinate spatial temporal location, or it fails to have some determinate set of parts (stages), or the parts (stages) fail to be connected to one another in any determinate temporal order. In Hume's terminology this would mean that a beginning of existence that is not subject to a rule would either fail to be determinate in its degrees of quantity or fail to be determinate in its degrees of quality. Hence, an uncaused beginning of existence would either fail to be determinate in its degrees of quantity or fail to be determinate in its degrees of quality. That is, an uncaused beginning of existence would be a beginning of existence that either fails to have a determinate spatial temporal location, or it fails to have some determinate set of parts (stages), or the parts (stages) fail to be connected to one another in any determinate temporal order.[20]

Kant and Hume argue, however, that no such indeterminate thing is a possible object of representations—that is, no such object "can appear to the senses." As we saw above, Kant rejects such a possibility because of the nature of objects of representations. Hume, however, rejects this possibility because of the nature of impressions. Hume simply states that "no impression can become present to the mind, without being determin'd in its degrees both of quantity and quality."[21] Since an uncaused beginning of existence would have to be just such an indeterminate object, on Hume's terms, there are not and cannot be any impressions of an uncaused beginning of existence. Hence, according to the derivability thesis, the suspicious philosophical term "an uncaused beginning of existence" is a philosophical term that is employed without any meaning or idea.

What exactly does this do for a demonstration of the causal principle? Well, in order for this to help with a demonstration that Hume would have

---

20. When discussing degrees of quantity and quality Hume's two main examples are "men of all sizes and all qualities" and triangles of various sizes and angles. In general, differences in degrees of quantity and quality of something amount to "every small alteration in its extension, duration and other properties" *Treatise*, Bk I, Pt. I § VII, 17.
21. *Treatise,* Bk I, pt. I, § VII, 19.

to accept, it must be shown that there is some contradiction implied by an uncaused beginning of existence. Showing that the *term* "an uncaused beginning of existence" does not have any meaning or idea is not the same as showing that an uncaused beginning of existence implies a contradiction. But should Hume find any contradiction involved in an uncaused beginning of existence? Given what we have found about the nature and possibility of an *impression* of an uncaused beginning of existence, I believe the answer is yes—Hume should find a contradiction involved in an uncaused beginning of existence.

If we suppose that we have an impression of a beginning of existence separated from all causes (that is, we have an impression of an uncaused beginning of existence), as we saw above, what we suppose is that we have in the mind an "impression, which in its real existence has no particular degree nor proportion."[22] Such a possibility, however, is, according to Hume, "a contradiction in terms; and even implies the flattest of all contradictions, viz. that 'tis possible for the same thing both to be and not to be."[23] Hence, with the contradiction we can give the demonstration that Hume requires. For the separation of a beginning of existence from all causes in reality implies a contradiction because what this amounts to is an impression that in its real existence has no particular degree nor proportion.

PROBLEM: DRAWING THE DISTINCTION BETWEEN A BEGINNING OF EXISTENCE AND A CAUSE OF EXISTENCE

If this proof is correct, then it seems that we should not be able to draw any distinction between a beginning of existence and a cause of existence. This follows from Hume's separability thesis.[24] For, according to the separability thesis, if objects are not separable, then they are not distinguishable.[25] Fur-

---

22. Ibid.
23. Ibid. I think Hume has an example such as the following in mind: Suppose I have a particular impression of a line that has no particular length. Of course, this doesn't mean the line has no length. It must have length, otherwise it would be a point rather than a line at all. It has length, but it has no particular length. This would mean, for example, the line does not equal one inch in length, because that would be a particular degree. This would also mean, for example, the line does not equal 1.1 inches in length, because that would also be a particular degree. Generally, for any particular value l, the line does not equal l in length, because then the line would have a particular length. What we find is that there is no length l such that the line is of that length. So on the one hand the line has length, but on the other hand there is no length the line has. This is a contradiction.
24. Of course, if we do not hold Hume's separability thesis, then we may not think there is any special problem with distinguishing between ideas that are inseparable.
25. This is the contrapositive of the second statement of the separability thesis. *Treatise*, Bk. I, pt. I, § VII, 18.

ther, according to the separability thesis, if a beginning of existence and of a cause of existence are not distinguishable, then they should not be different.[26] Now, this poses a problem because it seems we are able to draw a distinction between a beginning of existence and a cause of existence and a beginning of existence does seem to be different from a cause of existence. So in order for this proof to have a chance to be an answer to Hume we must be able to explain the distinction we draw between a beginning of existence and a cause of existence in a consistent Humean way.

The distinction we draw between a beginning of existence and a cause of existence would be explained by the same method Hume uses to explain "that *distinction of reason,* which is so much talk'd of, and so little understood, in the schools."[27] Under this label Hume explicitly includes the distinction between "figure and the body figur'd" and "motion and the body mov'd."[28] In his discussion the example he makes use of is when we distinguish the shape from the color of a globe of white marble. Hume, however, makes no specific mention of any other distinctions that are included under this label. Hume discusses "that distinction of reason" near the end of his discussion of abstract ideas.

As mentioned earlier, Hume's main weapon against abstract ideas[29] is the separability thesis. Hume himself realized that using the separability thesis, however, appears to create problems for certain pairs of ideas—in particular, those involved in distinctions of reason such as "figure and the body figur'd." For, according to Hume, in reality a figure is "neither distinguishable, nor different, nor separable," from the body figured.[30] From the separability thesis it follows that "if the figure be different from the body their ideas must be separable as well as distinguishable, [but] if they be not different, their ideas can neither be separable nor distinguishable."[31] From the separability thesis, then, it looks as if we should not be able to draw any distinction between the figure and the body figured, because they are neither distinguishable nor separable. Yet, Hume says, according to *a distinction of reason* there is a distinction between the figure and the body figured. Yet "since it implies neither a difference nor separation,"[32] we must be able to explain exactly what we mean by a distinction of reason.

---

26. This is the contrapositive of the first statement of the separability thesis. *Treatise,* Bk. I, pt. I,§ VII, 18.
27. *Treatise,* Bk. I, pt. I,§ VII, 24.
28. Ibid.
29. Again see chapter 1 footnote 45 on how to understand "argument against abstract ideas."
30. *Treatise,* Bk. I, pt. I,§ VII, 25.
31. Ibid., 24–25.
32. Ibid., 25.

According to Hume, a distinction of reason is drawn based on the different sets of resemblances objects have. When we see a globe of white marble we do not have two separate impressions: one of the color and one of the shape. Thus far we are not "able to separate and distinguish the colour from the form."[33] It is when we notice "a globe of black marble and a cube of white" that we realize the white globe is subject to two separate resemblances. Then,

> [a]fter a little more practice of this kind, we begin to distinguish the figure from the colour by a *distinction of reason;* that is, we consider the figure and colour together, since they are in effect the same and undistinguishable; but still view them in different aspects, according to the resemblances, of which they are susceptible.[34]

If we accept the proof of the causal principle presented here, then we would have to explain things this same way. So, for example, consider a cube of water changing from a solid state to a liquid state (of course, the beginning of existence in this case is the water in a liquid state—the water is beginning to be in a liquid state). We could argue as Hume does with color and shape that it is only when we notice water changing from a liquid state to a gaseous state, or water changing from a liquid state to a solid state, or water changing from a gaseous state to a liquid state, or even a cube of butter changing from a solid state to a liquid state that we realize that the change from solid water to liquid water is subject to a number of separate resemblances. After more practice, I am able to distinguish the parts of the change by viewing the change according to the resemblances it is susceptible to. So the method of resemblances that Hume uses to explain how we distinguish between shape and color could also be employed to explain how we distinguish between a beginning of existence and a cause of existence.

FINAL STATUS OF KANT'S ANSWER TO HUME

Kant correctly understood Hume's doubts concerning causation and Kant also correctly understood what a successful answer to Hume would have to do. Although in fact Kant understood Hume's position better than many others, he failed to understand some of the complexities of Hume's position on mathematics.[35] In light of this, Kant's explicit answer to Hume fails to live up to expectations. That is, there is no clear reason to think Kant's answer

---

33. Ibid.
34. Ibid.
35. See footnote 10 above in this chapter concerning the reasons for Kant's mistake.

would have to be acceptable to a properly instructed Hume. Given a proper understanding of Kant's arguments about causation, however, he had available an answer that Hume would have to accept as a consequence of his Copy Thesis conjoined with his Separability Thesis.

Conclusion

ON THE GUIDE(S) TO THE DISCOVERY OF THE ROUTE TO THE PRINCIPLE OF CAUSATION

When we first become interested in Kant's Second Analogy, we find ourselves faced with a number of difficulties. Of course, the difficulties begin with the text itself. Although we may believe that Kant had something interesting and important to say, it isn't always easy to put the pieces together, and so we find ourselves in need of an interpretive guide. Since the Second Analogy purportedly has something to do with causation, for many of us this is our first guide. After all, early in our philosophical training most of us have been exposed to a modern explanation of Hume's analysis of causation as well as modern criticisms of Hume's analysis. Further, most of us are familiar with some of the modern theories of causation developed in response to Hume's analysis. Since the Second Analogy is supposed to have something to do with causation, then this seems like an ideal place to start. So we often begin our examination of the Second Analogy by analyzing the text with an eye toward coming to grips with Kant's theory of causation. Well, this was, in large part, the way my investigation of the Second Analogy began at least. Even using this guide, however, it was still difficult for me to put the interpretive pieces together. Eventually, I came to think this first guide was part of the problem rather than its solution.

My study of modern interpretations of causation, as well as modern interpretations of Hume's analysis of causation, had created a set of expectations that I could not correlate with what I found in the text of the Second Analogy. Since I could see (from the case of Lovejoy in particular) how drastically a person's interpretation of the text of the Second Analogy could be affected by a person's expectations, I decided that, as much as possible, I needed instead to let the text alone be my guide to the discovery of the route to the principle of causation. That is, I tried to focus on the internal structure of the text itself while importing as little external baggage as possible. In particular, at this stage I would not worry about two of the most compelling external interests: the nature of Kant's theory of causation, and the way in which Kant's theory of causation is supposed to be an answer to Hume. I would worry about these only after I first attempted to make sense of the text on its own terms. In order to be a plausible interpretation, an interpretation must enable us to make sense of the text of the Second Analogy. One of the first interpretive litmus tests will be how an interpretation handles the Irreversibility Argument and the illustrative examples Kant introduces in that argument.

The house, the ship, and irreversibility

As we saw above, in the Irreversibility Argument Kant contrasts the case of the perception of an event (such as a ship floating down a river) with the case of the perception of an ordinary object (such as a house). The contrast between these two examples and the conclusion Kant draws from these two examples plays an important role in his argument for the causal principle in the Second Analogy, so it is important to make sure that an interpretation of his argument gets these examples and this conclusion right. As we saw in chapters 3 and 4 above, each of the first four possible routes to the principle of causation misses the mark in this regard. In fact, with the exception of Strawson's Event/Object Strategy, as interpretations of these two examples and the conclusion Kant draws from them, they miss the mark quite badly.

As we have seen above, when we examine the Irreversibility Argument and its two examples, it is difficult to see any indication that these examples illustrate how the causal principle is (or must be) utilized in order to distinguish between veridical and non-veridical perceptions. Lovejoy, however, does not allow any examination of the examples in the Irreversibility Argument to affect his antecedent expectation that Kant will be using the same strategy Wolff used in order to prove the causal principle—that is, that the causal principle is a requirement for being able to distinguish "between veridical representations and 'mere dream.'"[1] Lovejoy simply dismisses the house and ship examples as irrelevant to the conclusion Kant is "supposed" to be drawing. For, according to Lovejoy, Kant's discussion of the house, the ship, and irreversibility is precisely the point at which "with characteristic confusion of thought he allows this argument . . . to transform itself into something quite incongruous with the proof that he intends."[2] Given the first guide

---

1. Lovejoy, 296.
2. Ibid., 297–98.

to the discovery of Kant's argument for the causal principle, Lovejoy's lack of openness to taking the text at face value in indicating Kant's line of reasoning is a clear strike against the Veridical Strategy.

Although none of the Event/Event strategists seems to display the same disdain for a baggage-free interpretation of the text of the Second Analogy, the Event/Event Strategy still does not fare too well with regard to the Irreversibility Argument and its two examples. As we saw above, according to the Event/Event Strategy, we must utilize the causal principle in order to determine the temporal position of one event in relation to other events. Here we found the problem to be that in the Irreversibility Argument the examples Kant uses in order to illustrate his conclusion focus on particular individual objects—a house in the case of an ordinary object and a ship floating down a river in the case of an event. It is hard to see how the contrast between what happens in the house and ship cases could be taken to provide us with an illustration of the dating of an event in relation to other events, because in the case of the ship floating downstream we have only one event. Each of the four event examples Kant introduces in the Second Analogy (i.e., the ship floating downstream, the stove heating the room, the leaden ball denting the cushion, and the water filling the glass) deals only with one particular event. If Kant were arguing that the causal principle is required in order to date events in relation to other events, then we would expect his illustrative examples to help lead us to this conclusion, but they cannot, because in each case we are dealing only with a solitary event.

As we saw above in chapter 3, even the case of the cushion and the leaden ball, where it does seem that Kant makes a connection between temporal order and cause and effect, poses a problem for the Event/Event Strategy. For in this case Kant's clear conclusion is that we use the temporal sequence in order to distinguish the cause from the effect. This is, of course, just the reverse of what the Event/Event strategist is committed to, so the conclusion Kant draws from this particular example is particularly damaging to the Event/Event Strategy.

The fact that Kant's examples deal with only one event poses no special problem for the Justification Strategy. If utilizing the causal principle were a requirement for the justification that a particular event occurred, then we would expect Kant's event examples to focus on particular events. However, the way that Kant focuses on a particular event does present a problem for the Justification Strategy. In his examples, Kant discusses the perception that an event occurred, how this perception is different from the perception of an ordinary object, and what is important about this, but he does not bring up any question about the justification for the belief that this particular event has occurred. This, however, is precisely what we would expect to find if these examples are supposed to illustrate the need for invoking the causal principle in order to justify the belief that some particular event has occurred.[3]

Back in chapter 4 we have seen that in the Irreversibility Argument Kant concludes that in the case of an ordinary object (such as a house) we represent the order of our perceptions as being reversible whereas in the case of an event (such as a ship floating down a river) we represent the order of our perceptions as being irreversible. This is important to note for Kant because he wants us to see that, in contrast to the way things work in the case of the perception of the house, in the case of the ship floating downstream I represent the order of my series of perceptions as being controlled by the object that was perceived (i.e., by the succession of appearances or event that was perceived—the ship floating downstream). That is, I represent this succession of appearances as being responsible for the order of the series of my perceptions. This is what Kant means when he says that "in our case I must derive the *subjective succession* of apprehension from the *objective succession* of the appearances" (A193/B238). The reason Kant gives for the need to derive the subjective succession from the objective succession is that "otherwise the former would be entirely undetermined and no appearance would be distinguished from another" (A193/B238). This, of course, echoes Kant's discussion of objects of representations where he told us that

> appearance, in contradistinction with the representations of apprehension, can only be represented as an object distinct from them if it stands under a rule, which distinguishes it from every other apprehension, and makes necessary one manner of connection of the manifold. (A191/B236)

So whereas the first four strategies have problems dealing with Kant's examples here, the Object of Experience Strategy fits quite nicely with Kant's examples.

Now, of course, the mere fact that the Object of Experience Strategy deals well with the house, the ship, and irreversibility while the other strategies do not, does not automatically rule the other four strategies out nor

---

3. As I suggested above, Strawson's Event/Object Strategy does much better with the examples introduced in Kant's Irreversibility Argument, but that is not to say Strawson ultimately gets these examples right. Because Strawson's interpretation does do much better than the other three strategies, seeing exactly where he goes wrong requires a good deal of exegesis of the text. I have already discussed this in detail back in chapter 3, so rather than reproduce that discussion here, I will simply refer the reader back to that discussion of the problems with the Event/Object Strategy in connection with Kant's illustrative examples and the conclusions he draws from these.

does it automatically mean the Object of Experience Strategy is the right one. On the one hand, other interpretive considerations may override the difficulties that one of the first four strategies has here. On the other hand, the Object of Experience Strategy could run into interpretive problems of its own that negate its success here. I do take this to be an important guide to the discovery of the route to the principle of causation, but it is only the first hurdle an interpretation has to pass. A second such hurdle has to do with how a strategy interprets the nature of the causal principle itself.

The nature of the principle of the Second Analogy

No matter how well or how poorly a strategy does with interpreting particular aspects of the text of the Second Analogy itself, in order to be an adequate interpretation, then it must also be based on a proper understanding of the nature of the causal principle of the Second Analogy. I believe we do get some clear indications concerning the nature of the principle from the text of the Second Analogy itself, but as we have seen above in the various sections of chapter 1, the Second Analogy is not an isolated text. It stands in important relationships not only to other parts of the *Critique of Pure Reason,* but also to Kant's other works (in particular the *Critique of Judgment*). When we investigate the Second Analogy we must be careful to develop an interpretation that keeps this larger role in mind. No matter how plausible or philosophically desirable an interpretation seems, if it involves a causal principle that has a nature that is inconsistent with the role Kant has systematically delineated for a principle of understanding, then such an interpretation must be rejected. Unfortunately, this flaw goes unrecognized in too many interpretations. When dealing with proponents of the first four strategies this flaw shows itself in two ways.

Synthetic and a priori

Although, as we saw above, Strawson's Event/Object Strategy does better than the others when it comes to dealing with Kant's illustrative examples, his interpretation does not fare so well when it comes to the nature of the principle of the Second Analogy. As we saw above, Strawson interprets Kant as arguing that the causal principle is a requirement for using the irreversibility of perceptions as a criterion for distinguishing between successive perceptions of events and successive perceptions of coexistent objects. Ultimately, according to Strawson, Kant justifies this premise by arguing that "to conceive this order of perceptions as necessary is equivalent to conceiving the transition or change from A to B as *itself* necessary."[4] That is, conceiving the order of perceptions

---

4. Strawson, 138.

as necessary "is equivalent to conceiving the change from A to B as causally necessitated."[5] As we saw in chapter 4, basing the proof for the causal principle on this connection of concepts simply does not fit well with what Kant tells us about principles of understanding. A principle of understanding is supposed to be both synthetic and *a priori*. Conceptual analysis by itself would at best be able to provide proof for an *a priori* and analytic principle. This, however, would simply get the nature of the causal principle wrong. A synthetic *a priori* principle must be proven by means of a transcendental proof. A transcendental proof is not based on an appeal to conceptual analysis. Instead, a transcendental proof is based on an appeal to the conditions for the possibility of experience, which as Kant puts it, "are at the same time conditions of the *possibility of objects of experience*" (A158/B197).[6]

In basing the proof of the causal principle on the requirements for the possibility of an event's being an object of experience, it should be clear that the nature of transcendental proof is part of the inspiration for the Object of Experience Strategy. Grounding the proof of the causal principle in this way should also make clear the Object of Experience strategist's commitment to the causal principle's being a synthetic *a priori* principle.[7]

Constitutive versus regulative
When dealing with the nature of the causal principle, probably the most important guide is the distinction Kant draws between two types of principles: constitutive principles and regulative principles. One reason this is such an important guide is the fact that, although for Kant the requirement that principles of understanding be constitutive rather than regulative principles is just as fundamental as his requirement that principles of understanding be both synthetic and *a priori*, far too many commentators overlook this basic requirement. As we saw back in chapter 1, a regulative principle "is not a principle of the possibility of experience and the empirical cognition of objects of sense, consequently not a principle of understanding" (A509/B537). Whereas a constitutive principle of understanding deals with the requirements for the possibility of experience, a regulative principle of reason deals with "only the unique way in which we must proceed in the reflection about the objects of nature with the intention of representing a thoroughgoing

---

5. Ibid.
6. I should note here that one might still try to rehabilitate the Event/Object Strategy without using Strawson's conceptual analysis. Given the other problems discussed in chapters 3 and 4, however, I don't think such an attempt would be particularly fruitful.
7. Of course, I do not intend to imply here that the recognition of Kant's commitment to the synthetic and *a priori* status of the causal principle is unique to the Object of Experience Strategy. On the contrary, Strawson's version of the Event/Object Strategy is simply one of the exceptions in this regard.

connected experience" (*CJ*, 184). The causal principle of the Second Analogy is not supposed to be a regulative principle of reason, but instead it is supposed to be a constitutive principle of understanding. One of the main ways an interpretation can go wrong is in attempting to incorporate regulative features into this constitutive principle of understanding. We first saw this in chapter 2 with the SCSE formulation of the causal principle. In addition to requiring that every event has a cause, the SCSE interpretation of the causal principle includes a requirement that if one individual event causes a second individual event, then whenever any event of the first type occurs, an event of the second type will follow. That is, SCSE requires that for all sequences of events there is some true causal generalization covering other events of those same types. As we have seen in chapters 2 and 5, however, no matter how scientifically useful or philosophically satisfying such a regularity clause would be, such a clause would have to be adopted under the auspices of the regulative function of reason. It is not something that can be required by a constitutive principle of understanding. Kant is clear that such regularity is not required for the possibility of experience, but instead it is required for the comprehensibility, connectedness, and order of experience. However desirable these things are they cannot be part of a constitutive principle of the understanding and hence cannot be part of the causal principle of the Second Analogy.

In chapters 3 and 4 we saw how inattention to the distinction between constitutive and regulative principles creates problems in a slightly different but connected way. We saw there that by attempting to base the argument for the causal principle on its necessity for some regulative activity, both the Event/Event Strategy and the Justification Strategy would thereby transform the causal principle into a regulative rather than constitutive principle.[8]

On the one hand, according to the Event/Event Strategy, Kant's attempted proof turns on the causal principle's being required for determining the temporal positions of distinct events in relation to each other. As we have seen, however, the constitutive activity of understanding "is not that it makes the representation of objects distinct, but that it makes the representation of an object possible at all" (A199/B244). Unfortunately grounding the causal principle, as the Event/Event Strategy would have it, in our need to make an inference from features of events to the temporal ordering of events, would not ground it in something that is required to make the representation of an event possible. Instead it would be grounding it in something that is required

---

8. Although I did not discuss it in chapters 3 or 4 the same problem would arise with Lovejoy's Veridical Strategy. Distinguishing between veridical and non-veridical perceptions will be a regulative activity not a constitutive one. The reason I did not address this back in chapters 3 and 4 is that the textual problems associated with Lovejoy's Veridical Strategy alone amounted to insurmountable objections to his interpretation.

for making the representation of an event or events distinct. This in turn would inappropriately transform what is supposed to be a constitutive principle of understanding into a regulative principle.

On the other hand, according to the Justification Strategy, Kant's attempted proof turns on the causal principle's being required for our ability to justify the judgment that a particular event has occurred. If, however, I try to justify my judgment that a particular event occurred, I am attempting to justify something I have already represented to myself—namely, that some event has occurred. Justification is not a requirement for the possibility of experience or representation, so it does not play a role in a constitutive principle of understanding. Justification may play a role in the expansion, systematization, or regulation of our beliefs or judgments, but these go beyond what is required for the possibility of experience or representation, so they also go beyond the constitutive task with which understanding is engaged in the principles of understanding. As above, grounding the causal principle in this way would illegitimately transform a constitutive principle of understanding into a regulative principle.

In basing the proof of the causal principle on the requirements for the possibility of an event's being an object of experience, it should be clear that maintaining consistency with Kant's claim that principles of understanding are constitutive rather than regulative in nature is a crucial goal of the Object of Experience Strategy. The Object of Experience strategist makes it clear that the proof of the causal principle turns not on the requirements for the comprehensibility, connectedness, or order of experience—the hallmarks of the regulative activity of reason—but simply on the conditions for the possibility of objects of experience—the hallmark of the constitutive activity of understanding. In this way the Object of Experience strategist is able to carefully preserve the constitutive nature of the causal principle of the Second Analogy. The Object of Experience Strategy's focus on the conditions for the possibility of objects of experience is also what enabled me to find my third and final guide to the discovery of the route to the principle of causation. And that is the importance of Kant's discussion of objects of representations at the beginning of the Second Analogy.

Objects of representations

As we have seen above, it was back in the first edition of the Transcendental Deduction that Kant became interested in "what is meant by the expression 'an object of representations' " (A104). Kant takes up this investigation again in the Second Analogy and he realizes that

> admittedly one can call everything, and even every representation, in so far as one is conscious of it, an object, but what meaning this word

has with regard to appearances, not in so far as they (as representations) are objects, but rather only in so far as they signify an object, is a matter for deeper investigation. (A189–90/B234–35)

So what is the meaning of the word *object?* Kant tells us that "the object is viewed as that which ensures that our cognitions are not haphazardly or arbitrarily determined" (A104). As we have seen earlier, Kant's point is straightforward. The object is that which grounds the objectivity of cognition. If I take some set of my representations to have an object, then I represent my cognition in this case as having been constrained by the features of the object. In his investigation in the Second Analogy Kant does two things: first he uncovers the connection between events and objects of representations, and second, through his examination of the requirements for being an object of representations he forges a link between events and the schematized category of cause and effect.

We have already seen that through the Irreversibility Argument, Kant comes to the conclusion that in the case of an ordinary object, such as a house, I do not attribute the succession of my representations to the object— I attribute the succession of representations to my own subjective choices. In the case of an event, such as a ship floating downstream, however, I do attribute the succession of my representations to an object—I attribute it to an objective succession of appearances. That is, in this case, the ship floating downstream, this event (this succession of appearances) is the object of representations. So Kant has made the connection between successions of appearances and objects of representations. How does this help forge a connection to cause and effect? It is when we examine the requirements for being an object of representations a little more closely that the link becomes clear.

We have seen that the object is that which grounds the objectivity of our cognition, but how can objects, which are themselves representations, be "that which ensures that our cognitions are not haphazardly or arbitrarily determined" (A104)? Kant's answer is that in order for representations to be objects in this sense they themselves must not be associated in a haphazard or arbitrary way. That is, the representations must themselves be connected according to rules. Kant writes that

> appearance, in contradistinction with the representations of apprehension, can only be represented as an object distinct from them if it stands under a rule, which distinguishes it from every other apprehension, and makes necessary one manner of connection of the manifold. (A191/B236)

In other words, representations or appearances can be objects of representations only insofar as they are subject to a rule.

When we put this together with the ship's floating downstream being an object of representations what we find is the link Kant is looking for. For what we have found with the succession of appearances of the ship floating downstream, since it is an object of representations, is an example of "the succession of the manifold, in so far as it is subject to a rule" (A144/B183). This, of course, is the schema of cause and effect and so the ship floating downstream falls under the schematized category of cause and effect. That is, by making the connection between this succession of appearances, the ship floating downstream, and its being an object of representations, then Kant has found that the concept of cause and effect has application to experience.

The connection between successions of appearances and objects of representations also sets the stage for the completion of Kant's proof of the causal principle. For in order to prove that the causal principle is true (i.e., that successions of appearances must be subject to a rule), Kant once again looks to the requirements for being an object of representations. As we have seen, Kant argues that successions of appearances must be subject to a rule (i.e., the causal principle is true), because no succession of appearances that fails to be subject to a rule would meet the requirements for being a possible *object of representations*.

OBJECT OF EXPERIENCE STRATEGIES

In chapter 3 when I introduced the Object of Experience Strategy I noted there may be some variation on this strategy. I want to conclude by saying a little more about that here.

All of the Object of Experience Strategies agree that in the third paragraph of the Second Analogy Kant draws a distinction between two senses of the word *object*.[9] On the one hand Kant tells us that "admittedly one can call everything, and even every representation, in so far as one is conscious of it, an object" (A189/B234). Any object of consciousness is an object in this sense. This is the weak sense of the word *object*. In contrast to this weak sense there is also a strong sense of the word "object"—what we have all along been calling objects of experience. Although there is a good deal of agreement concerning objects of experience, it is, in the end, disagreement over the proper explication of the nature of these objects of experience that gives rise to the variations on the Object of Experience Strategy.[10]

---

9. Although in the end I disagree with William Harper's explication of one these two senses of "object," his discussion of Kant's use of these two senses of object has been helpful. See "Kant's Empirical Realism and the Distinction between Subjective and Objective Succession," especially Section II.

10. It is important to note that however we ultimately explicate the strong sense of "object," the distinction between the weak and strong senses of "object" should not be taken to correspond to the distinction for which Allison argues between *"Objekt"* and *"Gegenstand."* As I under

Conclusion

There are two things with regard to the nature of objects of experience on which all versions of the Object of Experience Strategy agree. First, the understanding plays a constitutive role with regard to objects of experience. That is, objects of experience are not simply given through sensibility and passively received by the understanding. Objects of experience have both an intuitive element and conceptual element.

Second, empirical objects are supposed to be objects in the strong sense. This is crucial for Kant's whole project in the *Critique*. If empirical objects are not objects in the strong sense, then this threatens to make the employment of the categories optional. If the categories are required for objects in the strong sense, but empirical objects are not objects in the strong sense, then we do not have proof that the categories must apply to empirical objects.

All versions of the Object of Experience Strategy agree on two additional points. The first is that successions of appearances are objects of experience. The second point is that the argument in the Second Analogy turns on the fact that successions of appearances are objects of experience.

As we have seen, on my reading objects of experience are best understood as being objects of representations. So when it comes to the nature of these objects, then it will include only those features required for the possibility of representation and nothing further. As we have seen, these requirements will be relatively sparse. As we saw in chapter 5, roughly speaking, the possibility of representation will only require that an object have some determinate spatial temporal location, that it be composed of some determinate set of parts, and that these parts be connected in some determinate way.

Some Object of Experience strategists, however, want objects of experience to be more robust than I have suggested. Ultimately, the main reason for this is that it would provide us with the ability to interpret Kant as adopting a more robust theory of causation within the Second Analogy itself than we can on the object of representations interpretation. William Harper, for example, wants to make a significant amount of regularity a constitutive part of an object of experience. With regard to successions of appearances his interpretation of an object of experience works in the following way:

> When it is empirically true that an alteration occurs consisting of A followed by B, there must, also occur an A' and B'[11] that are so related

---

stand the distinction Allison draws, an object in the weak sense and an object in the strong sense would both be *Gegenstände*. See *Kant's Transcendental Idealism*, chapter 7, especially pp. 133–36. We can also note, however, for what it is worth, that here in the Second Analogy when Kant is discussing both objects in the weak sense and objects in the strong sense, he sometimes uses *Gegenstand* and sometimes he uses *Objekt*.

11. A' "is a more determinate state of affairs ... that includes A and that obtained when A obtained in this instance," and B' "is a more determinate state of affairs ... that includes B and that obtained when B obtained in this instance." Harper, "Kant's Empirical Realism and the Distinction between Subjective and Objective Succession," 120.

that no possible object of experience is an instance of the alteration B' followed by $A.'$ This connection between A' and B' is a general constraint on possible objects of experience.[12]

It is clear that if such regularity were part of what it is to be an object of experience *and* if this were the interpretation Kant intended to adopt, then this would provide the Object of Experience strategist with a way to interpret Kant as adopting a more robust theory of causation within the Second Analogy itself. In particular, it would give the Object of Experience strategist a way to adopt the SCSE interpretation of the causal principle.

There are three reasons, however, for thinking it is a mistake to interpret the strong sense of object Kant introduces in the third paragraph of the Second Analogy in this way. The first reason is that throughout the Second Analogy Kant writes as if it is the possibility of representation that is at stake. In the third paragraph itself, Kant tells us that "appearance, in contradistinction with the representations of apprehension, can only be represented as an object distinct from them if it stands under a rule" (A191/B236). Here, when he introduces this strong sense of object, Kant is clearly concerned with the requirements for an appearance's being represented as an object. Then, later on, Kant tells us that

> understanding is required for all experience and its possibility, and the first thing it does is not that it makes the representation of objects distinct, but that it makes the representation of an object possible at all. (A199/B244)

Once again, Kant makes it clear that here in the Second Analogy he is concerned with what is required for the possibility of the representation of an object. So we should stick with interpreting objects of experience as being no more robust than objects of representations.

Secondly, as we have seen, Kant does indeed believe the second clause of SCSE is true, *but* he holds it to be a prescription of the regulative use of reason rather than a constitutive principle of understanding. So if we accept a more robust interpretation of objects of experience, for example Harper's, we will end up with a perfectly justifiable conception of objects of experience. *Unfortunately,* it is only the legitimate regulative interests of reason that provide us with justification for the conception of such robust objects of experience. It would be a mistake to base the proof of a constitutive principle of the understanding on the requirements for the possibility

---

12. Harper, 121.

of a type of object that itself can only be justified by appeal to the regulative function of reason.

Thirdly, as I said above it is important for Kant's project in the *Critique* that empirical objects are objects in the strong sense. If the categories are required for objects in the strong sense, but empirical objects are not objects in the strong sense, then we will not have proven that the categories must apply to empirical objects. It seems to me, however, that if we adopt an interpretation of objects in the strong sense that incorporates the sort of regularity Harper has in mind, then the claim that empirical objects are objects in the strong sense stands in serious need of justification. It is difficult to see why empirical objects must posses the regularity required by an object in Harper's strong sense. It is possible that empirical objects possess this regularity, but what are the grounds for holding that *all* empirical objects possess this regularity?[13] The search for such regularity may always guide my investigation of empirical objects. It may also be that I am never satisfied in particular cases until I am able to make out some regularity or other, but neither claim shows that there is a regularity to be found for every empirical object I might investigate. If we attempt to build regulative functions of reason into objects in the strong sense, then we have left open the possibility that empirical objects are not objects in the strong sense. This, in turn, means that we have not proven that the categories must apply to empirical objects.

Given these reasons we should stick with the version of the Object of Experience Strategy that interprets objects of experience as being objects of representations. Again, it may be that on the Object of Representations Strategy, what we find in the causal principle of the Second Analogy does not live up to our preexisting expectations for a modern theory of causation, but this is by design. A constitutive principle of understanding can only provide us with what I called in chapter 5, Kant's minimal theory of causation, because this is all that is required for *the possibility of experience*. When we want to find Kant's full-fledged theory of causation we must turn to the power of judgment and to regulative principles of reason. For a robust theory of causation is not required for the possibility of experience, but instead it would be required according to Kant for "the possibility of the unity of experience (as a system according to empirical laws)" (*CJ*, 183). To the constitutive function of understanding the possibility of the unity of experience is something contingent, but to the regulative function of judgment "such a unity must necessarily be presupposed and assumed, for otherwise no thoroughgoing connection of empirical cognitions into an entirety of experience would

---

13. As we saw above, Kant himself thinks we get this only from the regulative function of judgment. To the understanding, however, these are regularities that "can only be known empirically, and which in its view are contingent" (*CJ*, 184).

take place" (*CJ*, 183). Something more than Kant's minimal theory of causation may be a consequence of a legitimate *a priori* principle of reason, but according to Kant if we were to try to incorporate it into an *a priori* principle of understanding, such a use of our reason could only be described as dialectical.

BIBLIOGRAPHY

Allison, Henry E. "Kant's Refutation of Realism." *Dialectica*, 30 (1976): 223–53.
———. "The Non-spaciality of Things in Themselves for Kant." *Journal of the History of Philosophy* 14 (July 1976): 313–21.
———. *Kant's Transcendental Idealism*. New Haven: Yale University Press, 1983.
———. "Reflections on the B-Deduction." *The Southern Journal of Philosophy* 25 Supplement (1987): 1–15.
———. *Kant's Theory of Freedom*. Cambridge: Cambridge University Press, 1990.
Ameriks, Karl. "Remarks on Robinson and the Representation of a Whole." *The Southern Journal of Philosophy* 25 Supplement (1987): 63–66.
Bayne, Steven M. "Objects of Representations and Kant's Second Analogy." *Journal of the History of Philosophy* XXXII, no. 3 (July 1994): 381–410.
———. "Kant's Answer to Hume: How Kant Should Have Tried to Stand Hume's Copy Thesis on Its Head." *British Journal for the History of Philosophy* 8, no. 2 (June 2000): 207–24.
Beck, Lewis White, ed. *Kant Studies Today*. Chicago: Open Court, 1969.
———. *Essays on Kant and Hume*. New Haven: Yale University Press, 1978.
———. "A Prussian Hume and a Scottish Kant." In *Essays on Kant and Hume*, 111–29. New Haven: Yale University Press, 1978.
———. "Six Short Pieces on the Second Analogy of Experience." In *Essays on Kant and Hume*, 130–64. New Haven: Yale University Press, 1978.
———. "Kant on the Uniformity of Nature." *Synthese* 47 (June 1981): 449–64.
———. "Two Ways of Reading Kant's Letter to Herz: Comments on Carl." In *Kant's Transcendental Deductions*, ed. Eckart Förster, 21–28. Stanford: Stanford University Press, 1989.
Bennett, Jonathan. *Kant's Analytic*. Cambridge: At The University Press, 1966.
Bird, Graham. *Kant's Theory of Knowledge*. New York: Humanities Press, 1962.
———. "Kant's Transcendental Arguments." In *Reading Kant*, ed. Schaper and Vossenkuhl, 21–39. Oxford: Basil Blackwell, 1989.
Brand, Myles. *Intending and Acting*. Cambridge, Mass.: MIT Press, 1984.

Brittan, Gordon, Jr. *Kant's Theory of Science*. Princeton: Princeton University Press, 1978.
———. "Kant, Closure, and Causality." In *Kant on Causality, Freedom, and Objectivity*, ed. Harper and Meerbote, 66–82. Minneapolis: University of Minnesota Press, 1984.
Broad, C. D. *Kant: An Introduction*. Ed. C. Lewy. Cambridge: Cambridge University Press, 1978.
Buchdahl, Gerd. "The Kantian 'Dynamic of Reason' with Special Reference to the Place of Causality in Kant's System." In *Kant Studies Today,* ed. L. W. Beck, 341–74. Chicago: Open Court, 1969.
———. *Metaphysics and the Philosophy of Science*. Cambridge, Mass.: The MIT Press, 1969.
Butts, Robert, E. "Kant's Schemata as Semantical Rules." In *Kant Studies Today,* ed. L. W. Beck, 290–300. Chicago: Open Court, 1969.
Carl, Wolfgang. "Kant's First Drafts of the Deduction of the Categories." In *Kant's Transcendental Deductions,* ed. Eckart Förster, 3–20. Stanford: Stanford University Press, 1989.
Chisholm, Roderick. *Person and Object*. La Salle: Open Court Publishing, 1976.
Davidson, Donald. *Essays on Actions & Events*. Oxford: Clarendon Press, 1980.
Den Ouden, Bernard, and Marcia Moen, eds. *New Essays on Kant*. New York: Peter Lang Publishing, 1987.
Dryer, D. P. *Kant's Solution for Verification in Metaphysics*. Toronto: University of Toronto Press, 1966.
———. "The Second Analogy." In *Kant on Causality, Freedom, and Objectivity,* ed. Harper and Meerbote, 58–64. Minneapolis: University of Minnesota Press, 1984.
Engstrom, Stephen. "The Transcendental Deduction and Skepticism." *Journal of the History of Philosophy* 32, no. 3 (July 1994): 359–80.
Ewing, A. C. *A Short Commentary on Kant's Critique of Pure Reason*. Chicago: The University of Chicago Press, 1938.
Farr, Wolfgang, ed. *Hume und Kant: Interpretation und Diskussion*. München: Verlag Karl Alber, 1982.
Flew, Antony. *Hume's Philosophy of Belief*. London: Routledge & Kegan Paul, 1961.
French, Stanley. "Kant's Constitutive-Regulative Distinction." In *Kant Studies Today,* ed. L. W. Beck, 375-91. Chicago: Open Court, 1969.
Förster, Eckart. "How Are Transcendental Arguments Possible?" In *Reading Kant,* ed. Schaper and Vossenkuhl), 3–20. Oxford: Basil Blackwell, 1989.

———, ed. *Kant's Transcendental Deductions*. Stanford: Stanford University Press, 1989.
Friedman, Michael. *Kant and the Exact Sciences*. Cambridge, Mass.: Harvard University Press, 1992.
Gram, Moltke S., ed. *Kant: Disputed Questions*. Chicago: Quadrangle Books, 1967.
Guyer, Paul. *Kant and the Claims of Knowledge*. Cambridge: Cambridge University Press, 1987.
———. "The Failure of the B-Deduction." *The Southern Journal of Philosophy* 25 Supplement (1987).
———. "The Rehabilitation of Transcendental Idealism?" In *Reading Kant*, ed. Schaper and Vossenkuhl, 140–67. Oxford: Basil Blackwell, 1989.
———, ed. *The Cambridge Companion to Kant*. Cambridge: Cambridge University Press, 1992.
Harper, William L., and Ralf Meerbote, eds. *Kant on Causality, Freedom, and Objectivity*. Minneapolis: University of Minnesota Press, 1984.
Harper, William. "Kant's Empirical Realism and the Distinction between Subjective and Objective Succession." In *Kant on Causality, Freedom, and Objectivity*, ed. Harper and Meerbote, 108–37. Minneapolis: University of Minnesota Press, 1984.
———. "Kant on Space, Empirical Realism, and the Foundations of Geometry." *Topoi* 3: 143–62.
Hegel, G. W. F. *Phenomenology of Spirit*. Trans. A. V. Miller. Oxford: Oxford University Press, 1977.
Henrich, Dieter. "The Proof-structure of Kant's Transcendental Deduction," *Review of Metaphysics* 22 (June 1969): 640–59.
———. *Identität und Objektivität, Eine Untersuchung über Kants transzendentale Deduktion*. Heidelberg: Carl Winter Universitätsverlag, 1976.
Horstmann, Rolf Peter. "The Metaphysical Deduction in Kant's "Critique of Pure Reason." *Phil Forum* 13 (Fall 1981): 32–47.
———. "Transcendental Idealism and the Representation of Space." In *Reading Kant*, ed. Schaper and Vossenkuhl, 168–76. Oxford: Basil Blackwell, 1989.
Hume, David. *A Letter from a Gentleman to His Friend in Edinburgh*. Ed. Eric Steinberg. Indianapolis: Hackett Publishing Company, 1977.
———. *An Enquiry Concerning Human Understanding*. Ed. Eric Steinberg. Indianapolis: Hackett Publishing Company, 1977.
———. *A Treatise of Human Nature*. Second Revised Edition by P. H. Nidditch. Oxford: At The Clarendon Press, 1978.
Kant, Immanuel. *Kants gesammelte Schriften*. Ed. Königlichen Preußischen Akademie der Wissenschaften. Berlin: Walter de Gruyter & Co., 1902.

———. *Prolegomena to Any Future Metaphysics*. Trans. Lewis White Beck. Indianapolis: Bobbs-Merrill, 1950.

———. *Kritik der reinen Vernunft*. Ed. Wilhelm Weischedel, Wiesbaden: Insel-Verlag, 1956.

———. *Metaphysical Foundations of Natural Science*. Trans. James Ellington. Indianapolis: The Bobbs-Merrill Company, Inc., 1970.

———. *Logic*. Trans. Robert S. Hartman and Wolfgang Schwarz. New York: Dover Publications, Inc., 1974.

———. *Grounding for the Metaphysics of Morals*. Trans. James W. Ellington. Indianapolis: Hackett Publishing Company, 1981.

———. *The Critique of Judgment*. Trans. Werner S. Pluhar. Indianapolis: Hackett Publishing Company, 1987.

———. *Kritik der reinen Vernunft*. Ed. Raymund Schmidt. Hamburg: Felix Meiner Verlag, 1993.

———. *Kritik der Urteilskraft*. Ed. Karl Vorländer. Hamburg: Felix Meiner Verlag, 1993.

———. *Critique of Pure Reason*. Trans. Paul Guyer and Allen Wood. Cambridge: Cambridge University Press, 1997.

———. *Critique of the Power of Judgment*. Trans. Paul Guyer and Eric Matthews. Cambridge: Cambridge University Press, 2000.

Kemp Smith, Norman. *A Commentary to Kant's "Critique of Pure Reason."* New York: The Humanities Press, 1950.

Kim, Jaegwon. "Causes and Events: Mackie on Causation." *The Journal of Philosophy* 68 (1971): 426–41.

———. "Causation, Nomic Subsumption, and the Concept of Event." *The Journal of Philosophy* 70 (1973): 217–36.

———. "Events as Property Exemplifications." In *Action Theory*, ed. M. Brand and D. Walton, 159–77. Holland: D. Reidel Publishing Company, 1976.

Kuehn, Manfred. "Kant's Conception of 'Hume's Problem.'" *Journal of the History of Philosophy* XXI, no. 2 (1983).

———. "Kant's Transcendental Deduction: a Limited Defense of Hume." In *New Essays on Kant*, ed. Den Ouden. New York: Peter Lang Publishing, 1987.

———. *Kant: A Biography*. Cambridge: Cambridge University Press, 2001.

Lovejoy, Arthur O. "On Kant's Reply to Hume." In *Kant: Disputed Questions*, ed. Moltke S. Gram, 284–309. Chicago: Quadrangle Books, 1967.

Makkreel, Rudolf A. *Imagination and Interpretation in Kant*. Chicago: The University of Chicago Press, 1990.

Meerbote, Ralf. "Kant's Refutation of Problematic Material Idealism." In *New Essays on Kant*, ed. Den Ouden. New York: Peter Lang Publishing, 1987.

Melnick, Arthur. *Kant's Analogies of Experience*. Chicago: The University of Chicago Press, 1973.

Nagel, Gordon. "Substance and Causality." In *Kant on Causality, Freedom, and Objectivity,* ed. Harper and Meerbote, 97–107. Minneapolis: University of Minnesota Press, 1984.

Nussbaum, Charles. "Concepts, Judgments, and Unity in Kant's Metaphysical Deduction of the Relational Categories." *Journal of the History of Philosophy* 28, no. 1: 89–103.

Paton, H. J. *Kant's Metaphysic of Experience*. Two Volumes. New York: The Humanities Press, 1936.

———. "Kant on the Errors of Leibniz." In *Kant Studies Today,* ed. L. W. Beck, 72–87. Chicago: Open Court, 1969.

Penelhum, Terence, and J. J. MacIntosh, eds. *The First Critique: Reflections on Kant's Critique of Pure Reason*. Belmont, California: Wadsworth Publishing Company, Inc., 1969.

Pippin, Robert B. *Kant's Theory of Form: an Essay on the Critique of Pure Reason*. New Haven: Yale University Press, 1982.

Pollock, John. "Chisholm on States of Affairs." In *Grazer Philosophisch Studien* 7/8 (1979): 163–75.

Posy, Carl J. "Transcendental Idealism and Causality: An Interpretation of Kant's Argument in the Second Analogy." In *Kant on Causality, Freedom, and Objectivity,* ed. Harper and Meerbote, 20–41. Minneapolis: University of Minnesota Press, 1984.

Priest, Stephen, ed. *Hegel's Critique of Kant*. Oxford: Clarendon Press, 1987.

Robinson, Hoke. "The Transcendental Deduction From A to B: Combination in the Threefold Synthesis and the Representation of a Whole." *The Southern Journal of Philosophy* 25 Supplement (1987): 45–61.

———. "Two Perspectives on Kant's Appearances and Things in Themselves." *Journal of the History of Philosophy* 32, no. 3 (July 1994): 359–80.

Schaper, Eva, and Vossenkuhl, Wilhelm, eds. *Reading Kant: New Perspectives on Transcendental Arguments and Critical Philosophy*. Oxford: Basil Blackwell, 1989.

Strawson, P. F. *The Bounds of Sense*. London: Methuen & Co. Ltd., 1966.

Stroud, Barry. "Transcendental Arguments." In *The First Critique,* ed. Penelhum and MacIntosh, 54–69. Belmont, California: Wadsworth Publishing Company, Inc., 1969.

———. *Hume*. London: Routledge & Kegan Paul, 1977.

Suchting, W. A. "Kant's Second Analogy of Experience." In *Kant Studies Today,* ed. L. W. Beck, 322–40. Chicago: Open Court, 1969.

Turbayne, Colin. "Kant's Relation to Berkeley." In *Kant Studies Today,* ed. L. W. Beck, 88–116. Chicago: Open Court, 1969.

Van Cleve, James. "Another Volley at Kant's Reply to Hume." In *Kant on Causality, Freedom, and Objectivity*, ed. Harper and Meerbote, 42–57. Minneapolis: University of Minnesota Press, 1984.

———. "Comments on Paul Guyer's 'The Failure of the B-Deduction.'" *The Southern Journal of Philosophy* 25 Supplement (1987): 85–87.

Walsh, W. H. "Kant's Transcendental Idealism." In *Kant on Causality, Freedom, and Objectivity,* ed. Harper and Meerbote, 83–96. Minneapolis: University of Minnesota Press, 1984.

Wiener, Philip, ed. *Leibniz Selections*. New York: Charles Scribner's Sons, 1951.

Wolff, Robert Paul. *Kant's Theory of Mental Activity*. Reprint. Gloucester, Mass.: Peter Smith, 1973.

Yolton, John. "Hume's Ideas." *Hume Studies* VI, no. 1 (April 1980): 2–25.

INDEX

Allison, Henry E., 14n, 36n, 51n, 162n
Analogies, 1, 16n, 22–26, 106, 171
  mathematical versus philosophical, 23–24
Beck, Lewis White, 4n, 27, 36n, 51n, 58n, 122n
Bennett, Jonathan, 37n, 48n, 59, 82n, 87–89, 101–2
Causal Principle
  every-event-some-cause (EESC) interpretation, 36–39, 43–44, 51n, 116
  and necessary order, 46–47, 82–87, 93–94, 126–28, 130, 135–36
  and necessity, xi–xii, 83–87, 130–36
  and regularity, 129, 131, 159, 163–65
  repeatability requirement, 39–44, 60, 81, 84, 115–16, 120, 123–26, 128–31, 135–36
  same-cause-same-effect (SCSE) interpretation, 37–44, 51, 80–81, 84, 116, 124, 159, 164
Causation
  Hume's problem, xi–xiii, xv, 1–2, 26–34, 81
  minimal theory of, 136, 165–166
  theory of, xiii, 39, 44, 124, 126, 135–36, 153–54, 163–66
Critique of Judgment, xii–xiv, 19–22, 38, 41, 66, 132–3, 135–36, 157, 159, 165–66
Event/Event Strategy, 47–48, 51n, 58–67, 72–73, 89–90, 155, 159–60
Event/Object Strategy, 46–47, 55–58, 81, 86–87, 154, 156n, 157–58
First Analogy, 36, 57–58, 91, 104, 115n

Guyer, Paul, 14n, 37n, 48–49, 67n, 70n, 72n, 92–97, 99n
Harper, William, 37n, 51n, 58n, 122n, 162–65
Hume, David
  copy thesis, 5–6, 30–31, 146–47, 151
  derivability thesis, 146–47
  Hume's problem, xi–xiii, xv, 1–2, 26–34, 81
  Kant's answer to Hume, xi–xiii, xv, 1–2, 26–28 32–34, 43, 81, 137–151
  separability thesis, 30–31, 148–149, 151
Hypothetical use of reason, 40–41
Imagination, xii, 8, 11–12, 105, 134–35, 141
Irreversibility, 47, 51–52, 55, 57–58, 75–102, 112–14, 154–57, 161
Justification Strategy, 48–49, 51n, 67–73, 92, 96–97, 155, 159–60
Kant's examples
  house, xv, 41, 50, 54, 56–57, 60–62, 70, 75, 89, 97–103, 110–117, 121–22, 127, 154–156, 161
  leaden ball and cushion, 41, 61–62, 155–56
  ship floating downstream, xv, 41, 50, 54, 56–57, 60–62, 70, 75, 89–92, 94–102, 111–18, 121, 127, 130, 132, 137, 154–56, 161–62
  water filling the glass, 41, 155–56
  water freezing, xv, 50, 58, 60–61, 70, 95, 103, 117–18, 121, 123–25, 130, 137
Kemp Smith, Norman, 4n, 5n, 36n, 51n
Leibniz, Gottfried Wilhelm von, 2–5, 7–9

Lovejoy, Arthur O., 37n, 45–46, 52–55, 76–81, 90n, 153–55
Mathematics, 23, 33, 140n, 142–46
Meerbote, Ralf, 37n, 58n, 122n, 162n, 163n
Melnick, Arthur, 37n, 47–48, 59–60, 62–65, 80n, 89–92, 96
Metaphysical Deduction, 2, 13
Object of experience, 7–8, 50–51, 57, 103–104, 119, 127, 130, 139–40, 146, 160–65
Object of Experience Strategy, 42–43, 50–52, 60, 103–104, 146, 156–158, 160–65
Object of representations, xv, 42–44, 50, 54, 80, 103, 107–130, 137–39, 146–47, 160–65
Possibility of experience, 15–19, 24n, 33, 68–69, 73, 108, 120n, 130, 135, 140–42, 158–60, 165
Principles
  constitutive function of, 60, 69–70, 126, 133, 160, 165
  constitutive principle, xiv, 16–19, 21–22, 38–44, 59–60, 69–70, 126–27, 158–60, 164–65
  constitutive principle of reason, 19
  principles of understanding and principles of reason, 1, 16–22, 41, 67n, 158–60, 166

  regulative function of, 43–44, 60, 126, 133, 159, 165
  regulative principle, xiv, 16–22, 41, 66, 69, 126–27, 131, 158–60
Prolegomena, xi–xii, 29, 135, 142–43, 145
Schemata, 8–13, 15, 25–26, 105–107, 116, 162, 168
Schematism, 1–13, 15, 44, 104–107
Second Analogy's context within the Critique of Pure Reason, xiv, 1–16, 22–26
Strawson, P. F., 37n, 46–47, 55–58, 81–87, 154, 156–58
Subject to a rule, 43–44, 50–51, 103–130, 138–39, 147, 161–62
Transcendental Deduction, 1–2, 13–17, 24, 60, 70, 104, 109, 117, 133, 160
Transcendental proof, 32–34, 120, 130–31, 136–146, 158
Transcendental realism, 55
Van Cleve, James, 37n, 49n, 58n, 122n
Veridical Strategy, 45–46, 52–55, 76–81, 154–55, 159n
Watkins, Eric, 65, 72, 140
Wolff, Christian, 45, 53
Wolff, Robert Paul, 36n, 82n, 100–102, 154